A Guide to Nature on
Cape Cod and the Islands

A Guide to Nature on Cape Cod and the Islands

Edited by GREG O'BRIEN

Foreword by Robert Finch

PARNASSUS IMPRINTS

Cover Photographs © Jane Booth Vollers

Parnassus Imprints
270 Communication Way
Hyannis, MA 02601

Library of Congress Cataloging-in-Publication Data
A Guide to nature on Cape Cod and the islands / edited by Greg O'Brien
   foreword by Robert Finch
     p.   cm.
   Originally published: New York, NY : Penguin Books, 1990.
   Includes Index.
   ISBN 0-940160-61-7
   1. Natural History—Massachusetts—Cape Cod Region—Guidebooks.
2. Cape Cod Region (Mass.)—Guidebooks.
I. O'Brien, Greg
QH105.M4G85 1995
508.744'92—dc20

                        95-6373
                          CIP

Manufactured in the United States of America

Dedication

To my wife, Mary Catherine (McGeorge) O'Brien, the silent hero of this book, who for month after exasperating month patiently tolerated an absentee husband and distracted father of three small children. I owe you big time.

—Much love, the editor

Contents

Foreword *by Robert Finch*   ix

Acknowledgements   xv

Part I

About the Contributors   3

Introduction *by Greg O'Brien*   9

How Cape Cod and the Islands Were Formed   15
by Robert N. Oldale

The Forces of Erosion *by Greg O'Brien*   27

Part II

CHAPTER 1

The Nature Around Us—Its Mysteries and Marvels   35
by John Hay

    Question and Answer Section   46
    by Greg O'Brien, Robert Barlow, Mario DiGregorio,
    Robert Finch, John Hay, Peter Trull, Richard LeBlond,
    Craig Newberger, Verdie Abel, and Robert Prescott

CHAPTER 2

Birds of the Cape and Islands   55
by Erma J. Fisk and Greg O'Brien

    Question and Answer Section   61
    by Peter Trull, Robert Prescott, Greg O'Brien,
    Mario DiGregorio, Steve Morello, and Robert Barlow

CHAPTER 3

The Seashore *by Donald J. Zinn*   73
    Question and Answer Section   91
    by Donald J. Zinn, Greg O'Brien, Peter Trull,
    Robert Finch, Scott Hecker, Stephan Berrick, Robert
    Prescott, and the Cape Cod National Seashore staff

CHAPTER 4

The Wetlands *by Richard LeBlond*   107
    Question and Answer Section   124
    by Richard LeBlond, Greg O'Brien, Mario DiGregorio,
    Craig Newberger, and the Cape Cod National Sea-
    shore staff

CHAPTER 5

The Ponds *by John Portnoy*   133
    Question and Answer Section   146
    by John Portnoy and Greg O'Brien

CHAPTER 6

The Woodlands, Heaths, and Grasslands *by Robert Finch*   153
    Question and Answer Section   176
    by Mario DiGregorio and Greg O'Brien

CHAPTER 7

Cape and Islands' Weather   *by Robert Barlow*   191
    Question and Answer Section   200
    by Robert Barlow, Greg O'Brien, and Robert Finch

Part III

Everything You Wanted to Know about Nature and   213
Didn't Ask: A Guide to Intriguing Questions Pondered
at the Cape Cod Museum of Natural History and the
Cape Cod National Seashore
by Mary Loebig, Robert Cousins, and Greg O'Brien

Part IV

A Listing of Nature Trails and Sanctuaries on Cape Cod   229
and the Islands
by John LoDico and Greg O'Brien

Epilogue   *by Robert Finch*   247

Index   255

Foreword

Charlie Ellis, one of the last old dory lobstermen in Cape Cod Bay, once said to me, "Home is where you know what things mean." In this sense, the old Cape Codders felt at home here in a way most of us do not. It was not a matter of having seven generations of ancestors in the local cemetery or a 200-year-old house. Rather, it was a knowledge—often unarticulated—of what local things meant, what, in a more recent phrase, we might call a sense of place.

For the European settlers 300 years ago, and for the local native Americans seven or eight millennia before that, such knowledge was a matter of survival. They had no field guides or scientific vocabulary, but they could "read" a sky for weather, distinguish various habitats for hunting or agricultural use, and understand the behavior of local animals. Knowing the grazing habitats of deer, the medicinal and functional values of local plants, the seasonal comings and goings of fish and other marine life, the nesting habits of birds, the nature of tides, and a thousand other details and processes of the local environment was a pragmatic necessity. But it also produced an intimate association with the land and sea—one for which our present term "affection" might be inappropriate but certainly one that incorporated a satisfying sense of identity, of being "at home."

There were things, of course, that previous generations and cultures did not—could not—have known. Most obviously, the true geologic origins of Cape Cod and the Islands have only been understood for a little over a century. The local Wampanoag Indian myth of the Indian giant Maushop, who created Nantucket and Martha's Vineyard from sand emptied out of his moccasins, might be taken as a prefiguration of the glacial origins of our landscape; but it seems more accurately an imaginative expression of the human scale of these sandy hills and plains. We laugh now at the old Cape Codders' belief in an underground river from New Hampshire that supplied their local water. Yet our knowledge of the Cape's true hydrological nature is barely twenty years old, and our behavior has not yet fully adapted to it. Our predecessors gathered alewives—local migratory herring—out of our creeks and streams, much as we still do today. They did not know where the fish go during winter—and neither do we.

This is not to say that local residents in the past never made environmental mistakes. They did—and you will read about some fairly dramatic ones in the following chapters. The difference is that knowledge of the local environment was taken for granted as a requirement for living here, whereas today we regard it—residents and visitors alike— as *optional* knowledge, something we might choose to learn to increase our pleasure and understanding of what goes on around us. We listen to a lecture at the Cape Cod National Seashore or take a class at the Cape Cod Museum of Natural History or go on a bird walk at Wellfleet Bay Audubon Sanctuary or the Felix Neck Wildlife Sanctuary on Martha's Vineyard because we have the leisure to do so, because we wish to satisfy our curiosity and our pleasure in learning. There is nothing wrong with this; in fact, there is everything right with this. As the Wisconsin conservationist Aldo Leopold pointed out, environmental ethics will only be effective if they spring from love. We must love the land before we can learn about it.

But there is another motive at work in our curiosity about nature today and in such guides to it as this. For generations the Cape and Islands have been among America's premier summer playgrounds. Yet each year both visitors and residents alike encounter increasing restrictions on and diminishment of their enjoyment of our natural riches. More and more shellfish beds are closed by pollution, more and more areas of beach and dune are fenced off due to man-made erosion, more and more of our once-pristine kettle hole ponds are beginning to show signs of premature aging, more and more rare plants and archaeological sites are bulldozed to make way for construction, fewer and fewer migratory bird species return each year to nest on our cut-up forests and developed beaches, and less and less space is available to each of us for that sense of freedom and exploration that has always been at the heart of the Cape and Islands experience. We begin to sense that our love has too often been uninformed and our play has turned deadly. It is no longer enough simply to enjoy the mysteries and the marvels of these sea-and-ice-sculptured lands. We must begin to learn again what they mean.

This book, we hope, is one means to that end. It springs from the premise that, for most of us, an instinctive delight in the pleasures of the seashore and its associated environments leads to a desire to learn more about them—not only what and where but how and why. You will find here informed and entertaining writing on the major natural habitats, or ecosystems, of Cape Cod, Martha's Vineyard, and Nantucket, as well as specific answers to over 150 questions most often asked at our various natural history centers. In addition, it contains a guide to local natural areas.

The Cape and Islands are particularly rich, not only in natural beauty and diversity but in information as well, for they have long attracted people who have had a passionate curiosity about what things here mean.

In the 1870s Louis Agassiz, the famous Harvard geologist, established a natural history school on Penikese Island, one of the chain of the Elizabeth Islands off Woods Hole. This school was the precursor of the present Marine Biological Laboratory, which, with its sister organizations the Woods Hole Oceanographic Institution and the National Marine Fisheries Service, has become one of the world's great centers of marine research.

Agassiz was also the formulator of the modern theory of glacial geology, which provided the key to the Cape and Islands' geologic history. The Cape's geology, in fact, has contributed at least one term to the field's general vocabulary: "pamet," designating a stream bed covered with glacial drift, derived from the Pamet River Valley in Truro. A classic example of this formation can be clearly seen from Route 6.

In 1966 a landmark environmental study of the Cape's hydrology was published by Orleans resident Dr. Arthur Strahler, outlining for the first time the basic concept of the Cape and Islands' water supply as a single freshwater "lens," connected throughout a relatively porous, unconsolidated subsoil, that literally floats on top of a slightly denser layer of salt water. It was this study by a local resident, subsequently corroborated and refined by federal water studies, that resulted in the federal designation of our local water supply as a "sole source aquifer," a recognition that has shaped current water policies.

Woods Hole has drawn an international community of scientists, including dozens of Nobel Prize winners, and its research ships and expeditions study marine sites worldwide. Yet some of its most significant studies, and distinguished alumni, have deep local roots. Dr. Alfred Redfield, for instance, was a native of Barnstable. His boyhood explorations of the Great Marshes in that town eventually led to the first scientific study of the formation of salt marshes. This study has been used as a model for salt marsh research ever since.

Modern ornithology was pioneered in New England, and some of the most important work was done by those attracted to the Cape's shores and its abundance of birds—naturalists such as William Brewster, Edward Howe Forbush, and Ludlow Griscom. The landmark study of Cape Cod birds, however, is surely that of Dr. Oliver S. Austin and his son, Dr. Oliver L. Austin, who in 1930 established the Austin Ornithological Research Station in South Wellfleet. For nearly thirty years the Austins carried on extensive observation and banding work, and their published papers provided the first major studies on Cape Cod tern colonies, land bird populations, and migrating birds. Visitors today can see the site of these pioneering studies at the Massachusetts Audubon Society's Wellfleet Bay Sanctuary, which acquired the station in 1958.

Botanists have long been drawn to the Cape and Islands' unique community of plants, many of which are virtually restricted to the coastal plain of southeastern New England. One of these was the late Dr. Henry Svenson of Osterville, who first came to the Cape as a botany student in 1917. In 1979, *The Flora of Cape Cod*, an annotated list of local plants based on a lifetime of collecting, was published (with Robert W. Pyle) by the Cape Cod Museum of Natural History.

And finally, the Cape and Islands have attracted a long and impressive line of nature writers—including Henry David Thoreau, Henry Beston, and John Hay—who have interpreted both the natural and the human meaning of these sandy shores, producing a regional natural history literature unsurpassed in this country.

This rich tradition of informed and passionate curiosity about the local environment continues today, as represented by the individual contributors to this guide. In addition, research organizations such as the Center for Coastal Studies in Provincetown have continued the tradition of local marine research; their investigations of the natural history of offshore whale populations and the mechanics of coastal erosion have led to a greater understanding, not only of the local environment but of coastal ecology and systems in general. Other scientific communities, like the former New Alchemy Institute in Hatchville and Ocean Arks International in Falmouth, have experimented with novel applications of local resources—wind, aquaculture, organic recycling, and solar energy—aimed at developing models of more appropriate technology for such fragile ecosystems as ours. Research into wetland and pond systems within the Cape Cod National Seashore has led to greater understanding in the management of these critical resources. The Massachusetts Natural Heritage Program focuses on identifying and preserving critical habitat for this area's many rare and endangered plant and animal species. And with the development of a systemized archaeological artifact inventory at the Cape Cod Museum of Natural History, an accurate understanding of the long human past in this land is beginning to emerge.

In a sense we have now come full circle with those who first observed the nature of the Cape and Islands out of practical necessity, those who investigated it out of scientific curiosity, and the growing numbers who in recent decades have taken up nature study as a way of increasing their pleasure in the natural world. For now, by our sheer numbers and the disproportionate impact of our technology, our very affection for this place threatens our ability to live here and enjoy it.

We need to understand this land today in a way the older generations did not. It will still begin—or should begin—with spontaneous fascination or curiosity about a bright-winged bird, or a comically camouflaged crab, the mysterious comings and goings of broad, shallow tides over the flats, the grotesque form of a goose fish on the beach or the odd twisted shapes of trees on the sea cliffs, the sudden strandings of millions of squid or menhaden on the beaches, or the dramatic intensity of a line squall moving over the bay. It will begin with the universal wish to give a name to an unfamiliar animal, a plant, a shell, or a rock. Or the need to ask for simple explanations to small mysteries: why are Cape and Islands trees so small? Why are there so many ponds here? Why do whales beach themselves? Why does the ocean glow on some summer nights? Why do salt marshes smell like rotten eggs?

It may lead, in time, to the desire to investigate in depth the complex life cycles of marine species, the migration of birds or whales, the behavior of turtles, dragonflies, or horseshoe crabs. It may inspire some to seek more appropriate and benign solutions to the massive pressures we place upon these lands. It may even spark some imaginations to ask questions and explore mysteries for which we do not yet have adequate expression: why do we respond to the grace of a tern in flight? Why does the ocean at once so fascinate and terrify us? Why do our hearts lift with a rising shield of Canada geese over a frozen marsh or gladden with the antics of fiddler crabs? How is it that, barely a half century ago, we herded whales ashore to kill them for their oil, and today we strive with equal energy to save them when, for still unexplained reasons, they continue to beach themselves along our coasts? And why do these low, sandy peninsulas and islands—though we may be seeing them for the very first time—always seem so suddenly, powerfully, and nostalgically familiar?

The point is that, in our generation, the desire for such knowledge—at whatever level—has been led once again back to necessity, not simply to know, but to know why and how—why things are as they are, and how we must behave if we are to continue to enjoy them. Knowledge and love must become symbiotic, feeding off one another to the mutual benefit of both. That is the underlying aim and purpose of this guide. Only in this way will we once again come to understand what things here really mean, and so at last again deserve to call these irreplaceable places "home."

—Robert Finch
Brewster, Massachusetts

Acknowledgments

This revised and expanded edition of a *Guide to Nature on Cape Cod and the Islands* would not have been possible without the help and encouragement of many people. The book has been expanded to include more about the intriguing aspects of Cape and Island nature; it is meant to be an informative, entertaining, and useful guide to discovering the splendid—and at times, haunting—beauty that surrounds us on this fragile peninsula.

Special acknowledgments to Robert Cousins, who conceived of this book and who gave generous and thoughtful assistance to the editor during its revision, and to Mary Loebig, who has served the Cape Cod Museum of Natural History as a naturalist and educator. Her staff contributions are included in a section about answers to nature questions often asked at the museum in the pastoral Stony Brook Valley off Route 6A in Brewster. The section was edited by Cousins and O'Brien; some of the material was printed in the *Cape Codder* and the *Register* newspapers.

I also thank the following entities and organizations for their assistance: the Cape Cod National Seashore, the Massachusetts Audubon Society's Wellfleet Bay Sanctuary, the Center for Coastal Studies in Provincetown, the United States Geological Survey, the *Cape Codder* newspaper, the *Register* newspaper, and *Cape Cod Driftlines*, a Provincetown-based magazine dedicated to critical nature issues.

In addition, I thank Sue Orant; Alice Cousins; Fred Dunford; Steve and Terry Price; Frank and Virginia O'Brien; Bob Kelly; Greg McGrath; Nancy and Michael O'Malley; Barbara Hollis; Stephan Berrick, author of *Crabs of Cape Cod*; Ginger Carpenter and Martha

Bell of the Cape Cod Museum of Natural History's education staff; Sally Pearson; *Boston Magazine* for permission to adapt from an article on erosion previously published in the magazine; Tom Henze; Daniel Wilbur; Gordon Wright; Jack Weagraff; the late Paul Donham; and the late Arnie Manos, editor and publisher of *Cape Cod Driftlines*, for their various contributions and encouragements.

Special appreciation is also due my new publishers—Wally Exman and Walter Curley of Parnassus Imprints in Hyannis—for their fine direction and helpful suggestions on this project.

I thank my family: my wife, Mary Catherine, to whom I have dedicated this book and a partner with me in Stony Brook Press, and my three young children—Brendan, 11; Colleen, 8; and Conor, 6—whose love and understanding have sustained me this past year. And I acknowledge my parents, Frank and Virginia O'Brien, for introducing me to Cape Cod when I was a young boy and for instilling in me a deep respect for this land.

I express my enduring gratitude to the late Erma J. Fisk, known to her friends simply as "Jonnie," an author, lecturer, and friend of nature. Jonnie contributed to the chapter on birds and offered invaluable advice and expertise during the writing of the first edition.

And finally, I honor the late Malcolm Hobbs, former editor, publisher, owner, and soul of the *Cape Codder*—my mentor, my friend, and my inspiration for continuing the fight he began 46 years ago to preserve this Godly treasure surrounded by sea.

—Greg O'Brien
Brewster, Massachusetts

Part I

About the Contributors

This book was compiled and edited by a team of naturalists, writers, and researchers who have lived on Cape Cod for many years and who appreciate its beauty and desire to preserve it.

GREG O'BRIEN is editor and president of Stony Brook Press—a publishing and film production company in Brewster on Cape Cod Bay. He is former editor, publisher, and part-owner of Cape Cod Publishing Company, a group of 12 award-winning community newspapers, including the *Cape Codder* in Orleans and the *Register* of Yarmouthport.

O'Brien is former editor-in-chief and president of the *Cape Cod Business Journal* and has worked as senior writer at *Boston Magazine*, political reporter at the *Boston Herald American*, and investigative reporter at the *Arizona Republic* in Phoenix. He began his newspaper career in 1973 as a reporter at the *Cape Codder*. He also has contributed to the Associated Press, United Press International, and *USA Today*.

O'Brien is the editor of *An Insider's Guide to Cape Cod and the Islands* (Viking Penguin, 1988; a revised edition to be published by Parnassus Imprints), and editor and coauthor of *The Sea, The Land, The Life*, published by the Cape Codder Press. He is currently at work on a book about Cape Cod archaeology, and continues to contribute to *Boston Magazine, Cape Cod Life* magazine, and other regional and national publications.

He is a trustee of the Cape Cod Museum of Natural History in Brewster. He lives in the Stony Brook section of Brewster with his wife, Mary Catherine, and their three children.

ROBERT FINCH was principal advisor for this project and wrote the foreword, the chapter on woodlands, many of the answers to questions, and the epilogue. He assisted in every stage of this project.

A Harvard graduate, he is the author of several highly respected books on nature: *Common Ground: A Naturalist's Cape Cod* (David

R. Godine, 1981); *The Primal Place* (W.W. Norton, 1983); and *Outlands: Journeys to the Outer Edges of Cape Cod* (Godine, 1986). He is also co-editor of the *Norton Book of Nature Writing* (W.W. Norton, 1990) and editor of *A Place Apart: A Cape Cod Reader* (W.W. Norton, 1993).

Finch's articles and travel essays have been published in a wide variety of periodicals and journals, including; *Country Journal, New England Monthly, The New York Times, The Washington Post, The Boston Globe, Yankee, Cape Cod Compass, Family Circle* and *ORION Nature Quarterly*. In addition, his essays have been reprinted in several collections, including: *The Penguin Book of Contemporary American Essays* (Viking Penguin, 1984); *Barnet and Stubb's Practical Guide to Writing* (Little, Brown, 1985); *On Nature* (North Point Press, 1987); and *The Bread Loaf Anthology of Contemporary American Essays* (University Press of New England, 1989). He has also written the introductions to a number of books.

The civic-minded Finch is former co-chairman of the Brewster Conservation Commission and former co-chairman of the Brewster Land Acquisition Committee. He also has served as director of publications for the Cape Cod Museum of Natural History. He is the father of two children: Christopher and Katherine. He lives in West Brewster.

ROBERT COUSINS, who served as chief consultant for this book, is consultant to Stony Brook Press. He is a retired vice president of *Reader's Digest* and editorial director of the company's General Books division. He is a former executive editor at McGraw-Hill Book Company and editorial director of the *World Book Encyclopedia*, McGraw-Hill multivolume series, *Our Living World of Nature*. He is a former chairman of the Editorial Committee, National Council, Boy Scouts of America.

Cousins, a former contributor to the old *Saturday Review*, is an editorial consultant to major corporations here and abroad, and is a volunteer editorial consultant to the Cape Cod National Seashore, the U.S. Department of Interior, and the National Park Service.

He lives in Palm Coast, Florida, and East Orleans, Massachusetts, with his wife, Alice.

ROBERT OLDALE, a geologist for the United States Geological Survey since 1955, wrote the chapter on geology and is an expert on glaciers, glacial deposits, and sea-level history. He has conducted marine and land geological and geophysical studies of Massachusetts and the Atlantic continental margin. He has mapped the geology of Nantucket, Martha's Vineyard, and Cape Cod and has authored and coauthored more than 100 scientific publications. He is the author of *Cape Cod and the Islands—the Geologic Story*, published by Parnassus Imprints.

Oldale is a Fellow of the Geological Society of America and a member of the American Quaternary Association.

JOHN HAY, one of New England's most distinguished naturalists and the author of eleven books on nature, wrote the chapter on the mysteries and marvels of the Cape and Islands. He is the former president of the Cape Cod Museum of Natural History and one of the museum's founders. He has taught environmental writing at Dartmouth College each fall.

Hay's books, many of them focusing on Cape Cod wilderness and wildlife, include: *The Run, The Great Beach, The Undiscovered Country, A Private History, Nature's Year, A Sense of Nature, The Atlantic Shore, In Defense of Nature, The Primal Alliance: Earth and Ocean, Spirit of Survival,* and *The Immortal Wilderness.*

A Burroughs Award winner, he lives in West Brewster.

ERMA FISK, known to her friends as Jonnie, was the author of four books on birds, *The Peacocks of Baboquivari, A Birdwatcher's Cookbook, The Bird with the Silver Bracelet,* and *Parrots' Wood.* She wrote the chapter on birds.

She was a trustee of the Cape Cod Museum of Natural History and was active with the museum for many years. She lived in South Orleans.

DONALD ZINN, former president of both the National Wildlife Federation and the Cape Cod Museum of Natural History, wrote the chapter on the seashore. An enthusiastic collector of New England mollusks for more than fifty years, he has been a professor emeritus of zoology at the University of Rhode Island and former chairman of the university's zoology department. Zinn first came to the Cape in 1932 to take a course in invertebrate zoology at the Marine Biological Laboratory in Woods Hole, where he later conducted research in zooplankton and worked as a naturalist.

Currently a senior fellow of the Cape Cod Museum of Natural History and clerk of the New England Resources Center, headquartered in Boston, Zinn is the author of two books: *Marine Mollusks of Cape Cod* (published by the Cape Cod Museum of Natural History) and *The Handbook for Beach Strollers,* a popular guide to beachcombing.

Zinn lives in Falmouth where he is a member of the town's historical commission.

RICHARD LEBLOND, a former botanical researcher at the Center for Coastal Studies in Provincetown, wrote the chapter on wetlands. He is the former editor of *The Cape Naturalist*, a journal published by the Cape Cod Museum of Natural History, and has written a nature column for four weekly newspapers on the Cape: the *Cape Codder*, the *Register*, the *Advocate*, and the *Enterprise*. He is a former administrator for the National Park Service and contributes to various local and regional publications. He lives in Provincetown.

JOHN PORTNOY, chief biologist of the Cape Cod National Seashore, wrote the chapter on ponds. For the past ten years, he has conducted studies of lake and wetland ecologies for the National Park Service. He has researched and published many articles on zoology, wildlife, kettle ponds, mosquito biology, and salt marsh restoration. He lives with his family in Wellfleet.

ROBERT BARLOW, former president of the Cape Cod Museum of Natural History and a member of its board of trustees, wrote the chapter on weather. A scientist by training, he has supervised science, math, and environmental studies in the Dennis-Yarmouth school system on the Cape. He is also a botanist and lecturer and has worked as a seasonal ranger-naturalist at the Cape Cod National Seashore since 1966.

A free-lance writer, he contributes to many local and regional publications and has written a weekly nature column for the *Cape Codder*, the *Register,* and the *Valley Voice* in Middlebury, Vermont. He is the author of a self-guiding book on high school mathematics and is an incorporator of the Yarmouth Conservation Trust. Barlow lives with his wife in Yarmouthport.

MARIO DIGREGORIO, a former conservation administrator for the town of Brewster and an environmental consultant, wrote the answers to many of the questions in this book. He is the coauthor of two books: *Wildflowers of the Cape Cod Canal* and *A Vanishing Heritage, Wildflowers of Cape Cod.*

A botanist, DiGregorio has conducted field work for the Massachusetts Natural Heritage Program, a division of the Department of Fisheries and Wildlife, and has been a park ranger at many national parks throughout the country. He lives with his wife in Sandwich.

PETER TRULL, former education coordinator at the Cape Cod Museum of Natural History and a former warden for the Massachusetts Audubon Society, answered many of the questions in this book. He is an expert on birds and writes and has produced a local radio broadcast on the subject.

A free-lance writer, Trull has contributed to many nature publications, such as *American Birds, Massachusetts Wildlife,* and the *Cape Naturalist.* He lives in Chatham.

ROBERT PRESCOTT, director of the Massachusetts Audubon Society's Wellfleet Bay Sanctuary in Wellfleet, contributed answers to many of the questions in this book. He is former education director of the Cape Cod Museum of Natural History.

A biologist and free-lance writer, Prescott is an expert in marine animals and contributes to many local and regional publications, as well as scientific journals.

LARRY FOX provided assistance in editing this book. He is former managing editor of the *Cape Codder* and has written frequently on nature and environmental issues. He is former executive sports editor of the *New York Daily News* and before that was a sports columnist and writer for the *Daily News* and other major newspapers. He is the author of seventeen books and numerous magazine articles.

He and his wife, Kathryn, live in Brewster, overlooking a wetland.

DONALD G. SCHALL, who assisted in editing this book, is a wetland biologist with 18 years of professional experience in public education and conservation studies. As former director and educational curator for the Cape Cod Museum of Natural History, Schall directed an educational program that presented environmental issues, biological classes, and natural history programs. With an education in biology and forest science, Schall has served as an instructor at Cape Cod Community College and on local conservation commissions, and as a private wetland consultant. He is currently a wetland biologist for IEP, Inc. of Sandwich.

JOHN LODICO, who contributed to the section on nature trails, is a former staff writer for the *Cape Codder* newspaper. After attending college in Washington, D.C., where he edited George Washington University's literary and arts magazine, he covered Congress and the transportation industry for *Traffic World* magazine. He was associate editor at the *Register* on Cape Cod for two and a half years, and has contributed free-lance articles to a variety of publications.

KATHY ROLBEIN is the artist who drew the wonderful illustrations for this book. She is former art director of the *Cape Codder* and the *Cape Cod Business Journal*. Her illustrations have appeared in many publications and her work is displayed at art galleries on the Cape.

She also drew the illustrations for *An Insider's Guide to Cape Cod and the Islands*, published by Stephen Greene Press in May 1988. She lives in Orleans.

MARY LOEBIG has worked at the Cape Cod Museum of Natural History as a naturalist and educator. She is a teacher and lives in South Dennis.

THE CAPE COD MUSEUM OF NATURAL HISTORY, along scenic Route 6A in Brewster, has always stressed recognition and awareness of the local environment. Since the museum's beginnings in 1954, much of the world has come to realize the importance of this for its own survival. But the importance of recognition lies not only in protecting the land that supports us but in nourishing and enriching our own lives as well.

The museum was created to offer education in natural history for Cape residents and visitors to this peninsula; it is designed to encourage public understanding of the natural environment, to further its conservation and wise use, to provide a center for re-search in natural history, and to collect and display natural history exhibits.

The museum owns 80 acres in the Stony Brook Valley of Brewster and 132 acres in Osterville. Both properties, maintained in their natural settings, are home to wildfowl, wildlife, and several bird species. Guided field walks, open to the public, are regularly sched-uled at both locations.

Introduction

by Greg O'Brien

Cape Cod is indeed a place for children, or for those with the eyes and innocence of a child. For it takes a child's curiosity, desire for discovery, and sense of wonderment to appreciate fully the majesty of Cape Cod and its neighboring islands of Martha's Vineyard, Nantucket, and the Elizabeth chain—from the steep, clay cliffs of Gay Head on the Vineyard; to Nantucket's storybook harbor; to the clear, deep kettle ponds, round as a beach ball, of Wellfleet; to the sparkling salt marshes of Barnstable; to the tall pine forests of Falmouth and Sandwich. This is a book written for the questioning child in all of us.

I remember as a young boy marveling at the flats of Cape Cod Bay where the tide goes out in Brewster for almost a mile; it was as if someone had pulled a plug. I wondered where all the water went and why.

I can remember the first night I sat on a sand dune in the highlands of Truro and looked up at a clear moonless sky, a stark black canvas that had been flecked with a million specks of white. The sight was exhilarating, yet why did it make me feel so small?

I was always in awe of the graceful herring gull skimming the surface of the sea in search of another meal and ever amazed at the force of waves as they broke in steady rhythm on the lip of the beach. Where did these gulls nest? And what caused the ocean's soothing cadence?

I remember catching hermit crabs by the pail and watching in bewilderment as jellyfish slipped through the cracks between my fingers. Why did the crabs pinch and the jellyfish ooze?

Like many of my young friends, I also wondered about such things as: do fish sleep? How fast is a snail's pace? And why does the water often glow at night? The questions stumped my parents, too.

My universe, as a child, was the beach. But as I grew older I came to understand Cape Cod and the Islands as a collection of fragile and fascinating ecosystems—communities of related plants and animals dependent upon the same healthy environment. I grasped the wisdom of Henry David Thoreau who wrote, "Drink in the soft influence and sublime revelations of nature."

This book explores these revelations and focuses on ecosystems that include the seashore, ponds, wetlands, and woodlands; it highlights features of the Cape and Islands' environment, as well as plant and animal species that are common, conspicuous, and mystifying. It tells you what to look for and where to find it. It also contains listings of trails and sanctuaries on the Cape and Islands where the entire family can experience firsthand the nature described in these pages. At the end of each chapter are questions and answers that seek to satisfy the most inquisitive mind.

This guide reflects the research and writings of some of New England's foremost naturalists and scientists and the considerable educational resources of the Cape Cod Museum of Natural History in Brewster. Also contributing to the project were the Cape Cod National Seashore, the Massachusetts Audubon Society, the Center for Coastal Studies in Provincetown, and the United States Geological Survey.

Our goal, simple as nature itself, is to educate, stimulate, and entertain—to create interest and greater understanding in the fascinating natural world around us through the writings of our renowned contributors.

Naturalist and author John Hay unfolds the many mysteries and marvels of the region. Did you know, for instance, that codfish lay millions of eggs, while the common skate lays just one at a time in protective cases called "mermaids' purses?" Ornithologist Erma Fisk describes the Cape and Islands as a flyway for more than 300 species of birds. Donald J. Zinn, renowned zoologist and educator, describes the various zones of the seashore, from the dunes to the area beyond the tidal flats, and explains how waves are formed, shorelines are shaped, and plant and animal life survives. John Portnoy, chief biologist at the Cape Cod National Seashore, takes us through a year in the life of a typical Cape and Islands pond, detailing how sunlight is converted to food, how pond water is warmed, how algae can choke life, and how a pond transforms over many years to a marsh, swamp, and eventually upland. Richard LeBlond, former chief botanist at the Center for Coastal Studies in Provincetown, tells us the difference between a salt marsh and a freshwater marsh. He explains why wetlands are so biologically productive and hence why they must be protected, and he illustrates with graphic word pictures why our wetlands are among the finest in the world. Focusing on our woodlands, naturalist and author Robert Finch takes us back to the arrival of the Pilgrims in 1620 when the region was heavily forested. But the land, he notes, was clear-cut by settlers to the point in the 1800s that the Cape and Islands were almost barren. The forests, mostly pitch pine, gradually reestablished, but today the pitch pine, the most common tree on Cape Cod, is being muscled out by the oak, which will become the region's dominant tree in years ahead. Finch also tells us how plant and animal life have been affected by these changes. Robert Barlow, a scientist and teacher, provides a primer on Cape and Islands weather, which has more unexpected ups and downs than a Boston Red Sox team. Barlow describes the many factors that affect local weather—information helpful in making your day-to-day plans.

In his epilogue, Finch speaks of the need to appreciate and preserve our environment—a theme that dates as far back as the late 1500s when French essayist Michel Montaigne wrote, "Let us give nature a chance; she knows her business better than we do."

We start our journey through Cape and Island ecosystems at the very beginning, many thousands of years ago during the Ice Age. Geologist Robert Oldale gives us a scientific explanation of how the region was formed; we follow with an explanation of the forces that are carving it away.

Geologically speaking, Cape Cod existed before there was a Cape Cod, much as it can be said that Michelangelo's *Pietà* existed within the marble before the extraneous stone was chipped away or the way there is lurking in every mighty ash a baseball bat waiting to be delivered to the major leagues. Millions of years ago, the North American continent actually extended as a land mass approximately 100 miles farther east than it does now. The area resembled what is known today as a coastal plain. The exposed continental shelf was a patchwork of open pine forests and grasslands and 10,000 years ago was inhabited by Native Americans, according to Fred Dunford, an archaeologist at the Cape Cod Museum of Natural History.

But nature, as it does today, was to have its way. The vast expanse of continental shelf, according to Dunford, was laced with rivers and bogs that were soon to be drowned by the rapidly rising Atlantic, which ultimately will claim our islands and this entire spit of land we call Cape Cod.

How Cape Cod and the Islands Were Formed

by Robert N. Oldale

The Cape and Islands owe their existence to a continental glacier and to the sea. Continental glaciers characterize the Pleistocene epoch— the great ice age—that began about a million and a half years ago. Great masses of ice, called ice sheets, formed during glacial stages when the energy from the sun received at the Earth's surface was diminished. During an interglacial stage, the world climate was about what it is today. Variations in the amount of sun energy reaching the Earth are mostly the result of cyclical changes in the Earth's orbit and changes in the inclination of the Earth's pole of rotation. Thus, the present geological epoch, the Holocene, may not mark the end of the great ice age, was once thought, but may be only the latest interglacial stage.

As the Earth's climate cools, more snow falls during the winter than can melt during the summer. The snow accumulates layer upon layer, and the deeper layers are compressed to form ice. Ice will flow under pressure supplied by its own weight, and when the ice is thick enough to deform and flow, it becomes a glacier. The Laurentide ice sheet, the last of the great ice ace glaciers in North America, began to form in Canada about 75,000 years ago, at the beginning of the Wisconsinan Glacial Stage. For much of the Wisconsinan Stage, the Laurentide ice

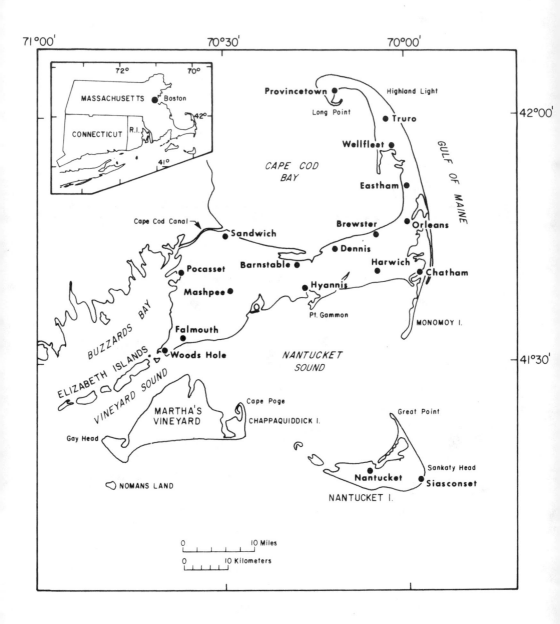

Index map of the Cape and Islands.

sheet was mostly confined within the borders of Canada, but about 25,000 years ago it advanced into New England, and reached the Cape and Islands about 21,000 years ago. Here, in a more temperate climate, the advance stopped. Thereafter, the retreat began, as melting at the glacier margin exceeded the rate of ice advance. As the glacier advanced, it scraped up soil and loose sediments and gouged and plucked fragments of the solid rock that lay beneath the ice. These materials were carried forward in the base of the ice and deposited along the glacier margin to form moraines, or carried beyond the edge of the ice by meltwater streams to form outwash plains. These landforms characterize the glacial Cape and Islands.

The glacial deposits on the islands of Martha's Vineyard and Nantucket were laid down earliest, at the maximum extent of the ice, and those on the Elizabeth Islands and Cape Cod were deposited somewhat after the Laurentide ice sheet had begun its retreat. At the close of the Wisconsinan Glacial Stage, the great continental glaciers retreated throughout the Northern Hemisphere, and water—formerly trapped in ice on the continents—returned to the ocean, where sea level began to rise (discussed in the section on erosion to follow).

During glaciation and for some time after the retreat of the ice, the sea level was about 400 feet lower than it is today. Much of the continental shelf south of Nantucket and Martha's Vineyard was exposed. Mastodon, mammoth, and other mammals of the Ice Age, and possibly early man, roamed the pine forests and meadows of this coastal plain, now submerged. About 6,000 years ago, the rising sea reached the glacial deposits of the Cape and Islands. Waves eroded the loose glacial sand and gravel to form sea cliffs. Waves and currents transported and redeposited this material to form beaches. Winds picked up the sand from the beaches and cliff faces and deposited it in the form of coastal sand dunes. Barrier beaches grew lengthwise, partly closing off embayments in the glacial landscape and forming lagoons protected from the open ocean. In these quiet shallow waters, salt marshes developed. The barrier beach, dune, and salt marsh together make up a barrier island. Barrier islands and sea cliffs are the dominant coastal landforms of the Cape and Islands.

Today, the sea continues to rise and continues to erode the glacial deposits. The barrier islands are migrating landward as sections of the barrier island are breached or washed over by storm waves, and new sections are built by longshore drift during more quiescent times.

This brief account has described only the most recent events in the geologic history of the Cape and Islands. We will now focus on the rocks and landforms that represent events in the geologic history of the region.

The Foundation

For the most part, the rocks that record events before the ice age are deeply buried by the glacial deposits, and their nature and origin are known from a few exposures and from a few drill holes. The glacial and marine deposits are underlaid by much older bedrock similar to the rock that can be seen in highway cuts and along the "rock bound coast" of New England north and west of the Cape Cod Canal, and by pre-glacial loose uncemented sedimentary rock that overlies the bedrock.

Bedrock beneath the Cape and Islands is more than 150 million years old. Some of the igneous rocks, such as granite, cooled and solidified deep in the earth's crust from molten material, whereas other igneous rocks are volcanic, formed at the earth's surface much like the rocks formed by the recent eruption of Mount St. Helens. Sedimentary rocks were laid down layer by layer in ancient lakes and seas. Many of these igneous and sedimentary rocks were later deeply buried and deformed by mountain building forces. Some had their appearance and mineralogy changed by heat and pressure. These altered rocks are called metamorphic.

On the Cape and Islands, the igneous, consolidated sedimentary rock and metamorphic rock lie hundreds to thousands of feet underground. However, the Laurentide ice sheet eroded and transported fragments of bedrock during its advance to the Cape and Islands; New England bedrock is abundantly represented by the stones that we find in the glacial deposits and on the beaches, such as Nauset Beach in East Orleans and Coast Guard Beach in Eastham on the Cape, Gay Head on Martha's Vineyard, and along Eel Point on Nantucket.

The largest glacially transported boulder known on the Cape and Islands is Enos or Doane Rock in Eastham on Cape Cod. This half-buried, greenish-gray volcanic boulder is 40 feet long by 25 feet wide and projects 15 feet above the ground. The boulder may have originally come from the vicinity of Boston, but is more likely to have been picked up by the glacier from somewhere to the east in the Gulf of Maine because it was deposited by ice that came from that direction. Doane Rock is located about a mile down Doane Road from the Cape

Cod National Seashore's Salt Pond Visitor Center. There is a parking lot at the site.

Loose, uncemented sedimentary rocks that are much younger than the bedrock and much older than the glacial deposits formed during the last part of the age of dinosaurs (the Cretaceous period) and the early part of the age of the mammals (the Tertiary period) perhaps 5 to 140 million years ago. These rocks are mostly found deep beneath Martha's Vineyard and Nantucket. But a few are exposed in the Gay Head Cliffs where they have yielded abundant plant fossils, fossils of fish including shark teeth, and fossils of mammals including ancient rhinoceros, elephant, seal, and whale. On Cape Cod, shelly limestone, fossilized wood, and shark's teeth can be found in the glacial deposits. The Cretaceous and Tertiary rocks were deposited on the continental shelf and coastal plain, and are similar to rock layers that underlie the Atlantic margin in New Jersey.

Ice Age deposits older than the glacial deposits that form the Cape and Islands are exposed in the Gay Head Cliffs and in Sankaty Head cliff on Nantucket. Deposits on Nantucket include both glacial and warm water marine interglacial deposits that represent the next to last glacial stage that ended about 130,000 years ago, and the interglacial stage that followed and ended with the beginning of the Wisconsinan Glacial Stage, about 75,000 years ago.

The Glacial Deposits

Ice at the base of a glacier contains abundant rock debris that consists of an assorted mixture of boulder-sized fragments to microscopic-sized clay particles. The debris is carried forward as the ice advances. Some is plastered onto the surface beneath the ice. Later, any debris remaining in the base of the ice is deposited when the ice melts. Rock debris deposited directly from the ice is called till. Till can be seen in sea cliffs in Eastham on Cape Cod, in the Gay Head Cliffs on Martha's Vineyard, and at Sankaty Head cliff on Nantucket.

Most of the debris carried by the glacier is transported beyond the ice margin by meltwater streams. Meltwater deposits are layered and called outwash. Meltwater flows through the glacier by way of crevasses and tunnels within and beneath the ice. As it flows, it gathers rock debris from the base of the ice and carries it to the ice front. Beyond the ice front, the meltwater forms glacial streams that enter glacial lakes or the sea. Meltwater streams transport rock fragments of all sizes from boulders to clay. Changes in the speed of the water flow sorts the debris, leaving behind fragments too big to carry. Generally the streams flow fastest near the ice and slow gradually with increasing distance from the ice margin. Thus, outwash is coarsest near the ice, where it includes large boulders and coarse gravel, and becomes progressively finer grained downstream (where it is mostly sand and gravel). When meltwater streams enter a lake or the sea, the current slows rapidly and sand and gravel is deposited in the standing water near the shore to from a delta. Weaker currents carry the finer particles, mostly silt and clay, offshore to where they are deposited on the lake bottom or sea floor.

Meltwater streams are shallow and broad, with numerous channels that are separated by sand and gravel bars in a braided pattern. As they form, the braided streams sweep back and forth across a relatively flat surface. The streams are braided because they have rapid changes in flow. Glacial streams carry large amounts of water during the afternoon and early evening, as the temperature rises and melting increases; they carry relatively low amounts of water at night and early morning, when the temperature falls and melting slows. As the volume of water diminishes, the streams drop much of their sediment load; later, as the amount of water increases again, the stream finds a new course around the previously deposited material. In this way, they construct broad gently sloping outwash plains or outwash fans.

Glacial Landforms

The most common landforms on the Cape and Islands that owe their existence to the glacier are ridges known as end moraines and broad gently sloping surfaces known as outwash plains.

Prominent end moraines occur along the northwest side of Martha's Vineyard (Martha's Vineyard Moraine); in the eastern part of Nantucket (Nantucket Moraine); along the shore of Buzzards Bay, including the Elizabeth Islands chain southwest of Woods Hole (Buzzards Bay Moraine); and on inner Cape Cod parallel to Cape Cod Bay (Sandwich Moraine).

Many end moraines are composed mostly of till, formed when debris carried in the ice melts out and is dumped along the stationary front of a glacier, in roughly the same manner that a conveyer belt carries material and dumps it at its end. However, the great moraines of the Cape and Islands were not formed in this way. They were formed

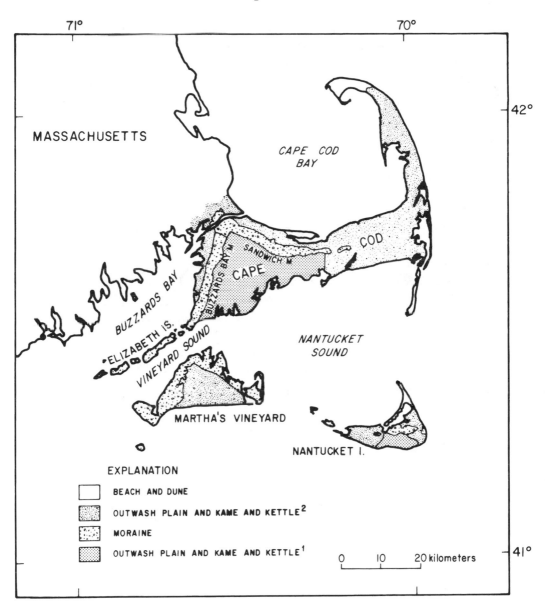

Generalized geologic map of the Cape and Islands showing the distribution and relative age of the moraines and outwash plains and the distribution of beach and dune. [1]Outwash plains and kame and kettle terrain older than the adjacent moraine. [2]Outwash plains and kame and kettle terrain younger than the adjacent moraine.

when the glacier advanced and deformed the deposits that lay ahead of it. Blocks of material were pushed forward and upward to form ranks of ridges that together make up the moraine. In this way they are more like a mountain range. The displaced and folded layers can most easily be seen in the Martha's Vineyard Moraine, where a cross section of the moraine is exposed in the Gay Head Cliffs. There blocks of Cretaceous and Tertiary age sediments are overlaid and underlaid by layers of till. Elsewhere on the Cape and Islands, the moraines are underlaid by glacial stream deposits and glacial lake deposits that have been pushed and folded to form the moraines.

The moraines form segments of two moraine belts that loop across the islands from western Long Island, New York, to Nantucket (the southern belt) and across the southern New England mainland from Connecticut to Cape Cod (the northern belt). The looping moraine segments show that the southern margin of the Laurentide ice sheet was characterized by glacial lobes that formed in broad bedrock basins. The positions of the lobes and the angles between them are the cause of the roughly triangular shape of Martha's Vineyard and Nantucket and the flexed arm shape of Cape Cod.

The end moraines on Martha's Vineyard and Nantucket represent the greatest advance of the ice sheet. The Buzzards Bay and Sandwich moraines were formed during the overall retreat of the ice when the glacier temporarily readvanced.

Outwash plains, gently sloping flat surfaces, are the most common glacial landform on the Cape and Islands. They were formed by braided meltwater streams that deposited sand and gravel beyond the glacier front. The upstream end of the outwash plains was underlaid by the glacier. When the ice melted, the surface collapsed forming a hummocky area, called an ice-contact head, that sloped steeply toward the glacier. There are few ice-contact heads of outwash preserved; many were overridden when the moraines were formed and others have been eroded by the sea. A preserved ice-contact head can be seen on the south side of Route 6A in the towns of Dennis and Brewster on inner Cape Cod. The outwash plain surfaces are, in places, interrupted by holes that formed when large blocks of ice left behind by the retreating glacier and buried by the outwash plain deposits melted away, causing the surface to collapse. These holes are called kettles. In some places, parts of the outwash plain were underlaid by numerous ice blocks so that when the ice melted, the surface collapsed completely to form a hummocky surface called kame and kettle. Many

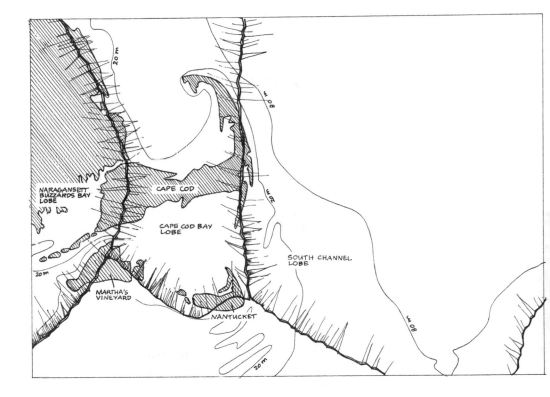

Map showing the approximate limit of the Laurentide ice sheet, the glacial lobes, and the approximate location of the interlobate angles during ice retreat. Depths of ice below sea level (in meters) shown by thin lines.

kettles are deep enough to reach the water table and contain kettle lakes and ponds. Others, breached and drowned by the sea, form salt ponds such as Salt Pond in Eastham, adjacent to the Cape Cod National Seashore visitors center.

The Marine Deposits

The encroachment of the sea during the Holocene epoch is the other major factor in the formation of the deposits that make up the Cape and Islands. Waves have eroded the glacial deposits and moved them to the sea. The beach deposits are formed when the waves return sand to the shore to build narrow strands at the base of sea cliffs and barrier beaches across bays and estuaries. The waves transporting the sand rush up the beach obliquely and the water returns to the sea directly down the slope of the beach. In this way, sand grains are transported along the beach following a saw-tooth path, a process known as longshore drift. When an embayment in the coast is encountered, the longshore drift deposits sand across the mouth of the embayment to form a barrier beach. Sand, silt, and clay have been transported into the bays by the tides where they are deposited to form sand flats and mud flats. Carried farther into the bays, these sediments are deposited along with decaying salt marsh vegetation to form the salt marsh deposits. Salt marsh plants grow near sea level and thus the salt marsh deposits preserve a record of sea-level rise that on the Cape and Islands covers about the last 6,000 years.

Although not strictly a marine deposit, dune sand is closely associated with the sea. The beaches and sea cliffs provide the source of the dune sand. Strong onshore winds pick up sand from the cliff face, carry it upward, and deposit it at the top of the cliff or pick up sand from the beaches and carry it inland. During its passage inland, the wind slows and drops its load of sand to form dunes that cap the barrier beach.

Coastal Landforms

The sea cliff is perhaps the most dramatic landform created by the environment of the sea. Rising abruptly above the sea, the cliffs are more than 100 feet high in many places and reach heights of more than 150 feet along the east shore of the Great Outer Beach in Wellfleet and Truro. This great cliff is more than fifteen miles long and would be an impenetrable barrier except for the hollows or valleys that interrupt the cliff in places. Today, the hollows provide access to the beach for swimmers, windsurfers, and fishermen. In the past, they were the only way rescuers could reach vessels stranded on the beach. Most of the cliffs are exposed to the sea, and from time to time they are eroded by storm waves. In other places they are protected from the sea by barrier islands. These inactive or fossil sea cliffs are usually covered by vegetation (for example, High Head in Truro), or built upon—as is the sea cliff in the village of Nantucket. The protection offered by the barrier islands may be temporary and the inactive cliffs may again be attacked by the sea.

Beaches occur as narrow strands at the bases of sea cliffs or as barriers; long, low, narrow peninsulas bordered by the sea and by bays and salt marshes. Barrier beaches are recurved or hooked at their ends. The hooking is the result of wave refraction around the end of the barrier, which changes the direction of the longshore drift and consequently the trend of the barrier beach. Good examples of recurved barrier beaches include Race Point and Long Point on Provincetown spit, Cape Pogue on Martha's Vineyard, and Great Point on Nantucket.

Coastal dunes that cap the barrier beaches and top the sea cliffs are dynamic landforms that have many shapes. The dunes are shaped by the prevailing wind and have gentle upwind slopes and steep downwind slopes. In this way, they are similar to snow drifts. They are shaped by the winds in other ways. On the Provincetown spit, there are "U"-shaped dunes with the open end facing the wind. They are formed when the wind blows away the sand in the middle, sometimes exposing the underlying beach deposits, and drops it downwind along the advancing face of the dune. Other dunes form gently curved ridges that may have been deposited on ancient recurved spits. The most seaward dune atop barrier beaches parallels the shore and is called a foredune. During storms, the foredune acts to preserve the barrier island by protecting it from overwash. Clifftop dunes form a narrow band along the coast. Youthful unstabilized dunes are on the move as sand is transported by the prevailing wind. Older dunes become stablilized by vegetation including dune grass and forests. However, if they lose the protective vegetation, they will be on the move again. This can be seen along U.S. Route 6 in Provincetown, where once stabile dunes are advancing on the forest and highway and are filling Pilgrim Lake.

Salt marshes are flat horizontal surfaces that lie at about mean high tide and are covered by salt tolerant grasses and reeds. Tidal creeks meander across the marsh and carry the tidal waters that cover the marsh twice each day. They form in areas sheltered from the open ocean by barrier islands, in drowned outwash plain valleys, and in kettles that have been breached by the sea.

Man as a Geologic Agent

Today, man himself is a geologic factor in the development of the Cape and Islands. Through his activities natural processes are influenced and the landscape is modified. Some examples: the creation of sand and gravel pits—an eyesore to many but a delight to geologists because they provide exposures to help us understand the nature and origin of glacial deposits; public works—such as erosion control, harbor maintenance, schools and hospitals, roads, water and sewer facilities; the construction of power lines, telephone lines, and gas lines. Few would argue that these intrusions by man are not necessary, but equally important is an understanding of whether they are good or bad for the natural environment.

Consider this: efforts to control the erosion of sea cliffs and to control changes in the barrier islands through construction of sea walls, jetties, and hardening or filling breaches may limit the sand supply necessary for the survival of the barrier islands. The construction of houses or condominiums on coastal land comes with risks—risks that should be recognized and accepted by property owners, because ultimately these structures are likely to suffer damage or be destroyed by northeast storms or hurricanes. Thus, arguments in favor of protecting these structures from flooding and wave attack should be carefully weighed.

In addition, the quality of the water supply can easily and quickly be degraded. Leaking fuel tanks; inadequate handling of dump, septic, and hazardous wastes; and the uncontrolled loading of nutrients, such as nitrates and other fertilizers, into the ground are all serious threats to the water supply and to the quality of our lakes, ponds, bays, and marshes.

The best time to recognize man's adverse impact on the natural landscape and water supply may already have passed; however, much can be done now to preserve what is left and, in many cases, to restore the natural environment and to begin a much-needed process of healing.

The Forces of Erosion

by Greg O'Brien

The old summer house was falling into the sea. The timbers of the building groaned as the crowd watched in anticipation from the beach. The house, its clapboards gray from decades of weathering, inched forward on its foundation, then fell back again as the rolling surf pounded the entryway and climbed the wall to the roof.

The wind was blowing hard from the northeast, and the building shivered with each gust. The cold January air was heavy with a salty mist that caked the windows and coated the shutters. There was speculation that six other homes, mere feet from the shoreline, would soon fall victim to the elements. It was just a matter of time.

Finally, late in the afternoon, the ocean's appetite grew to house-sized proportions, and, after one last assault, the old structure that had been home to generations of fishermen and their families lurched forward again. There was a loud snap, then twenty tons of timber, shingles, and nails collapsed into Cape Cod Bay.

The scene was not Chatham, where homes have been sliding into the Atlantic with frightening regularity. It was Billingsgate Island in the 1880s, a sixty-acre patch of land off Wellfleet that was lost to the sea. Houses that weren't swamped were floated on barges to Wellfleet, Truro, and Brewster where they remain today, a memorial to the destructive forces of nature here.

Billingsgate was once a fishing village off Jeremy's Point that harbored thirty-five families, a lighthouse, a school, and even a base-ball team. Now all that is left of this island, first explored in 1620 by the Pilgrims, is a sandbar that surfaces at low tide.

The forces of nature have for thousands of years carved away at Cape Cod and the Islands and will continue to whittle this narrow land until there is nothing left. The good news is that every home eventually will have a water view. The bad news is that many generations from now the Cape and Islands will be worn to a few sandy shoals. No number of man-made jetties, rock revetments, or sandbags will stem this inexorable tide.

Parts of the Cape and Islands are losing five acres or more a year to marine erosion. But a greater threat to the shoreline is the rise in sea level brought on by a global warming trend, called the greenhouse effect by some, which will melt polar ice caps at alarming rates. Scientists predict that in the next forty years the shoreline from Provincetown to Bourne will retreat approximately 100 feet, and by the year 2100 more than 1,200 feet of shoreline may be underwater. The warming trend is also expected to cause more storms, which in turn will result in greater erosion. Adding to this problem is the fact that while the sea level is rising, some coastal areas of the Cape and Islands, formed from silt sediments, are actually sinking—slowly compressing under their own weight.

The center of Provincetown, at the Cape's slender fist, faces the most immediate crisis. "And I think you can measure it in tens, not hundreds of years," says Robert Oldale, a geologist and erosion expert with the United States Geological Survey office in Woods Hole and author of the previous chapter. Oldale predicts the center of town, with its scores of shops and fine restaurants, will flood soon with every major storm. "They are either going to have to dike it, as the Dutch did in Holland, or they are going to have to raise the whole town," he says.

Provincetown and Chatham aren't the only areas on the Cape facing severe erosion. Others include Falmouth Heights, where the cliff is falling into Vineyard Sound and undermining the coastal road above it; Sandwich and West Barnstable, where beaches like Sandy Neck can lose 15 feet in one storm; Mashpee, where the shoreline is eroding from Waquoit Bay to Popponesset Bay and exposing high-priced homes to the sea; Dennis on the bay side, where the popular Corporation and Cold Storage beaches are losing ground; and Eastham, Wellfleet, and Truro on the ocean and bay sides, where homeowners are moving their houses back from the bluffs. The tower site in Wellfleet from which Guglielmo Marconi sent the first transatlantic cable message, eight decades ago, from President Theodore Roosevelt to England's King Edward VII, is now more than 200 feet out to sea.

The same uncompromising forces are at play on Nantucket, Martha's Vineyard, and the neighboring Elizabeth Islands, all part of the same moraines and outwash plains that formed Cape Cod. Time is running out for Nantucket: on the east, south, and west shores, from Great Point to Siasconset to Madaket, beaches of this low-lying sand spit are losing an average of ten to thirty feet a year. That's impressive when you consider the island is only about three and a half miles wide and fourteen miles long.

"I would give this island a life expectancy of 700 to 800 years," predicts Wes Tiffney, a geologist and botanist who has directed the University of Massachusetts field station on Nantucket. The "old gray lady," as the island is often called, will be under the sea before the year 3000, he says.

Martha's Vineyard, which is losing shoreline at the same rate on its northeastern, eastern, and southern shores, faces a similar fate. "But I would anticipate that Martha's Vineyard would last quite a bit longer than Nantucket," says Tiffney, noting the island is more sheltered and twice the size of Nantucket.

But in the end, nothing will stop the advancing tides. "What can be done?" asks Graham Giese, an oceanographer with the Provincetown Center for Coastal Studies who has studied Chatham's North Beach cut extensively. "There may be temporary and partial answers of varying complexity and practicality, but the single final answer is very simple: nothing," Giese has written. "Nothing can be done to prevent the erosion of the shore of Cape Cod. To the person whose house sits imperiled at the edge of the sea, this may be a distressing state of affairs. He is unlikely to realize that the Cape is merely a temporary deposit of glacial sediment, pausing briefly in the geological sense on its way to inevitably being washed into the sea."

On Martha's Vineyard, of particular concern to the locals is the area of State Beach fronting Sengekontacket Pond, one of the island's richest shellfish beds and a popular spot for young families and windsurfers. In summer, the pond is framed by a blanket of the pink and red flowers of the rugosa rose; on the south side is the Massachusetts Audubon Society's 350-acre Felix Neck Wildlife Sanctuary. This area is one of the most delightful on the island, but there is concern that this might all change.

Much of the beach has washed into the pond. Wind and wave erosion has carried the sand across the shore road, leaving a bed of pebbles behind. The shoaling has threatened the tidal pond's prolific scallop and quahog grounds by preventing an adequate circulation of salt water, which is needed to cleanse and nourish the shellfish. The shoaling also impedes navigation into the pond, which empties into the sound. It is difficult for even small boats to maneuver under the access bridge. There is even an area you can walk across at low tide.

Dredging the pond and dumping the spoil on the beach to replace sand that has washed away is only a temporary solution. In time, the spoil will be carried by currents down toward Edgartown Harbor and the pond will fill with sand again.

What is happening to State Beach and Sengekontacket Pond is happening throughout the Cape and Islands. This stretch of beach offers a textbook study of erosion patterns and man's futile attempt to control them.

The stone spurs that stick out like fingers along the beach were put there, as they have been in many places, to slow the east-to-west flow of tides, which carries sand down the beach. But, as has happened elsewhere, this has interrupted a natural nourishing process, a continual breaking down and building up of the shoreline.

About two of the five acres a year Cape and Islands beaches lose to marine erosion are dumped on nearby sand spits or beaches along the mainland. But for each acre lost, less than half an acre is gained, and ultimately the forces of nature win out. To think otherwise, a research geologist for the United States Geological Survey told islanders fifteen years ago, is to suffer from "delusions of omnipotence." The best way, in fact, to preserve what we can of these beaches, scientists say, is to do nothing, although local officials find this difficult, often politically suicidal, in the face of pressure from property owners whose million-dollar houses are tumbling into the sea.

Erosion of the shoreline has caused many to think twice about living on the exposed ocean. This has caused real estate agents—as a species more adaptable than any fish or animal on the Cape and Islands—to adopt a new selling strategy: buy a block away from the shoreline; it's cheaper and each year you'll get closer to the water.

In the case of State Beach, this type of accelerated erosion is precisely why so many environmentalists over the years have denounced the use of spurs, jetties, and groins (all of which run perpendicular to the shore) and rock revetments or seawalls (which run parallel to the shore). In 1973 after several failed attempts to hold back the ocean at storm-ravaged Coast Guard Beach in Eastham, the Cape Cod National Seashore adopted a policy against the use of jetties and revetments. Said then Seashore Superintendent Leslie Arnberger, "We need to learn to live with erosion as a fact of life." On Martha's Vineyard a year earlier, the Army Corps of Engineers adopted a similar policy in deciding to take no action to preserve the eroding Gay Head cliffs, a registered national monument.

To appreciate just how futile these erosion-control methods can be is to understand the process scientists call barrier island migration. Simply put, Martha's Vineyard and Nantucket are slowly moving toward the mainland. As oceanographer Orrin H. Pilkey, Jr., an expert on shoreline erosion, pointed out in a 1985 lecture: "The world's rising sea level causes erosion on the front side of the island and growth on the back—or bay—side. In effect, the island migrates landward to assure its own survival."

This point is best illustrated by the fact that many years ago, before the Vineyard's outer beaches began drifting back in earnest, it was possible to sail from Gay Head to Edgartown, a distance of several miles, on coastal ponds behind the dunes. Today, you would have to sail on choppy Atlantic waters.

Edgartown, the island's commercial hub, has indeed felt the effects of erosion. Beaches are washing away at what seems to be record rates. Scientists also fear a storm surge from a powerful hurricane will flood the center of town because there is no stable dune system to protect it. The adjacent island of Chappaquiddick, the least inhabited yet most exposed part of the Vineyard, has taken some of the worst beatings. A few years ago, the United States Coast Guard in a last-ditch effort to save historic Cape Pogue Lighthouse at the northeastern tip of Chappy (as the natives call it) moved the ninety-five-year-old white-shingled lighthouse 500 feet back from the eroding cliff where it was precariously perched after years of being battered by storms.

Old Great Point Lighthouse, on Nantucket's northern shore, was not so lucky. The stone structure was toppled in March 1984 by a winter storm. But the most endangered stretch of shoreline on the island is the extraordinary cliffs at Sankaty, which face the full force of the Atlantic on the southeastern side of Nantucket. The cliffs are receding 30 feet a year on the average, but winter storms have taken bigger bites from them. And, as in Chatham, Sankaty homeowners are unprepared for the pending destruction of some of Nantucket's most expensive real estate. It baffles scientists why people seem so bent on building their homes on a moving cliff or sand dune.

It's really quite an old story. Man has witnessed the erosion of the

Cape and Islands since the region was first settled in the 1600s. Often damage comes in cycles. In the case of Chatham's North Beach, which breached on January 2, 1987, it's about every 140 years. The history books are filled with such accounts. Thoreau even made note of it in 1850, writing that the cliffs a Highland Light in Truro had lost about forty feet a year. But erosion wasn't such a problem then because no one lived on the shoreline. Land along the shoreline was used for farming and grazing.

In all, about thirty homes in Chatham are now threatened by the encroaching seas; many will be moved back from the shoreline with funds from a bill signed in 1988 by then president Ronald Reagan. But more cut-throughs are expected on the Cape and Islands. There will be more homes falling into the sea, there will be more homes to try to save.

Geologists predict that in time currents could cut from the Atlantic, through Nauset Inlet on the Orleans-Eastham line, all the way to Cape Cod Bay—making outer Cape Cod an island. The currents, scientists say, would likely follow the path of the old Jeremiah's Gutter—a man-made canal since filled in that was used briefly by small ships in the early 1800s to make their way from the bay to Town Cove and out to sea.

Truro is the site of another possible cut-through some generations from now, thus creating a second island on the Outer Cape. "In the case of Ballston Beach (on the Atlantic) at the head of Truro's Pamet River, striking evidence of the sea's advance upon the land was given in the winters of 1972 and 1978 during severe easterly storms," oceanographer Giese wrote in a booklet on erosion. "Waves washed over the dwindling barrier dune onto the paved road connecting North and South Pamet roads and threatened the waters of Pamet River (which runs in from Cape Cod Bay.)"

"Wash-overs" have happened here before. A spectacular wash-over in 1896, in fact, prompted the *Provincetown Advocate* newspaper to predict that outer Cape Cod would "be made an island" some day. And after a much publicized wash-over in 1933, the *Boston Globe* predicted in a headline: "Cape Cod an Island Ten Years from Now."

While Giese says a permanent cut-through at Ballston Beach is unlikely because the dunes will migrate inland, he stresses that this place we call Cape Cod is just temporary—or doomed, as the locals say—to become the Atlantis of the Northeast. "And nothing," Giese says with authority, "that man can ever do, intentionally and unintentionally, will change the fact that it is slowly submerging."

Part II

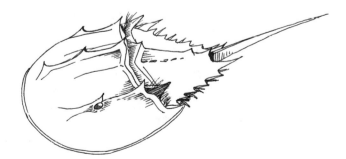

Chapter 1

The Nature Around Us—
Its Mysteries and Marvels

by John Hay

It may be surprising, in our age of information, to hear that nothing in nature is finally known. There is always more to be discovered about the most commonplace things we see around us, or pick up, like colorful stones or shells on the beach. The novelty lasts for every individual and from generation to generation. We are all instinctive collectors, just as a bowerbird in New Guinea selects bits of colored glass, flowers, and broken snail shells, which it lays out on a bed of green moss at the threshold of its nest. The practice is as old as the world and as new and exciting as any child seeing things for the first time.

The most basic elements in nature are part of a world that is highly complex. Such simple creatures as the moon snail, a predator often detected plowing its way just beneath the surface of Cape and Island tidal flats, or the little dark-shelled common periwinkle, making trails on the surface of the sand, have secrets that still defy us. We know, for example, that the periwinkle was not originally a native of North America but an immigrant from Europe, like many of us. When and how did these snails arrive on our shores? It is assumed they came over in the longboats of the Norsemen, but moving at a snail's pace they did not cross the Gulf of St. Lawrence to Nova Scotia until the mid-nineteenth century. Periwinkles were found in Portland, Maine, in 1870, and by 1928 they had reached Cape May, New Jersey.

The natural world of the Cape and Islands and its many elements—the seashore, wetlands, ponds, woodlands, and the weather around us, all discussed in chapters to follow—are full of open-ended questions and answers everywhere you look: in blades of grass, the wings of an insect, the eyes of a spider. Who has any more than a fraction of the knowledge needed to understand the several million species of insects catalogued so far, with their strange sensory equipment and their enigmatic ways? Who can see deeply enough into the lives of trees, each kind with its own mode of survival over millions of years of geologic change?

It can never be said, however, that there is an end to discovery; scientific research is continually finding out more about the behavior and senses of plant and animal organisms. Did you know, for instance, that the chemical ingredients of the light of a firefly are now being used in medical tests to detect certain infections; that the blue, copper-based blood of the horseshoe crab is used in analyzing certain blood clots and cancers; that scientists are now studying the woodpecker's head—hoping to gain some insight for improving sports and safety helmets?

The nature around us is infinite and in a state of constant change. Storm surf breaks through barrier beaches, as it has, for instance, in Chatham, on the northeast side of Nantucket, and on Chappaquiddick Island off the east end of Martha's Vineyard. Currents have undermined sandy banks and once majestic cliffs. Farms, towns, and development, roads and highways, have also caused drastic and disturbing changes in the original character of the Cape and Islands.

Yet there are many long-term rhythms and consistencies, like the tides and the timing of the seasons, that are acting on the life in nature just as they always have. And there are forms and structures that have remained much the same throughout recorded history. This is certainly true of the horseshoe crab, *Limulus polyphemus*, not a crab at all but belonging to the family of arthropods, which claims scorpions and spiders as kin. Its cast shells can often be found along protected beaches of the Cape and Islands. Its body shield, like some martial helmet, helps to keep the animal free from overturning as it explores the mud and sand of tidal flats for its food. Its spinelike tail is not a defensive weapon but a device, not always successful, to turn the horseshoe crab right side up after it has been tipped over. The females, larger than the males, and followed by them, move out of deeper water in early summer to lay eggs along the shore. The vast number of these eggs might account for the extraordinary fact that this animal has survived for 350 million years with little change. It is more likely, however, that it has existed for that incredible length of time because the shallow seas surrounding the continents have endured as a stable environment for it.

The eggs of the horseshoe crab are very important for thousands of shorebirds on their spring migration to nesting grounds in the Arctic. Beaches where countless of these eggs have been laid provide a precious store of food, enabling the migrants to put on another layer of fat to provide the necessary stamina to fly the next long lap of their journey.

While mysterious, many aspects of the natural world of the Cape and Islands are often predictable. It is not too difficult, for instance, to anticipate local events such as the singing of the *Hyla crucifer*, the spring peeper, or pinkwink, a shrill chorus that rises out of pond edges and bogs at much the same period of time each year, after the ice melts. These tiny tree frogs, only an inch long, make the first mating calls of early spring.

It is another matter when migratory birds appear in the spring at much the same time every year, almost to the exact day. The phoebe returns to the same nest box under the eaves of a house. Warblers of many different kinds start to fly in, starting in late April or early May, a few to nest on the Cape but more to continue on.

Bird Migration

Roseate, common, and least terns, plus a few Arctic terns, breed on the Cape and Islands, arriving about the beginning of May from wintering grounds as far away as Brazil, although the Arctic tern has a more spectacular migration. Far more numerous in nesting areas farther north from Canada to Greenland, this bird travels over the coast of Europe after its young are fledged, then flies down the coast of Europe to southern Africa, from which it makes another flight to the Antarctic, where it spends the winter feeding on krill between ice floes. It returns north in the spring by a more westerly route up the mid-Atlantic, flying fairly low over the surface of the water, and diving in for its principal food of fish as it goes. This makes a great round-trip journey of up to 22,000 miles a year. How a tern may nest in the same sandy area, often within inches of the little scraps or hollow where it nested a year before, is truly mind-boggling.

It is not only that birds know where to return to but their timing that is so surprising. How do they know when to leave their wintering territories, which may be a very long distance away, and head north? What guides them on migration? A shorebird, like a sanderling, may fly all the way from the tip of South America to reach its nesting grounds in the Arctic.

Biological Clocks

Through experiment, it has been shown that birds can find their way on migration by means of the earth's position with respect to the sun, by the stars on a clear night, and by the earth's magnetic field. Now it has been learned that what sends the birds north in the spring and south in the fall comes not from outside them but within. There is an annual rhythm in the migratory birds that results in a strong impulse to set forth at the appropriate times and also guides them on their way. They know their main destination, how far to go, and when they have arrived through a rhythmic inner timekeeper—or biological clock—coordinated with the seasons of the hemispheres.

A biological clock is a built-in behavioral mechanism in plants and animals by which the timing of certain activities is programmed. Much of the behavior of all organisms occurs in cyclic fashion, and such behavioral rhythms are often synchronized with some physical cycle. For example, numerous plants and animals have a twenty-four-hour rhythm—one that is geared to the solar cycle of the day and night, together with the accompanying cycle of temperature. Many coastal organisms also display behavior synchronized with tidal cycles.

The fiddler crab, for example, has a rhythmic response that is exactly timed to the ebb and flow of the tides. When the tide is out and the shore is uncovered, these little creatures come out of their burrows in a salt marsh to feed. On the incoming tide, they close the door behind them, so to speak, plugging up the entrance hole with mud, and wait. These rhythms persist in spite of changes in the environment—at least for a period of time. Fiddlers, for example, flown in dark chambers to similar environments on the West Coast exhibit cyclic color changes according to tides on the Atlantic. These crabs, however, eventually synchronize with tides on the Pacific coast and thus become accustomed to their new surroundings.

Timing, in terms of temperature, is behind the extraordinary performance of the snowy tree cricket in late summer, when it can be found, though with difficulty, in shrubby areas. After dark a flashlight is helpful in locating them. They are slender, pale green little insects with a shrill, pulsing chorus that sounds not unlike the spring peepers. Their song speeds up or slows down in response to heat and cold at such regular intervals that you can tell the temperature by it. Divide the number of notes per minute by four and then add forty, and you will get the approximate temperature in degrees Fahrenheit.

An example of biological rhythm in plants is the daily opening and closing of flowers. Plants are especially receptive to the influence of graduated, changing daylight through much of the year and blossom at the appropriate period for each variety, from the white flowers of wood anemones and starflowers in early spring to the purple, white, and pink asters in the fall. And bees learn that certain flowers on which they feed are open at specific times, and their inner timekeeper enables them to return to the flowers daily at the same hours.

We all have biological clocks. They are common to our wakefulness and sleep. But sometimes our inner biological mechanism is thrown out of whack, and our adjustment to changes in the environment isn't always smooth or comfortable. Overseas air travel, for example, is marked by abrupt time changes. Anyone who has departed at about noon from Heathrow Airport in London or DeGaulle Airport outside of Paris and arrived in Boston or New York at 2:00 P.M. local time (7:00 P.M. London time) can tell of feeling desynchronized, fatigued, and longing to catch up with sleep—a condition known popularly as jet lag. Bodily functions and rhythm take different lengths of time to correlate with the changes in time schedules.

A Point of Passage

Cape Cod is a way station or point of passage for mammal and fish migrants as well as birds, since its bended arm stands out so far into the Atlantic. The islands, too, provide shelter, rest, and a ready source of food.

WHALES

Interest in whales and their habitat has given birth to one of the Cape's fastest growing cottage industries: whale watching, operated primarily out of Provincetown and Barnstable harbors.

The finback whale—second only in size to the mighty blue whale with its maximum length of some seventy-nine feet—is fairly common in waters off the Cape and Islands. While some finbacks winter near the Cape, others range over the continental shelf between Labrador and New York. Occasionally, a finback is stranded and dies on a beach along Cape Cod Bay. But the most dramatic and mysterious strandings are those of pilot whales. Schools of pilot whales, hundreds of these mammals in recent years, periodically beach themselves along the bay for reasons that are not entirely clear and die in what appears to the casual observer to be a mass suicide ritual. There are many theories; the most likely, according to Cape cetologist Charles Stormy Mayo of the Center for Coastal Studies in Provincetown, suggests a bacterial infection may attack the inner ear and interfere with the whale's natural sonar system that bounces high-frequency sounds off objects in the water to determine distance and direction. Since whales travel in herds, or pods as scientists call them, mass strandings can be caused by the disorientation of a single leader. Another theory holds that small disturbances in the earth's magnetic field cause the disorientations.

Pilot whales are easy to spot; they are also called pot heads because of their bulbous heads and blackfish because of their jet black color. Pilot whales can reach a length of twenty feet, though the average is about thirteen. The less-common humpback whale, with a size of thirty to sixty feet, may be seen in waters off the Cape and Islands. It has a great range—from the West Indies to Greenland. The smallest whale in this region is the minke. It measures up to twenty-eight feet in length, wintering south as far as Puerto Rico and summering from Cape Cod north. The smaller white-sided and white-beaked dolphins, members of the whale family, too, arrive off the Cape and Islands in the spring to feed on fish and squid.

SEA TURTLES

Sea turtles that originate in warm or subtropical waters occasionally strand on Cape and Islands beaches in early winter. The two most common are ridleys and loggerheads, the first being the smaller in size. These animals move into the waters of the northeast in early summer when the temperature of the surface water rises. Being cold-blooded reptiles, they are unable to alter their body temperature, so they swim where the surrounding water approximates it. They feed primarily on crab and clams, and when they range in off the ocean into shallow Cape Cod Bay and surrounding waters—where the average depth is 100 feet—they may be seriously affected by the cold as the autumn months progress. The bay cools rapidly because of its shallow water and exposure to frontal systems from the northwest. The sea turtles experience severe loss in body temperature when they meet colder waters and are stunned; they land on the beaches and soon die. The ridleys cannot survive temperatures below forty-one to forty-two degrees Fahrenheit and the loggerheads no lower than thirty-five degrees.

BOX TURTLE

BOX TURTLES

The box turtles of the Cape and Islands, once much more common than they are today (due to a loss of habitat and because people cart them away), bury themselves in the ground over the winter under a few inches of leaf litter and soil, a burrow the box turtle may deepen as winter advances. In winter, turtles lie buried below the frost line in the mud of ponds or streambeds, their bodily processes having been greatly slowed down. These turtles are able to supercool to seventeen degrees Fahrenheit, though in an exceptionally cold winter of deep frost and ice, with little snow for insulation, they often die.

The dusty black or brown markings of their broad, blocky shells are contrasted with specks of yellow and orange. The term box comes from the fact that the turtle—when threatened or for convenience—will close up its shell like a box. The box turtle's head, neck, and squat legs are also mottled with yellow, orange, and often red. The turtles average four to eight inches in length and live in open woodlands, although they prefer to be near ponds, bogs, or brooks. They usually do not wander more than 150 feet from their homes. Female turtles lay their eggs in late May through June—often, for some unknown reason, on a drizzly evening. The preferred site is loose, sandy soil.

Fish Migrations

ALEWIVES

As early as late February or March, when the water temperature of inland rivers and streams begins to warm up relative to the still colder waters offshore, the alewives—or freshwater herring—in small numbers at first, begin to move inland from the sea to spawn. It is not entirely understood how they are able to find their way from out in the Atlantic to a particular stream that may be only a few yards wide and then into an adjoining freshwater pond. But it is known that they tend to come back to the same freshwater systems, their home streams, where they were hatched out. They are very sensitive to differences in temperature, which helps guide them on their entry from salt water. Alewives are able to recognize the home stream through their sense of smell, since every stream, brook, river, or salt-marsh channel meeting the sea has its own distinctive chemistry. A more detailed description of alewives is covered in the ensuing question and answer section.

EELS

Another dramatic migration, but in reverse, is that of the common eel. Eels grow in fresh water, rather than salt, as with the alewives, and migrate out all the way along the Atlantic coastline when they are sexually mature—at seven years old or more. They journey far out into the ocean, many of them laying their eggs in the region of the Sargasso sea where they die. After the larvae, the color of clear glass, are hatched out in those distant waters, these glass eels are carried by ocean currents across the Atlantic, changing the shape of their bodies into elvers as they go. The American eel spawns in midwinter; it takes up to two months for the species to reach the spawning grounds. One of the most fascinating aspects of this migration is that the breeding areas of the American and European eel overlap—their larvae can hardly be distinguished from each other. The European variety moves over to Europe, a journey of two to three years, where it enters the Mediterranean at Gilbraltar. The American eel, taking only a third of the time, migrates to the eastern side of the Atlantic.

OTHER FISH MIGRANTS

The story of marine fish migration is worldwide in extent and very complex in nature, having to do with the presence of food for different species at different times of the year, as well as the nature of water currents in the oceans.

The winter flounder spawns on sandy bottoms off the Cape and Islands between January and May, often when the water is the coldest of the year. Other types of flounder, or flatfish, such as the yellowtail and the summer flounder, spawn in the spring or during other seasons of the year. A female winter flounder lays as many as a half million eggs, which sink to the bottom and stick together in clusters. Other fish lay floating, or buoyant, eggs in often prodigious quantities. Great numbers of eggs are necessary to keep fish populations in being. Eggs and larvae die from disease, while vast numbers are eaten; they also tend to drift away from the spawning beds and nursery grounds to areas where they are unlikely to survive. In areas where tidal currents take them away, the mortality rate of some flounder has been 99.98 percent.

In mackerel it has been estimated that one to ten fish survive from each million eggs that are laid, and in some years the rate is even more unfavorable. Codfish, which range between Cape Cod and Newfoundland, may lay between 3 to 4 million eggs, depending on the size of the fish, which can be very large—well over seventy-five pounds.

The common skate—which you often see lying dead along the beaches, with thin bodies and long tails—lay their eggs in unusual, leathery black cases called mermaids' purses. But instead of thousands or millions of eggs, the female skate lays only one, which is enclosed for its protection. Each mermaids' purse is equipped with four hooks, one at each corner, that attach it to offshore beds of seaweed. When dislodged by storms and ocean currents, they often litter the beaches.

The Senses and Behavior

The most wonderful aspect of the natural world lies in its wealth of sensitivity, displayed in all the responses of living things to the earth and the elements. It amounts to a continuous exchange of senses and awareness, from a squid with its nearly human eye, to a hawk that can see a mouse in the grass from high in the air, to a starfish whose sight comes from a spot at the end of each of its arms, or rays, that is sensitive to light, to a bat that sends out rapid bursts of ultrasonic sound, with frequencies of up to 80,000 vibrations a second—so high the human ear is incapable of hearing it. These sounds are reflected off the smallest of insects and are detected by a bat's large ears, so that it can catch its prey in the dark.

Since our eyes, ears, nose, and taste buds are all located in our heads, many people are inclined to think that other animals must be equipped in much the same way. So it comes as a surprise to learn that crickets and grasshoppers can hear with their legs, having auditory equipment there or on their abdomens.

SIGHT

Eyes are located in all kinds of places, depending on the organism. Some creatures have eyes, or light-reflecting organs, on their backs, so they can retreat to safety when the light strikes them. Tube worms, commonly found on Cape and Island tidal flats, have eyes on the tips of their tentacles that act like sentries, enabling them to retreat into their shells at any disturbance. Scallops have little blue eyes all along the mantles of their shells, so that they can keep on the lookout for an approaching enemy, such as a starfish. The scallop also has tentacles that extend outward between its eyes, and when these tentacles smell a starfish, the animal swims speedily away by clapping the two sides of its shell together.

The highly mobile squid, swimming by jet propulsion, has very efficient and complex eyes, with unusual power to discriminate between shapes and forms, as well as being able to detect different planes of polarized light. They have the ability to change in color and often mimic, or reflect, objects on the water, such as jellyfish, floating sponges, or seaweed. They can also express strong feelings of nervous fear and hostility. They even engage in courtship behavior; streaks, stripes, and bars show on their bodies when expressing emotion.

One of the special senses of a fish is the lateral line, a canal filled with mucus that runs under the skin of its body. An alewife running upstream can keep stationary in the current by means of its eyes. But how does it manage in the dark? The lateral line sense enables it to detect currents in the water, to know when it is nearing the bank, and where it is with relation to its many companions swimming beside it.

Those shiny, black little whirligig beetles we see in freshwater streams, twitching and spinning together, are equipped with eyes that see both over and under the surface of the water. Each whirligig has the means, though packed tightly into a raft with hundreds or thousands of individuals, not to bump into its neighbors. Its antennae receive an echo of its own ripples as it bounces back from the others in the crowd. This is not unlike the echolocation of bats, as they read the sound waves coming back to their great ears.

SMELL

Guided by a sense of smell in its antennae, the butterfly finds ripe fruit on the ground. Then, relying on a sense of taste located in the soles of its front legs, it sips the juices with its feeding tube. A male moth, with very large antennae, has an extraordinarily acute sense of smell, an attribute that enables moths to distinguish their own species from hundreds of others. The male in finding its mate is guided by the fact that each female of his species emits a unique and delicate scent—called a pheromone—so faint that the human nose is unable to detect it. Salamanders and eels are guided by their sense of smell, whereas frogs are guided by sight. Bats, too, as we mentioned earlier, have extraordinary smelling abilities.

Lights Beneath the Sea

Although we invented artificial light, and there is hardly a region on earth without it, the living world, especially in the oceans, has always been full of a natural light known as bioluminescence that still baffles scientists. Bioluminescence, or the emission of light by a living creature through a complex chemical process, is found in a few plants and several species of animals and insects, but reaches its peak in the marine community. Natural light occurs in some squids, in bacteria, marine worms, jellyfish, deep-sea fish, and others, though not in birds, mammals, and reptiles.

At times, the open sea can be ablaze with light caused by organisms in the plankton. Along our beaches on a summer night, the wet sand, or the water itself, is often full of phosphorescence that sparkles underfoot or runs like starlight along a swimmer's arms. Open your eyes beneath the surface on such a night and you will experience an underwater light show. This is caused by a one-celled organism with some of the characteristics of both plants and animals called noctiluca, or nightlight.

Such light shows are not limited to the sea. Fireflies, one of the beauties of a summer night, have complicated light organs located under their abdomens. In our latitude, where we watch them slowly dancing like tiny lamps over the grasses and across the midlevels of trees, the females rest on the ground and flash only in response to the signals of the male of their own species. Watch for this. The insects that engage in these mating flights are not flies, incidentally, but soft-bodied beetles called *Lampyridae*, a word stemming from the ancient Greek from which the English word lamp came.

To Open Young Eyes, As Well As Old

Cape Cod and the Islands belong to the natural world. Each one of its distinctive environments—sandy beach, salt marsh, oak and pine wood, grassland, pond, or bog—is made up of plants and animals that are not just here as passive residents but contribute to the region's character and existence. We are not the only explorers. Everything in nature discovers and rediscovers its environment, using an astonishing variety of senses to do it. The Cape and Islands are a dynamic center for migratory life from afar—one that is also being explored before our eyes, and in the ground under our feet, by life that we should never idly refer to as unimportant or insignificant.

Q & A

Q How far can a monarch butterfly fly?

Monarch butterflies are the premier long-distance migrants of the insect world. Few birds can match their long-distance travel. Millions of them fly 2,000 miles or more cross-continent from as far north as Canada's Hudson Bay to a small mountainous region in central Mexico where they roost and breed in the hillside groves of bright ovamel trees. They fly at a cruising speed of about ten miles per hour, roughly twenty feet above the ground, and cover about eighty miles a day. The monarch has a short life. Few make the round-trip; returnees are descendants of the migrants. How monarchs find their way over such great distances without landmarks continues to baffle man.

Q What are fireflies? Where do you find them? Why do they blink?

Fireflies, one of the Cape and Islands' favorite summer attractions for children and grown-ups alike, can be found on warm summer nights in just about any meadow, woodland, or lawn. Armed with peanut butter jars or empty milk cartons with holes punched in the lids, children (young and old) scramble to catch these so-called "fairies' lanterns," more often than not missing their targets.

The light of the firefly (the firefly is actually a member of the beetle family) is mystifying. Behind each millisecond of light is a complex chemical process stimulated (if theorists are correct) by a need to reproduce. The creation of light by a living organism is known as bioluminescence. The process occurs in bacteria and other simple animals, as well as in more complex organisms. The process, simplified here to the extent it can be, works as follows:

The light-producing chemical present in these organisms is called luciferin. For light to be produced, two things must happen. First, the firefly must take in oxygen, which makes its way to where the luciferin is stored. Second, the firefly's body must contain a special enzyme called luciferase. The enzyme makes it possible for the luciferin to absorb an extra molecule of oxygen. The extra oxygen, in turn, adds electrical energy to a molecule of luciferin. That extra energy, released simultaneously by many molecules, produces the light burst that so delights us. The process is continuously repeated.

The special light gland of the firefly is far more efficient than the most effective light bulbs in common use. For example, if you touch a working light bulb your hand will burn. Most of the electrical energy that goes into a bulb is wasted making heat. The firefly's lamp, by contrast, is cold. No energy is wasted; it is all used to produce light. Scientists are studying this process with the hopes of developing a more efficient light bulb. They are also closely studying luciferase—an oxidizing enzyme that acts with luciferin to produce light. Luciferase is being used in medical tests to detect infections and for measuring ingredients in certain pharmaceuticals.

It all sounds coldly scientific, but there is a warmer purpose to this flashing. Male fireflies, searching out females, flash their beacons about once every six seconds in a matching cadence. If the light appeals to the female, she will flash back two seconds later, a signal inviting his attention. If she is not interested, she will not respond. Some insects are able to mimic the flash as a way of preying on fireflies.

Q *What is a horseshoe crab? Is it true the species is more than 350 million years old?*

Predating the dinosaur, the horseshoe crab can easily lay claim to the title "living fossil." The most ancient relative of the horseshoe crab crawled along our shoreline about 350 million years ago. The crab's unmistak-

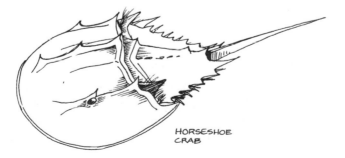

HORSESHOE
CRAB

able body structure—its spiny tail, martial helmet of a shell, and long thin claws—has remained unchanged for more than 200 million years. Initially an inhabitant of brackish water, the horseshoe crab evolved into a saltwater creature.

When surrounding water temperatures reach fifty degrees Fahrenheit, you can expect to see horseshoe crabs in the shallow waters off the Cape and Islands. The larger females wander around unattached for only a short time. The males, which outnumber the females two to one, latch onto the first female they see. Using specially modified front claws or claspers, the smaller males may latch onto a male-female pair, forming a threesome.

Each spring with the full moon spring tide, the crabs crawl to the shoreline in large groups. The females lay 200 to 300 eggs in three of four separate nests buried under the sand along the high-tide line; the males fertilize the eggs. The horseshoe crabs then depart, leaving the eggs to mature. The blue-green egg mass can easily be seen with the naked eye. Twice a day, high tide—with its nutrients—will wash over the eggs. This is essential to their growth. In three to four weeks, the embryos are ripe for hatching. Coarse sand grains will rupture the egg cases and the newly born crabs will begin life in the ocean. The young crabs measure about one inch in length and take seven years to reach maturity (a shell width of six to eight inches). Horseshoe crabs are thought to live at least thirty years.

Although it's called a crab, the horseshoe crab is an arthropod, a distant relative of scorpions and spiders. The crab does not have true jaws. Instead, its mouth parts are attached to its legs so that it walks and eats at the same time. It literally eats on the run. Its four eyes are useful in determining its position but not in locating food. The horseshoe crab's breathing apparatus, called a book gill, is located just in front of its tail. The book gill consists of six overlapping plates that move back and forth taking oxygen from the water that passes over them.

The horseshoe crab eats small clams, marine worms, and organic particles. Though its habit of feeding on seed clams does not endear it to shellfish wardens, the horseshoe crab does feed on the clam worm, a major shellfish predator.

Gone are the days when the horseshoe crab was ground up, along with lobsters, for fertilizer. Today it plays a key role in medical research. The horseshoe crab has blue, copper-based blood that contains only one type of cell, which is used in analyzing certain infections such as spinal meningitis and all E. coli infections, as well as certain blood clots and cancers.

The future of the horseshoe crab unfortunately is not as bright as its past. Pollution, destruction of its habitat, and pressure to destroy it because of its shellfish predation threaten the crab's existence. But with the proper understanding and protection, the horseshoe crab, scientists say, may be allowed to continue its ancient evolutionary path instead of becoming another casualty of man.

Q   What is a moon snail?

Moon snails, a form of shellfish, can grow to the size of softballs, and they often wash up on the beach after a powerful storm. The two most often found here are the northern moon snail and the shark-eye snail. They look much alike but the shark-eye snail has a brown or purple callus next to its body opening. The shark-eye is the more colorful of the two, with its bluer, glossier tone and flatter spire. The common northern moon snail is rounder, more moon-like, and blue-gray in color.

Both are voracious feeders; they eat a variety of food from clams and mussels to each other when bivalves are scarce. Patrolling the bottom on its expanded foot, this snail will expel water when it retreats into its shell. Known locally as sweet meat, these snails are delicious eating, but be careful not to overcook them or you will wind up with seafood chewing gum. We suggest you tenderize them, pound them with a wooden mallet, then let them sit in the refrigerator for twenty-four hours before frying or steaming them.

Both snails are responsible for the sand collars found in shallow water in the summer. They will cement grains of sand together with a mucus and embed their eggs in this matrix.

The shark-eyes are at their northern limit here and are common on tidal flats. The northern moon snail is more abundant along the outer ocean beaches.

Q   Are there any bats on the Cape and Islands?
Are they really blind?

There are 853 species of bats worldwide, 39 in North America, and 6 are regularly seen on the Cape and Islands—3 species inhabit local cliffs and abandoned buildings, and 3 species live in trees. The cave dwellers include Keen's bats, little brown bats, and big brown bats (appropriately named for their size). Tree dwellers include red bats, hoary bats, and silver-haired bats.

Despite Hollywood's depiction of bats as blood-sucking vampires, dirty, and loathsome, bats on the Cape and Islands serve a purpose. Bats help to keep the insect population down. They can be found feeding in and around shopping centers, ponds, baseball fields, or tall structures—like Provincetown's Pilgrim Monument—that attract insects, beetles, and moths. They are by no means unclean. In fact, scientists claim they are as clean as cats.

You are more likely to see bats at night than during the day. Blind as a bat, they use their built-in ultrasonic signaling system, a process called echolocation, which is used both for navigation and to detect their prey at night. Bats have notoriously poor eyesight.

Q How fast is a snail's pace?

This is another favorite question of children that usually stumps parents. A snail on a flat surface can travel three inches in one minute. That is the equivalent of a yard in twelve minutes and a mile in fifteen days, according to scientist William Beebe, who did a laboratory research study of the snail and published his findings in *Natural History* magazine.

Q What is an opossum?

The opossum is a strange composite sort of creature. It possesses the general shape of a pig; the nose of a fox; the fur of a raccoon; thin, papery batlike ears; the pouch of a kangaroo; a rat's tail textured like snakeskin (from which it can hang like a monkey from tree branches); the size of a cat; the walking gait of a skunk; and rear feet with nailless thumbs that look uncomfortably human.

The female's pouch, in which its prematurely born young are carried for nearly two months, is its most distinguishing characteristic, for the opossum is North America's only native marsupial. How it arrived here originally is still a mystery. How it managed to survive and increase is somewhat puzzling, for marsupials in general, and the opossum in particular, are regarded as primitive mammals. Opossums are relatively new arrivals on the Cape. The first reported trapping of an opossum on the Outer Cape was in 1976 at Brewster's Nickerson State Park.

Scientists believe the opossum evolved in South America and migrated northward millions of years ago.

ALEWIFE

Q *What are alewives? Where do you find them? Why are they so fascinating?*

Alewives are members of the herring family, and their arrival each March in Cape and Island herring runs on their way to freshwater spawning grounds is a sure and welcome sign of spring. Related to the sea herring, menhaden, and shad, alewives can grow fifteen inches in length but usually measure ten to eleven inches, the female being larger than the male. The alewife has the characteristic silvery scales of the herring family, a small mouth, large eyes, a slightly projecting lower jaw, and primarily feeds on plankton. Unlike the sea herring, its body has greater depth and sharper serrations, or scutes, along the underside of its belly, hence the nickname "sawbelly."

Alewives often first appear each year in Brewster's Stony Brook run, with public access not far from the intersection of Route 6A and Stony Brook Road—perhaps the best place on the Cape and Islands to view them fighting their way against the current up a series of stone ladders into the ponds. The first herring are usually spotted making their way upstream from Cape Cod Bay to the spawning grounds of Upper Mill and Lower Mill ponds shortly before March 15, but the majority—hundreds of thousands—arrive during April and early May. Early colonists described the spring run of alewives as being so thick in the water that it looked as if you could walk upon the backs of the fish. The same holds true today during the late April height of the run. The annual spawning migration provides one of the Cape and Islands' biggest tourist attractions. Many runs are on private land or in conservation areas, but other good public viewing places include the Herring River in Harwich off North and Bells Neck roads, Herring Pond in Eastham off Herring Brook Road, and in the Bournedale section of Bourne off Route 6, approaching the Sagamore Bridge on the mainland side of the canal.

Alewives are not endemic to the Cape and Islands; their spawning migration takes place in the headwaters of many inlets, streams, and tidal rivers all the way from Newfoundland to the Chesapeake, the time of entry being progressively later from south to north. Alewives are anadromous migrants in that they grow up in salt water and spawn in fresh. The female alewife lays up to 100,000 eggs, which hatch out in freshwater ponds in a week or less, depending on the temperature. After attaining a certain size, the young alewives head out toward the sea, led by currents. Those that survive reach maturity in three to four years, when most of them seem to return to the same freshwater ponds they were hatched in through a sense of smell (olfactory).

It is not true, as some have thought, that all adult herring die during this migration, like the West Coast salmon. But many do, having been attacked by gulls or exhausted by the stress of swimming upstream. Surviving adults return to coastal seas shortly after spawning and may come back to spawn again the following year. As far as scientists know, seven years is about the longest alewives will live. Their age is determined by reading their scales, much like rings on a tree; these scales record their entry from salt to fresh water and their return.

Alewives, it should be said, are in need of protection from encroachment by the public. Let them follow their life's mission without interference.

Q What are spring peepers? Where do they go in summer?

Spring peepers, sometimes known as pinkwinks or pinkletinks, are tiny tree frogs whose ringing mating chorus in March is one of the most eagerly awaited signs of spring.

The high-pitched singing of the tiny male suddenly stops in late April, leading many Cape Codders to ask, where do all the peepers go in summer? The answer is, probably up.

SPRING PEEPER

As tree frogs, peepers are equipped with adhesive toe pads and have been found as high as sixty feet up in the red maples and tupelos of their native swamplands in the warmer months. This vertical migration, combined with the amphibian's cryptic coloration (which renders it practically invisible even when singing), gives rise to the mistaken belief that the peepers simply vanish after mating season.

This great disappearing act is all the more incredible when the total estimated Cape peeper population is taken into account—about 100 million!

Q *What are "no-see-ums" and why do they so aggravate visitors and residents alike?*

A "no-see-um," as locals call it, is one of nature's most effective weapons in its war against man for control of this land. These flea-like, barely visible pests have a tiny set of teeth and the minimum wingspan necessary to dart around. Officially called cullicoides, no-see-ums are the bane of sunbathers and campers. A member of the family of mosquitoes, midges, blackflies, and deerflies, the female no-see-um can lay 700 eggs at one time. Particularly fond of shallow still water and hollow stumps, no-see-ums can make areas virtually impassable.

Man has three ways of fighting back: On damp, muggy days, avoid Cape and Islands beaches, ponds, lakes, and wetlands in the early morning or late afternoon (times of feeding frenzies for no-see-ums); stock up on insect repellent and be sure to cover every inch of exposed skin; and enlarge your family medicine chest to include medications that will take the sting out of insect bites.

Q What is a goose fish?

The ocean is filled with strange and mysterious creatures. Observing some of these aberrations firsthand, it is easy to see how sailors of old came up with chilling tales of sea monsters.

If there were an award for the ugliest fish, the American goose fish would surely win the prize. Its enormous mouth extends all the way across its large flat head, which is grossly out of proportion to the rest of its body—a body that tapers from head to tail. Both jaws are equipped with numerous long slender teeth of various sizes. The lower teeth can be seen even when the mouth is closed because the lower jaw projects far beyond the upper jaw. Large fleshy flaps of skin

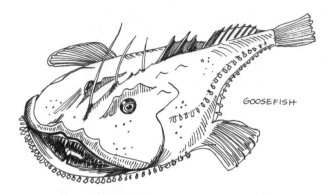

GOOSEFISH

fringe the upper jaw, while smaller flaps of skin extend along its lower side.

The goose fish is our only local representative of a tropical fish group known as anglers. Lurking on the ocean floor, the large green eyes of the goose fish are constantly on the lookout for a good meal. Remaining in the same spot for days at a time, the goose fish assumes the stationary appearance of a sponge coral or small rock. Occasionally, it will use its paired fins for crawling along the bottom or digging in the sand.

Many divers have watched goose fish engulf their prey, but all they observed was a quick blur. It has been estimated that a goose fish can consume its prey in less than six milliseconds, perhaps making it the fastest feeding fish in the sea.

The diet of the goose fish is anything but selective. Although it is doubtful one could consume a goose, as its name implies, this unusual fish will eat anything and everything from seabirds to sharks. Hundreds of fish species have been found in their stomachs, along with sea turtles, squid, lobsters, gulls, cormorants, sea ducks, loons, and murres. A large goose fish, weighing about fifty pounds, was once found with twenty-seven flounder and a spiny dogfish in its stomach. Another devoured seven ducks in a single meal.

It is unlikely you will find a goose fish sold in Cape and Islands fish markets. The locals don't care much for them. Goose fish caught in local waters are usually shipped to the mid-Atlantic states where the white flesh of the tail is sold as monkfish. The meat has the taste of lobster.

Chapter 2

Birds of the Cape and Islands

by Erma J. Fisk and Greg O'Brien

It doesn't take much to make birders out of visitors to the Cape and Islands. You don't need to know anything about ornithology or even know how to spell it. You don't have to look studious, wear frumpy hats, know the mating call of the elusive *Rallus limicola* (Virginia rail), or cart around an expensive pair of binoculars. All you really have to do is slip back into your hammock and soak up the view. Of course, you can get more scientific about it.

The Cape and Islands are a flyway, a point of passage, for more than 300 species of birds, many of them migrants not easily found along parts of the East Coast. You can view birds in every ecosystem on the Cape and Islands—on the beach, on the shore of a pond, along the edge of a wetland, in a meadow, or in our woodlands.

It's easy to get hooked. "Birding is hugely important to many Cape Cod residents and visitors; before moving here many people were content with spotting spring's first robin or the blue jay flying from pine to oak, but once surrounded by the variety of species that inhabit the region, they've become passionate bird watchers," explains local writer John LoDico.

The Cape and Islands have attracted hundreds of bird watchers, amateur and professional alike. There are a number of bird clubs here, frequent bird lectures (announced in the local press), and guided tours sponsored by the Massachusetts Audubon Society's Wellfleet Bay Sanctuary, the Cape Cod National Seashore in Eastham and Provincetown, and Brewster's Cape Cod Museum of Natural History and Nickerson State Park, both along Route 6A, to mention just a few. Some opt to trudge off on their own through woodlands, marsh, and along the beach, carrying with them the highly recommended Roger Tory Peterson's *A Field Guide to the Birds.*

If you go it alone, we have a few words of advice, passed along from Mike O'Connor of the Bird Watcher's General Store off Route 6A in Orleans. "The best hours for finding songbirds in the spring and summer are just after sunrise when the males are most likely to be singing. Early morning is also a good time to start out in summer; many of the better beaches for shorebirds also attract vacationers who drive away the birds," advises O'Connor, who writes about birds for *Cape Cod Driftlines,* a seasonal monthly journal about nature.

"Another important variable is the tides. Shorebirds feed on the flats at low tide and rest at high tide. Unfortunately, at low tide the birds are so far out and widespread that it is hard to see them. The best thing to do is to look for birds on the incoming tide. The rising water forces them to move toward the shore and to bunch up in tidal pools. Another thing to consider is the direction of the sun. Try to keep the sun at your back, especially at sunrise and sunset when it is at eye level. Bird watching right after a storm can be very rewarding. Strong winds can force seabirds into protected bays or close to shore and will force migrating birds to land and rest for a day or so."

O'Connor urges caution when watching for birds. "Try to be aware of times of stress for birds," he says. "A hard freeze in the winter forces many birds (ducks and heron, for example) to crowd into small unfrozen pools. It is tempting to visit these pools, for it is an easy way to see a lot of birds. But weather-weakened birds that are constantly forced by intruders to fly may become even weaker."

Another time to avoid disturbing birds, he says, is during nesting. "The most obvious example is the terns (which nest in the dunes). When they fly up and scream at well-meaning onlookers, they are leaving their nests unprotected. Eggs left exposed to the sun for very long may actually cook, while young chicks left unguarded will become an easy meal for the ever present gulls."

Oh, one more word before you trek off. Take along insect repellent, wear long pants if weather permits, and bring sneakers or old shoes to muck around in. Now you're ready.

Where to See Them

And there should be plenty to see. It's a testimony to nature that so many species can be viewed here. A century ago, shorebirds of the Cape and Islands were shot by the thousands for sport. The feathers and bright wings of many of these birds adorned ladies' hats as far away as Great Britain and France; robins sold for ten cents apiece in Boston.

What the hunters didn't shoot, developers chased away. But still, the Cape and Islands are especially rich in birds, particularly water birds: great white gannets diving offshore in winter storms; varied flotillas of scoters, eiders, and ducks; and small sanderlings and peeps that scoot along the tide lines, twisting and turning in the slanting light above the waves before settling in at water's edge to probe the sand.

Bird species vary with the seasons, although many birds are present year-round. The variety is apparent if you look along the mud flats and the shores of beaches, bays, harbors, marshes, and ponds. There you'll find ducks (both sea and freshwater), cormorants, gulls, terns, loons, herons, egrets, kingfishers, shearwaters, willet, plover, horned larks, snow buntings, owls in some places, ospreys, oystercatchers, skimmers, and occasionally an immature bald eagle. In summer and winter, these birds can be found wherever public access permits; follow roads to town landings or to any shore, pond, or bird sanctuary, respecting signs posted to protect fragile areas. Most town beaches charge a fee for parking in summer, but if you arrive early enough (by 7:00 A.M.) you can avoid the fee and enjoy some prime bird watching, too.

Land birds (resident, breeding, or migrant) can be found just about anywhere, although sightings are not predictable. Search for them by walking in wooded areas, along ponds, and near edges of streams, cemeteries, open fields, and wherever development offers them food and shelter. Conservation holdings and public parks throughout the Cape and Islands (shown on detailed maps available at many local bookstores) are also good places to look for land birds. Among the better-known spots on the Cape and Islands (shorebirds can be found there, too) are the Beech Forest Nature Trail of Provincetown, the Wellfleet Bay Sanctuary, Cape Cod Museum of Natural History trails, Nickerson State Park, the Harwich Conservation Area, Chatham's Monomoy National Wildlife Refuge and Morris Island, Fort Hill in Eastham, as well as other Cape Cod National Seashore trails (maps available at National Seashore visitor centers), The Yarmouth Botanic Gardens off

Route 6A behind the Yarmouth Post Office, Beebe Woods in Falmouth, the Audubon's Ashumet Holly Reservation in East Falmouth, and the Lowell Holly Reservation in Mashpee.

Other good sighting spots for land birds and shorebirds are Race Point and MacMillan Wharf in Provincetown; the area around Corn Hill in North Truro; the Wellfleet Harbor area; First Encounter Beach on Cape Cod Bay and Hemenway Landing on Salt Pond Bay, both in Eastham; Nauset Light Beach and Coast Guard Beach in Eastham; Nauset Beach in Orleans; the Harwich Conservation Area in North Harwich and Bells Neck Road off Great Western Road in Harwich; Swan Pond in Dennisport, the woods behind the fish hatchery in Dennis, and West Dennis Beach along Bass River; Sandy Neck in Barnstable and Sandwich; Sider's Pond behind Falmouth Town Hall and Nobska Point in Falmouth; South Beach in Mashpee; and the entrance to the Cape Cod Canal in Sandwich.

On Martha's Vineyard, good sighting spots include Cedar Tree Neck Sanctuary off Indian Hill Road; Felix Neck Wildlife Sanctuary off the Vineyard Haven-Edgartown Road; the Martha's Vineyard State Forest off Airport Road; Long Point Wildlife Refuge off the Edgartown-West Tisbury Road; and the Wasque Reservation and Cape Pogue Wildlife Reservation, both on Chappaquiddick, a short ferry ride from Edgartown Harbor.

On Nantucket, the viewing is good at Great Point, north of Wauwinet; Nantucket Harbor; the meadows and beaches of Siasconset, on the east side of the island; and Madaket Beach, Madaket Bay, and Eel Point, on the west side of the island.

Birds of Winter

Many species, as we've noted, are seasonal. In winter, look for seabirds in harbors from Woods Hole to Provincetown, particularly Falmouth, Hyannis, Barnstable, Rock Harbor in Orleans, Chatham, Hatches Harbor in Provincetown, and Provincetown Harbor. On Martha's Vineyard, look for seabirds along State Beach, South Beach, Long Beach, Vineyard Haven Harbor, and the beaches of nearby Chappaquiddick. On Nantucket, try Sankaty Head, Dionis Beach, Tom Nevers Head, Cisco Beach, and Surfside Beach.

If you are willing to brave the bitter northeast winds of the Cape, Sandy Neck and First Encounter Beach are known for sheltering unexpected species during winter storms. On ponds and marshes, and in sheltered coves and salt bays, look for assorted water birds: mergansers, scaup, old-squaws, scoters, buffleheads, goldeneyes, the ubiquitous mallard, black ducks, and occasional loon, snow buntings, Lapland longspurs (a cousin of the snow bunting), and sanderlings.

Backyard feeders attract the local resident birds: woodpeckers, titmice, cardinals, mourning doves, and perhaps a covey of bobwhites, although these are scarcer as their habitat has declined. Often you can spot wintering flocks of goldfinch and juncos, an occasional wintering song sparrow, yellow-rumped warblers or catbirds, and always the abundant house finch (sharpshins and kestrels may be on the lookout for an easy meal of these).

In winter, crows will harass great horned owls and screech owls prospecting for nesting holes. Saw-whet owls are present in winter months but difficult to spot. This is not the case with snowy owls, who will often sit immobile on a beach dune, or a great blue heron flapping over a marsh, a red-tailed hawk soaring over a road, or a lingering black-crowned night heron, hunting by an ice-free creek.

Birds of Spring

The spring is heralded by robins, red-winged blackbirds, grackles, and song sparrows singing from a shrubby branch. As the trees regain their leaves and begin attracting insects, warblers come in waves, along with orioles, catbirds, flycatchers, tanagers, swallows, and a rare bluebird or two. These migratory birds are blown in by winds from the south; they pause here to feed and build up reserves needed to carry them farther north. A scattering stays to nest, although with the lack of rural, open barns, sheds with rafters, and old trees (many have been felled by the bulldozer), their numbers are fewer every year.

Still, orioles weave their hanging nests on tall, slender branches where the most adventuresome red squirrel will not dare venture; phoebes find a ledge, even a quiet windowsill; kingbirds establish territories on pine boughs, fiercely defending their nests against crows and other predators. Where the vegetation is thick, pine and yellow warblers, common yellowthroats, sparrows, and often mockingbirds will build nests.

In May, herring gulls noisily nest on the beaches of Provincetown and on the beaches of the Vineyard, Nantucket, and the Elizabeth Islands. By now, the laughing gulls and terns (common, least, and roseate) have flown up from the Caribbean Islands and South America; they are vulnerable to storm, tide, and natural predators—skunks, raccoons, weasels, crows, and hawks. These small birds cannot survive the human disturbance either—the family picnics, dogs, Frisbees, and beach buggies that often clutter the shoreline. In an effort to protect these colonies, the Massachusetts Audubon Society has posted nesting areas with signs and thin (symbolic) string. The preservation effort receives greater public acceptance each year, especially now that the piping plover has been declared an endangered species by the federal government.

By June, egrets and heron are common in ponds and marshes; a few willet will nest there too. Horned larks will run in beach grass, and songbirds will feed their fledglings.

Birds of Summer

The summer, for most, is the season for bird watching, and Mike O'Connor offers the following suggestions on where the birding is best.

The Audubon's Ashumet Holly Reservation off Route 151 in Falmouth is a great place for the family, with its trails and mixed habitats that offer shelter for a large number of birds; in the summer nesting months, swallows can be seen raising their young. For songbirds, Beebe Woods at Highfield in Falmouth is a good bet. On Sandy Neck on the Sandwich-Barnstable line, terns and piping plover can be found in abundance. And West Dennis Beach along Bass River is a good place to see shorebirds, particularly along the bordering marsh.

In Harwich, if you drive down Bells Neck Road off Great Western Road, you will arrive at two bodies of water, brackish on your left and fresh on your right. The salty area is the most productive, offering wigeons, teals, pintails, loons, rails, and occasional gallinules. The most regular visitors of note are the osprey, who do not seem to mind an audience as they splash down for an unsuspecting bass.

Outer Cape Cod, many believe, is the best area for general bird watching, particularly Chatham's Monomoy National Wildlife Refuge on Monomoy Island, accessible by boat, and Morris Island, accessible by land. Morris Island is great for migrating warblers, and flats have plenty of shorebirds, including the fascinating oystercatchers; Monomoy, more difficult to reach but worth the trip, is a nesting area for virtually thousands of birds, more than any other sanctuary on the Cape and Islands. The Cape Cod Museum of Natural History in Brewster offers regular trips to Monomoy.

A local favorite is Fort Hill in Eastham, with its spectacular views of

Coast Guard Beach in Eastham and Nauset Beach in Orleans. In summer from the top parking lot, one can see swallows, meadowlarks, bobolinks, and mockingbirds. Forty or more great blue herons may be seen in the marsh below, along with plenty of egrets. Fort Hill, part of the Cape Cod National Seashore, is also an excellent place to spot birds of prey, including the rare peregrine falcon. During late spring and early summer, the lowly woodcock may be seen just after sunset; try to catch the courtship display.

Just before the woodcocks come out, the night herons leave their roosts, from nearby Hemenway Landing. As many as 100 herons may be seen leaving the trees around the parking lot.

The concentrations, however, of songbirds and shorebirds are more visible on the islands of Nantucket and Martha's Vineyard, primarily because there is less development there.

Hawks are also more visible on the Islands, the last landfalls before Europe; so are merlins, peregrines, kestrels, red-tails, harriers, and short-eared owls.

Birds of Fall

Fall migration on the Cape and Islands lasts into mid-October, sea ducks, a few thrush, and other songbirds lingering. Then interest shifts to the birds of harbors and ponds, and the cyclical miracle of nature begins anew.

Q & A

Q What is a piping plover? Where can you find it?

A small, stocky bird, dovelike in appearance, the piping plover is indigenous to the sandy shore. It is so well camouflaged with its color of dry sand that it is often difficult to spot. The upper parts of its body are sand colored, its breast is white, and its legs and feet are an orange yellow. In spring its bill is orange and black, but it turns darker in winter. The piping plover's call is a melodious "peep-lo," supplemented by a series of sweet, piping whistles. The Atlantic population of piping plovers breeds from the north shore of the Gulf of St. Lawrence and southwest Newfoundland through the Maritime Provinces of Canada and down the East Coast from northern New England

PIPING PLOVER

to Virginia. They winter on the South Atlantic coast, with some birds migrating as far south as northern Mexico.

Each year piping plovers migrate to the Cape and Islands between the end of March and the end of April. They nest on local beaches from late March to August. These gentle birds eat marine worms, fly larvae, and beetles. When feeding, they run a short distance, pause to survey the sand with neck outstretched and head tilted, snatch their food, then run and pause again.

When intruders come too close to their nests, adult piping plovers are known to coax then away by feigning injury or crying plaintively.

The piping plover was formerly listed as an abundant bird. In the 1920s, Edward Howe Forbush, writing in *The Birds of Massachusetts,* said the piping plover was getting "too numerous for its comparative safety." But like other shorebirds, the piping plover has over the years been a favorite of hunters and predators who have drastically thinned out the ranks. In 1977, the Massachusetts Audubon Society estimated there were only 125 breeding pairs of piping plovers left in the state, and although up-to-date estimates are not available, it is feared the piping plover population on the Cape and Islands is still threatened, due to a loss of habitat rather than hunting.

Several agencies and organizations have adopted special management protection programs for the piping plover. Among them: The Cape Cod National Seashore, the U.S. Fish and Wildlife Service, the Massachusetts Audubon Society, Tufts University, and the Trustees of Reservations on Martha's Vineyard.

Q Should I pick up a baby bird lying on the ground?

Spring is a time when many birds that commonly nest in the trees and shrubbery near homes and cottages are incubating eggs and feeding chicks. Species like house finches, robins, blue jays, mourning doves, and mockingbirds all nest near dwellings.

The young of these species, blind and featherless at hatching, are barely able to lift their heads and open their beaks when the parent arrives with food. They develop quickly, however, and most are ready to fly within fourteen days of hatching.

On a great many occasions, these baby birds, in their zeal to fly, end up stumbling over the edge of the nest and tumbling to the ground. This is normal. Parent birds still feed their babies in and out of the nest. But during the short period a baby bird spends on the ground, a human often comes along and picks up the fledgling, putting it in a box and taking it to a nearby nature center for care. It's a well intentioned move, but humans should leave baby birds alone. If a baby bird is found on the ground, it is also possible the parent has rejected it for reasons we do not understand. Obviously, a blind, naked chick cannot climb out of a nest by itself. Baby birds either live or die; natural selection and predation determine this. The average mortality rate for nestling birds is about 50 percent but may be as high as 90 percent.

Nature takes care of itself. So, during the days when young birds are leaving their nest—some a bit prematurely—keep this in mind. Let their parents care for them; certainly they are most competent.

Q What is a gannet?

Gannets resemble large gulls from a distance but are related to a species of tropical birds, called boobies. They have a stately white plumage with black wingtips and yellow head coverings, wingspans of up to six feet, and are streamlined like a custom jet. Considered seabirds, gannets have been found hundreds of miles out to sea.

Gannets are gliders; they always seem to be flying uphill. They are fascinating to watch. They are also divers. Their eyesight is exceptional. A gannet can spot a school of fish as deep as fifty feet below the surface while flying at a height of fifty feet or more. They hit the water traveling at speeds up to sixty feet per second. Their bodies are equipped with special cushioning air sacs and a hard skull to absorb the impact. Their dives create such a splash they are often mistaken for whale spouts.

Gannets nest in enormous colonies on coastal islands in the Canadian Maritimes. They are seen on the Cape and Islands mostly during fall and spring migrations.

Are woodpeckers found on the Cape and Islands? How do
Q they search for food? How do they manage to pound their
heads against trees without damaging their brains?

Downy woodpeckers and flickers are common year-round residents of local forests. Dressed in striking black-and-white, gray, or brown garb, downy woodpeckers and flickers spend most of their lives on the side of a dead tree, pecking away for insects and grubs. Their strong feet, with two toes in front and one in back, help them grasp and hold onto the bark, while their stiff tail provides additional support. The woodpecker is well equipped with a remarkable tongue, which it uses to pierce its food. The tongue dominates a woodpecker's mouth; two rear extensions reach behind the jaw, up the back of the skull, over the top of the head, and back down into the woodpecker's right nostril. This unique apparatus, called the hyphoid, enables the woodpecker to stretch its tongue great distances when it feeds. It can thrust its tongue through a tree cavity with amazing speed and agility.

Many people have often wondered how a woodpecker manages to pound its head against a tree without damaging its brain. Scientists, in fact, are now studying the woodpecker's head, hoping to acquire some insight for improving the construction of safety helmets. Preliminary research indicates that woodpeckers have protective air sacs in their heads.

Woodpeckers are always rapping on wood for one reason or another. The sound of their hammering is soft and muffled when looking for food. In early spring, however, the hammering produces an entirely different sound—the sound of love. When the woodpecker is searching for a mate, the hammering is loud and resonant. For this reason, flickers will often peck on house trim in spring. Trees caught in the path of migrating dunes are also perfect for producing this sound; they ring with a quality all their own. Often the downy woodpecker pounds on these old sand-blasted trees for the sheer enjoyment of the music they produce. When the bird shifts its position, the tree changes pitch. The woodpecker seems to enjoy belting out as many different sounds as possible. Like songbirds, the woodpecker feels a compelling urge to express its feelings, especially in spring when thoughts, even for a woodpecker, turn to love.

SCOTER
HARLEQUIN
EIDER

Q   How fast do birds fly?

At a regular pace, most birds fly at speeds between 20 and 50 miles an hour, but they can attain much higher speeds. Red-breasted mergansers, for instance, have been clocked at 80 miles an hour, while the white-throated swift (not found on the Cape and Islands) flies at speeds of up to 200 miles an hour. Sandpipers, common to the Cape and Islands, reach speeds of up to 100 miles an hour, and the peregrine falcon dives for its food at an estimated 175 miles an hour.

Q   What is the current long-distance record for a shorebird migrant?

The sandpiper also holds the long-distance record for a shorebird migrant. A semipalmated sandpiper (shot on its arrival in Guyana, on the north coast of South America) was identified through a band on its leg to have been released August 12, 1985, by the Manomet Bird Observatory in Plymouth (just over the Cape Cod Canal). The bird was picked up on August 16, having flown 2,800 miles in four days.

Q   When do the sea ducks arrive each year? How long do they stay? Where can you find them?

If you are walking the beach in the late fall, you cannot mistake the arrival of sea ducks flying south from Canada. You can spot them flying in tight formations no more than a foot above the surface of the water. Often they can even be seen riding the waves. Sea ducks stay through the winter, and of particular interest are the eiders, scoters, and harlequins (discussed in the following questions and answers).

Cape Cod Bay, especially at low tide, seems to confuse the newly arriving ducks. It is as if they hate crossing land, even such a narrow peninsula as ours. These ducks wheel and circle back and forth waiting for the tide to cover the mud flats, and even then, they don't cross land just anywhere. They seem to prefer the Brewster-Orleans corner near Skaket Beach or a little farther north near Boat Meadow Creek and First Encounter Beach in Eastham as jumping-off points for their cross-Cape flights. First, the ducks gain altitude as if to take a peek across to the Atlantic, just to make sure there is water on the other side. Then off they go, most of them flying over Jeremiah's Gutter, which runs from Skaket through the Orleans-Eastham rotary and into Town Cove. From there they fly across Nauset Spit to the Atlantic, just south of Eastham's Coast Guard Beach and north of Orleans's Nauset Beach. Some of the ducks linger to feed on the rocks at Nauset Beach, one of the better spots to view sea ducks. Most, however, head for Nantucket Sound to an area bounded by Monomoy Island off Chatham's east shore, Nantucket, and Martha's Vineyard. More than 500,000 eiders spend the winter here. Most of the scoters and harlequins migrate farther south to winter.

Q What is an eider?

Eiders are the most numerous of our wintering sea ducks and the largest of our North American ducks, greater than twenty inches in size. There are two types of eiders: the common eider and the king eider. The common eider is predominant here. The eider's large size gives it an awkward and ungainly appearance, but as any beach-goer who has seen flocks of these ducks wheeling and banking back and forth above the waves knows, the eider is anything but awkward. Male eiders are an excellent example of reverse coloration; they are white on top and black on the bottom. Sitting on the water, tossing in the waves, eiders often look like whitecaps from a distance. The female, equal in size to the male, is a somber, russet brown with a heavily barred feather pattern. Eiders breed from Labrador to southern Maine and winter from Massachusetts to Virginia. During their winter on the Cape, they feed extensively on mollusks (shellfish), with blue mussels their favorite. In fact, no other duck is as dependent on a single source of food as the eider. As you can see, the elimination of shellfish beds has consequences far beyond the restaurant business.

Q What are scoters?

Next to eiders, scoters are the second largest species of sea ducks found on the Cape and Islands. Three types of scoters can be seen here: the white-winged scoter, the surf scoter, and the black (or common) scoter.

The white-winged scoter is the most common of the wintering scoters, especially near the shoals of Nantucket and Martha's Vineyard. The males are all black with a small comma-shaped white mark over their eyes and broad white wings. Females are brownish black, with the same broad white wings. The white-winged scoters nest in western Canada, more than 90 percent of them in Manitoba. About 60 percent of the population migrates east and winters in an area from Maine to New Jersey. They feed mostly on dog welks, yellow periwinkles, sand launces, blue mussels, and wedge clams.

The surf scoter, or shunk head, as it's called down east in Maine, can also be found on the Cape and Islands but in fewer numbers. The black male surf scoter is distinguished by its outrageously colored bill and by the striking white patches on its forehead and back of the head. Females are more difficult to identify. They are brownish black in color and have two indistinct dark patches on their head and one on their nape.

Surf scoters breed in the boreal forests of Canada and Alaska; the majority of them come from Labrador and Quebec. Unlike the white-winged scoters, surf scoters favor the West Coast three to one. They tend to congregate in fall and winter from Barneqat Bay in New Jersey to Norfolk, Virginia.

Black (or common) scoters can often be seen rafting with other scoters and eiders; they spend winters diving beneath the water surface in search of mussels and invertebrates. The male is pure black, with a bright orange knob on his beak. The female is grayish brown, with a paler face and throat. Black scoters can be found off the shores of Cape Cod and the Islands—mostly on the bay and sound sides—from September through April.

Q What is a harlequin?

Harlequins are the least common of our wintering sea ducks but the most spectacular. A small dark duck, the male is blue gray and the female is a dusky brown with white patches on the face, giving it almost a clown-like appearance. The males are often called lords and the females ladies. Harlequins spend most of their time in open waters; they breed in western Canada. A good place to spot harlequins is on the rocks at Nauset Beach in Orleans.

Q Are there owls on Cape Cod?

There are six species of owls that breed on Cape Cod and a seventh that wanders into our area in the winter. The nesters include the great horned, long-eared, short-eared, barn, screech, and saw-whet owls. The winter visitor is the snowy owl.

Dusk and dawn are the best times to look for these elusive night fliers, whose silent, mothlike flight, acute hearing, and large, light-sensitive eyes, a hundred times sharper than ours, make them uniquely suited for nocturnal hunting. Owls are known as lords of the night.

Most owls need good-sized tracts of deep woods unsegmented by development, though screech, barn, and saw-whet owls can occasionally be seen in suburban settings, seemingly unperturbed by human presence. They eat rodents mostly, thereby helping—along with hawks—to control the rodent population. The great horned owl will go after much larger prey, such as cats, porcupines, and skunks. Their weapons are long powerful claws and hooked beaks.

Two exceptions to the forested, nocturnal habits normally associated with owls are the short-eared and snowy. These diurnal, or day-flying, owls inhabit open country such as dunes, sand plains, and salt marshes.

While the snowy's presence in places like Sandy Neck can be considerable in some winters when the vole population is low in northern New England, it can be entirely absent in other years. The rarest owl on the Cape and Islands is the short-eared, a species listed as endangered by the State Division of Fisheries and Wildlife. The expansive, open grasslands needed by this owl are being developed and fragmented by a growing human population. There are an estimated twenty-five breeding pairs left in the state, most of which are located on Martha's Vineyard, Nantucket, and the Elizabeth Islands. A few breeders cling to existence inside the Cape Cod National Seashore and on South Monomoy Island off Chatham, inside the Monomoy National Wildlife Refuge.

Q What is a black skimmer?

A black skimmer is a coastal bird often in the company of terns. Black on top and white on the bottom, the skimmer is unmistakable. It is the only bird whose lower mandible (beak) is longer than its upper mandible, giving its bill a strange appearance. The name skimmer is derived from its method of feeding. This long-winged bird cuts (or skims) across the water with its lower beak, snapping its head down to snare a fish. You can watch skimmers from the shoreline; a pair of binoculars will greatly enhance your view.

Q Are there any eagles on the Cape and Islands?

Golden eagles are extremely rare. Only immature (up to four years old) bald eagles with dark brown heads and mottled dark coloring can be spotted on the Cape and Islands with any regularity. They can be seen just about any month of the year, flying over dunes and town landfills. Mature, white-headed adult bald eagles are not found here.

Q What is the large gray bird I see standing like a statue at the edge of salt marshes?

The graceful bird you are seeing is the great blue heron. It is the largest and most common of our coastal herons, with a wingspan reaching some 70 inches.

A great blue heron when hungry is a study in coordinated effort. Stalking its prey of fish, amphibians, and crustaceans in quiet salt marshes, mud flats, and inland freshwater shores, it barely ripples the water as it carefully lifts one leg at a time, gazing intently for a potential meal. Standing motionless for what seems an eternity, the great blue uncoils its long neck in a flash towards it prey, spearing it with its long bill, then quickly tossing the unlucky catch down head first.

Very little energy is wasted in this effort, which is valuable in rough winters, when great blues suffer high mortality rates.

GREAT
BLUE
HERON

CORMORANT

Q *What is a cormorant? Why does it hang its wings out when perched?*

Cormorants are large fish-eating birds about three feet in size, marked by a long, snakelike neck, fully webbed feet (all four toes), and a hook at the end of a long beak. Cormorants have a propensity to sit on pilings, piers, rocks, and trees with their wings held open in spread-eagled fashion.

The unusual posture is due to this bird's lack of the waterproofing oil that protects most other aquatic birds (cormorants lack oil glands). When a cormorant dives from the surface in pursuit of fish, it comes up thoroughly drenched and ready to "hang out" to dry. It also feeds on moths and crustaceans.

Sitting atop a piling or pier, the cormorant will raise its wings and turn its dark back to the sun, a warming drip-dry technique that gives the bird a somewhat regal air.

There are two species of cormorants on Cape Cod, which appear to have increased greatly in recent years: the great cormorant seen in winter and the more common double-crested cormorant of the summer. The great cormorant is blackish brown in color, or black with white markings, with a light yellow chin pouch. The double-crested cormorant is dark and has an orange throat pouch.

Q *What is a towhee?*

Named by an early colonist naturalist who thought its call resembled the word "towhee," this small ground-feeding bird, which looks like a sparrow, is common throughout most of the continental United States and Canada. The female has a brown head and upper body, white underparts, and rust-colored patches on the flanks. The male is similarly marked, but its head is black. A towhee's calls vary in different locations and distances, a fact that confused early birdwatchers into believing they were listening to different species.

The towhee, a relative of the sparrow, finch, and grosbeak, is rarely found in the deep woods. Towhees, fond of thick brush and dense cover, thrive in meadows at the edge of the woods. Junglelike tangles of blackberry and catbrier offer perfect nesting areas. The towhee rarely abandons its shelter for the open trees and forest canopy. As a result, you are more likely to hear a towhee scratching in the brier than see one. Since most of its food searching is in areas that are cool and well protected from the extreme temperatures of midsummer, you will often hear the towhee's vibrant song, "drink your tea," in the middle of a day so hot and uncomfortable that it has driven other birds to cover. Towhees are often heard scratching in leaves for food; they sound like squirrels digging.

Q What is an osprey?

The eaglelike osprey is a rare bird of prey that feeds almost exclusively on fish. Its plumage is glossy brown on top and white below with a brown band across its breast and a brown stripe through its eyes. A mature osprey is about two feet long, has a wingspan of about six feet, and builds nests six to eight feet in diameter. Ospreys usually nest in large dead trees, but because such trees have become scarce, man has erected poles with wide platforms on top to encourage nesting. Such poles have been erected in many areas; the easiest to spot is the osprey nesting area in the Pleasant Bay section of Chatham, Harwich, and Orleans off Route 28 on the Cape and inside Martha's Vineyard's many nature sanctuaries.

Ospreys decreased in numbers in the 1950s and 1960s because of the use of the toxic chemical DDT. Their numbers today are slowly increasing, thanks to these man-made nests.

OSPREY

Chapter 3

The Seashore

by Donald J. Zinn

On a clear, cloudless summer day—the kind that has defined the essence of Cape Cod and the Islands—you can stand at the top of a long flight of wooden stairs leading down to Nauset Light Beach in Eastham, look out to the horizon where the sky meets the Atlantic along a broad sweep of deep blue, and sense the curving of the earth. Your attention is now drawn toward the shore by the graceful ripples of water rolling in from the horizon. Even at a distance you can hear the steady, soothing, almost reassuring pounding of the breakers as water slides up the slope of the beach. The beach itself is a wide swath of white sand, framed by the ocean and by a steep slope of glacial deposits that retreats inland several feet each year. At the crest of the slope is the old lighthouse that has guided fishing boats plying the waters of the horizon through many a winter blow.

But the seashore is more than just a beach, a cliff, and a lighthouse; it is a world of intricate interrelationships and interdependencies, a complex web that binds all living and nonliving things to one another. While wetlands, discussed in Chapter 4, are the most productive of our ecosystems from a biological point of view, the seashores of Cape Cod, Martha's Vineyard, Nantucket, and the Elizabeth Island chain are home to more species of plants and animals than any other local habitat. It is estimated that more than a thousand different marine animals and plants inhabit the seashore. Some are extremely rare, while others are so small that a magnifying lens is required to detect them.

Seashores have fascinated man since the beginning of time. Whether it is the restlessness of tidal water forever altering the shoreline; the on-slaught of angry and destructive winds and storms; the amazing variety and ways of plants and marine organisms that populate the beaches; or the simple curiosity about this environmentally varied and ever-changing coast; a visitor to the shoreline of the Cape and Islands cannot help being physically and spiritually drawn to it.

In her book *The Edge of the Sea*, Rachel Carson writes, "Like the sea itself, the shore fascinates us who return to it, the place of our dim ancestral beginnings. The edge of the sea is a strange and beautiful place . . . always it remains an elusive and indefinable boundary."

In the pages ahead we endeavor to detail the most common species visible to observers walking along or wading at the water's edge—from beach to rock outcrop to groin to dock to pier. Emphasis is placed on the physical characteristics and ecology of the shoreline, describing plants and animals to be found in the various zones of the beach. Explaining all this can get technical, but if you pay close attention you will come to understand much about the seashore.

Rhythms of the Tides

Simply put, the tide is the daily (diurnal) rising and falling of the surface of the ocean and connected bodies of water, such as bays, inlets, and gulfs. Tidal movement is caused by the gravitational pull of the sun and moon, which is exerted unequally on various parts of the earth, particularly on water since it occupies approximately three-quarters of the earth's surface. Near the times of a new and full moon, the earth, moon, and sun are aligned (scientists call this *in phase*), and the range from high to low tide is greatest because of the multiplying effect of these gravitational pulls on the earth's waters.

This rise and fall of the water level stimulates an alternating landward and seaward water movement to and from bays and harbors. As the tide level rises, the landward flow of water sets up a flood current. When the water level begins to fall, this current comes to a standstill (called slack water), after which the flow starts again, but this time in reverse. This is the ebb current or ebb tide, which carries the water back out. The ebb tide flows until the water reaches another slack water point and the start of another tidal cycle. Extreme high tides and extreme low tides are called spring tides because the coastal waters appear to spring up, or accelerate, back up the beach after a low tide. However, when the alignment of the earth, sun, and moon forms a right angle, the tidal range is smallest—10 percent to 30 percent below the average. This is known as a neap tide.

Tidal cycles on the Cape and Islands occur twice a day (semidiurnal), meaning there is a tidal pattern of two high tides and two low tides every twenty-four hours and six minutes. The strong influence of the moon in these tides—much stronger than the sun because the moon is closer to the earth—causes the observable tidal cycles to be based on a lunar rather than solar day. Twice a month during the full and new moons of the twenty-nine-day lunar cycle, the tides develop into extreme high tides and excessively low tides. Since the tides are so closely allied with the moon—its cycle and gravitational pull—tidal cycles occur fifty minutes later each day, a fact easily verified by a glance at the local tide tables. For example, if a peak high tide on Cape Cod Bay occurs at noon on a particular day at Brewster's Breakwater Beach, the following day the peak tide will occur at 12:50 P.M. It is important to understand this principle if you or your children enjoy swimming in Cape Cod Bay because you cannot swim there at low tide; the flats in some places extend out for nearly a mile, making them the perfect spot for shell collecting.

Although the high and low water points of the two daily tide cycles on the Cape and Islands are roughly the same, there are some variances in tidal ranges largely because of differences in the shapes and depths of straits and embayments and variations in local topography. For example, high water occurs earliest at Gay Head on Martha's Vineyard, where the mean (average) range between the two high tides is 2.8 feet. At Monomoy Point the mean average is 3.7 feet; near Falmouth Heights it is 1.3 feet; at the foot of Buzzards Bay off Cuttyhunk Island (the outermost of the Elizabeth chain) it is 3.4 feet, while at the head of the bay it is about 4.1 feet; and north of Muskeget Island off Nantucket it is 2 feet. At the head of Buzzards Bay, where it meets the southern end of the Cape Cod Canal, the mean tidal range is 4.1 feet; while at the northern end of the canal where it meets Cape Cod Bay, the mean range increases to 9.5 feet. A relatively similar situation exists on the eastern shore of the Cape and on Nantucket (facing the Gulf of Maine and Nantucket shoals, repectively), where the mean tidal range is 7.6 feet at Cape Cod Lighthouse in Truro, but at Tom Nevers Head on the southeast corner of Nantucket it is only 1.2 feet.

Knowing the tidal range or an approximation of it will enable you to plan a visit to the shore where exposure is greatest at low tide. Most local newspapers will furnish tide table information. However, weather conditions also affect tidal ranges, particularly in shallow bays, sounds, and straits. Offshore winds can counteract the normal rise of high tides and increase the lows, while onshore winds may have an opposite effect.

The shoreline, like all of nature's ecosystems, has specific zones, which are discussed later in detail. The area between the high and low tide lines is called the intertidal, or littoral, zone. The area above the high tide line is called the splash, or spray, zone; the area below the low tide line is called the subtidal zone. The subtidal zone is accessible by wading or swimming when the tide is relatively low or by rowboat or small craft when the tide is high.

The Power of Waves

Because of the impact a wave has on the beach, we think of it as a volume of water relentlessly propelling a surfboard to shore. But what appears to be a wave of water moving shoreward is in reality a wave of energy made visible by its action in the water. A wave is actually a pulse of energy flowing both beneath the surface of the ocean and through water that remains relatively stationary on the surface. A seagull or a piece of driftwood or a beach ball floating out beyond the surf zone (where waves break) remains fairly stationary after each passing wave. Only the wind or a current will move it and then not necessarily toward the beach.

The source of wave energy is wind, which transfers energy from air to water. Offshore waves are lower in height but longer from bow to stern than their near-shore form. As a wave approaches the shore, its "bottom" comes in contact with the slope of the submerged portion of the beach. The front of the wave is slowed, but the back continues to move forward at a greater rate of speed, causing the wave to pile up on itself, increasing its height. When the back of a wave finally overtakes the front, the wave crests into a breaker; the wave has, literally, tripped on the beach. Waves commonly strike the shore with a pressure of about two tons a square foot. If a pocket of air is trapped (and compressed) inside a curling wave crest, the force can be as great as eight tons a square foot.

But the energy flow does not stop here. The breaker creates a rush of water—the swash—that runs up the slope of the beach until it slows down and stops, depositing whatever material it has been carrying, such as seaweed and bits of flotsam, in a row of marine debris that is called the tide line. Most of the water sinks into the sand. The rest courses back down the beach (the backwash). The wash and backwash move sand, gravel, and even cobbles up and down the slope (foreshore) of the beach, sorting these sediments. The degree of distribution depends on the strength of the swash and the slope of the beach. This is the main reason for changes in the character of many beaches—one day a beach may be covered with sand, then several days later it may be partially or completely covered with pebbles and cobbles. Sometimes at the base of the foreshore there is a rounded step-shaped deposit of large pebbles and coarse gravel.

Where flood and ebb (low) tide currents flow rapidly in entrances to narrow bays and harbors, they tend to scour the bottom, molding the loosened sand and pebbles into low ripple marks. Scouring the bottom, a natural dredging process, keeps bays and harbor entrances open and provides a supply of nutrients for the organisms living in these inlets.

Beyond the foreshore is the offshore. The offshore slope is more gentle, has relatively fine sand, and is exposed only during peak low tide. On the beach above the foreshore there is often a slightly raised terrace of sand, called the summer berm, which is subject to the onslaught of storm waves. Higher up the beach is the winter berm, a more pronounced terrace built by winter storms; and landward of the winter berm, often in the spray zone, are the sand dunes, which are formed by wind rather than by waves.

Many visitors to the Cape and Islands are curious about the scalloped appearance along the water edge of the beach. These beach cusps are the result of wave action, longshore currents, and tidal movement working in concert. While at times strikingly displayed, these cusps usually disappear after a few days, leaving the beach in its original form. A longshore current arises when waves approach the shore obliquely—at an angle, rather than head on. These currents drag sand parallel to the beach but rarely reach a speed of greater than three knots (3.45 miles an hour).

Special mention should be made of the marine cliffs or scarps of clay and sand (of glacial till) you'll find along the shoreline at such places as Pilgrim Heights in Truro, the Truro Highlands, Eastham's Nauset Light Beach, Succanesset Point on Popponesset Beach, and Falmouth Heights on the Cape; Gay Head, the Highlands, and Nashaquitsa Cliffs on Martha's Vineyard; and Nantucket Cliffs, Squam Head, and Sankaty Head on Nantucket. Virtually no animals or plants live on these cliffs because the steep, often unstable slopes do not remain undisturbed for a sufficiently long period to permit the growth of organisms. Every time there is a storm, the swash of breaking storm waves rides up the sloping beach, cutting into the base of the cliff and sweeping the sand and clay seaward in the backwash. It is estimated that in the area between Highland Light and Nauset Light on the Cape there is an average loss of about three feet a year. In this fourteen-mile stretch it amounts to an average loss of about 750,000 cubic yards of land annually. There are also many miles of less spectacular wave-eroded cliffs up and down the Cape Cod Bay shoreline.

When storm waves undermine cliffs containing clay and silt layers of glacial till, the clay and fine silt particles are carried by currents into bays and estuaries by the flood tide. At slack water, the sediment sinks to the bottom and over a period of time builds up into a mud flat, aided by eelgrass that traps additional sediment particles. When the mud builds up to sea level, the flat is submerged at high tide and exposed at low tide. Salt-loving plants such as cord grass now take root and help trap even more silt and clay until the surface of the mud flat is eventually level with high water. At this point, the flat has become a salt marsh. Throughout this gradual growth, plants and animals that inhabit the area change both in variety of species and in abundance, keeping pace with this transition.

When glacial sand, cobbles, and gravel eaten from marine cliffs by storm waves are carried in the longshore current across the mouth of an inlet or bay, rather than into the estuary itself, these particles usually settle in the deeper water beyond and another transition begins—the gradual buildup of an underwater sandbar. The sandbar over time grows in length and height until it builds above the water level into a sand spit. Sand spits—for example, at Nauset Beach, on Monomoy Island, at Long Point in Provincetown, and on the Outer Beach at Nantucket Harbor—invariably curve toward the land at their outermost tip.

Life Along the Shoreline

Throughout the year, the sandy shores of the Cape and Islands are lined with all manner and size of marine invertebrates (animals without backbones) and their remains are strewn among the flotsam and jetsam of the beaches. Among the windrows (ridges) of live, dying, and dead seaweeds can be found communities of beach hoppers and other insectlike amphipods; the shells and cast-off tests of molted crabs and echinoderms (starfish, sand dollars, and sea urchins, to mention a few); varieties of marine sponges; transparent masses of jellyfish; pieces of coral skeletons; tough masses of sea pork and bulbous sea squirts;

molts of horseshoe crabs; driftwood filled with galleries of shipworms or holes made by gribbles; and so on.

Of all the invertebrate animals, however, no group is more characteristic of the seashore or has more appeal for the amateur and professional beachcomber than the shelled mollusks. Even the mere dining room zoologist, who knows animals primarily as gastronomic delicacies, is familiar with the oyster, the quahog, the scallop, and the mussel. Whether or not we are serious collectors, few of us who walk the beaches or the tidal flats can resist picking up a colorful moon snail, a well-turned whelk shell, or an elegant angel wing. To the seaside naturalist, mollusks have special appeal. Some, like the scallop, have developed extraordinary means of locomotion. Others, like the periwinkle, have managed to live on the edge of two radically different environments, while still others, such as sea slugs and squid, appear at first glance not to be mollusks at all.

Mollusks are not only one of the most obvious groups of invertebrates along the shores of the Cape and Islands, but they are also one of the most important groups in the animal kingdom. They include more described species of multicellular marine animals than almost any other major division in the animal kingdom, with more than 110,000 known.

The general distribution of mollusks and other organisms along the shorelines of the Cape and Islands depends on the nature of the sea bottom, the influence of waves and tides, the salt content of the water, and the water temperature. Animals and plants survive in their habitats usually through adaptations to these environmental factors that have evolved over varying periods of time.

These plants and animals are usually categorized by the broad general habitat in which they live, and it is important to know the limits of their native environments; although there are always exceptions, like the blue crab that both swims in open waters and prowls in beds of eelgrass.

Plants and animals (from the large to the microscopic) that live in open waters are called pelagic. Plants and animals that live on the bottom below the low tide zone make up what is called the benthos. In addition to microscopic algae, benthic plants include the larger algae—the brown, red, and green seaweeds—and the marine seed plant commonly known as eelgrass. Eelgrass is ecologically important as a nursery and shelter for many animals, as a stabilizer of sediments, and, when dead and disintegrating, as a food source for many organisms.

Benthic animals—mostly mollusks, worms, and crustaceans—burrow into the mud and sand; creep, crawl, or glide along the bottom; or attach themselves to hard surfaces, such as rocks, pilings, shells, bottles, or ropes. Usually the rougher the surface, the greater the number of organisms you'll find on it.

Sand Beaches

When people think of the Cape and Islands, they generally think of the beach. Sand beaches make up the largest habitat here. Most of our sands were carried by currents and tides from the continental shelf and deposited on the beach by waves; some were carried by rivers and estuaries to their mouths and deposited along the shore by prevailing coastal currents; and the rest had glacial beginnings—gleaned from the broad floodplains of glacial meltwater streams. Sand beaches are unstable habitats whose surfaces are at the mercy of every storm, tide, and wave, which constantly stir, sift, and redistribute the sand, continually reshaping the beach. This repeated roiling grinds the sediments into smaller particles and scatters the lighter elements to the higher parts of the beach where the wind carries the powdery, drier sand away to form sand dunes, leaving the coarser, larger grains behind. Below the low-tide line, waves also sort the sand grains, sending the finer particles to the bottom and washing the others seaward.

Beach sands along our shores consist mainly of eroded granite or granite-type rocks, composed of quartz particles of various colors occasionally infiltrated with minerals such as biotite—a dark brown to black or dark green mica—and chips of semiprecious gems such as garnets. There are also shell fragments of mollusks and crustaceans, as well as bits of detritus from many sources. A handful of beach sand viewed under a microscope reveals an attractive granular landscape of many hues and variously rounded shapes.

Our quartz sand tends to be fine and hard packed, an observation readily attested by all beach strollers. It is the home of exciting and little-explored microscopic animals and plants that live in the water-filled spaces between the sand grains. This group of unique organisms that live within these spaces is known as meiofauna (pronounced may-o-fawna). They glide, swim, or crawl through these spaces without displacing the particles. Meiofauna can be found from the surface of the sand to a depth of several meters. The area is more extensive than you might think; although the sand grains touch each other, the space between their irregular shapes provides ample living room. For a given volume of Cape beach sand, about 80 percent is sand and 20 percent is space.

The only plants growing in this area are algae, yeasts, and bacteria that are attached to the sand grains or live between them. These microscopic plants provide food for tiny but far more varied animals: protozoa, flatworms, roundworms, segmented worms, mites, sea slugs, and sea squirts. Many species display an amazing structure, having withstood the rigors of tides, waves, storms, extremes in temperature, and changes in salinity.

Beaches that are exposed to the ocean tides, winds, and waves of the Outer Cape from Nauset Beach in Orleans to Race Point in Provincetown are particularly unstable habitats. For this reason only the larger animals are able to survive—those that can burrow into the sand or move up and down the beach with the tide.

From a biological perspective, the more protected bay beaches are far more interesting between the tide lines than ocean beaches. Here you can see ripples from currents and the readily recognizable tracks of gulls, sandpipers, and other small birds—sometimes even those of crows and starlings. Occasionally along protected bay shores, like Barnstable's Sandy Neck, you can detect the alternating scratches of the scarce diamondback terrapin turtle. In the wet intertidal area or tidal flats, you will find the tracks, burrows, and holes of hard clams, razor clams, trumpet worms, clam worms, and sandworms, to name a few.

Farther up on the beach you will find sand fiddlers and beach hoppers but very little else, since most of the plant and animal life here is on the surface of the sand. Often the most commonly encountered materials are rows of live, dying, or dead seaweeds, termed black wrack, along the upper part of the beach, each row left behind at the level of high water. The rows of wrack are usually composed of species found immediately offshore: eelgrass, Irish moss, sea lettuce, kelp, and sponge. In the rows of wrack live several kinds of flies, like the eelgrass fly and biting green head. If rotting wrack is disturbed, often many tiny beach animals will emerge, like sand fleas or beach hoppers. On some beaches you'll find thin, sandcolored collars, a few inches high. These are egg masses of the moon snail, whose eggs are embedded in jelly in the sand collars. Other strange-looking sights include empty black rectangular cases with curled or horn-shaped extensions at the corners. These are mermaids' purses, or egg cases of the common skate, which have cut loose from their underwater nursery and drifted to the beach. Do not expect to see all of these animals at once; the habits, appearances, and migrations of marine beach fauna depend on temperature, tides, time of day, wave action, and season.

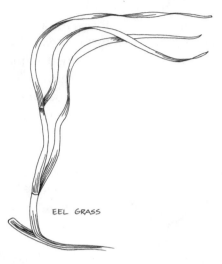

EEL GRASS

Sometimes the perfect shells of molted crabs and horseshoe crab skeletons, cast during growth, are carried onto the beach by the tide. Of course, parts of dead crabs and other invertebrate animals are often scattered about. Mollusk shells are also found in all stages of fracture and decay—color may be bleached by the sun, chips and breakage are common, edges may be dulled by rolling in the surf and by abrasion. These factors often make positive identification difficult. Usually the best collecting in terms of variety is accomplished directly after an onshore storm.

Sand Dunes

Amateur geologists have often described the Cape and Islands as one big sand dune. While this is an exaggeration, sand dunes—along with sandy beaches—dominate the picture postcard image of our region. In many places along the shoreline, you will find clusters and ridges of great and small sand dunes—from the great dunes of Provincetown to the minor dunes of Waquoit on Nantucket Sound on the south side, to the complex dunes of Sandy Neck in Barnstable on Cape Cod Bay and the small dunes of Black Beach bordering Great Sippewissett Marsh and Buzzards Bay in Falmouth on the north and west sides, to the rolling dunes of Chappaquiddick on the Vineyard.

In many cases small foredunes (as they are called) are backed by larger and more massive dunes that gradually merge into the typical pitch pine and scrub oak environment of the Cape and Islands. Often between the dunes are hollows or swales, which—if they cut below the water table—

become brackish or freshwater ponds. The dune water table is highest in winter and lowest in summer due to greater evaporation and less rain.

The highest coastal dunes on the Cape and the Islands occur where the coastline is at right angles with the prevailing winds, which carry sand landward from the beach and from the intertidal sand flats. The finer sand particles are carried farthest inland and become characteristic of inland dunes.

The growth rates of dunes are directly related to the density and growth of beach grass, which helps to hold dunes in place, although this is often a losing battle. On the Cape and Islands, the vertical dune growth rate varies from twelve to eighteen inches a year, but erosion and dune migration often blunt this growth.

Your first trek through dunes will reveal a physical environment severe in several respects—shifting sand, strong winds, salt spray, intense light, and nutrient-poor soils. This environment is virtually uninhabitable for most species of plants and animals; indeed, those few that do occur must be well adapted to weather the harsh conditions. Plants such as American beach grass grow best when they are buried by sand. This and other beach grasses, by trapping sand and stabilizing the surface on which they grow, play a major part in the development and maintenance of coastal dunes.

PLANTS

Important plants that may be associated with the American beach grass are dusty miller; the beach pea; seaside goldenrod; beach heather, or

SALT SPRAY ROSE

SEA HEATHER

poverty grass; the pesky cocklebur, or sea burdock; and the seaside pin-weed. These are all herbaceous (green-leaved) plants. Among shrubs that may be present are beach plum; poison ivy (see question and answer section); bayberry; the salt spray rose; scrub oak; the red cedar, or juniper; and the sea myrtle, or goundsel tree. Plants such as red fescue grass, wormwood, and seaside spurge usually grow in dune areas that are protected from wind and salt spray.

A few lichens (moss) including old man's beard can be found on beach plum and bayberry twigs; in boggy hollows between dunes are such mosses as sphagnum and hairy cap. Where water is highly acidic in dune bogs, for example at Chappaquoit Beach in West Falmouth, in the Province Lands dunes of Truro and Provincetown, and on Monomoy Island, plants such as the round-leafed sundew, cranberry, peat moss, steeplebush, and sensitive fern abound.

ANIMALS

The animals of the sand dunes are apparently more sensitive to the physical extremes of this environment than the plants. Many are nocturnal. Consequently, you will be more successful finding them on a slightly overcast day or when it is cooler in the early morning, late afternoon, and evening. It is little wonder it seems hot on the dunes; around the noon hours on a clear summer day, the sand surface temperature may pass 120 degrees Fahrenheit! However, just below the surface, the temperature drops surprisingly.

Insects are prominent and pesky, particularly near dune wetlands. There may be predatory robber flies; biting horseflies; small shore flies; sand flies, or punkies; mosquitoes; mole crickets; digger wasps; and tiger beetles. Near the upper intertidal zone look for scavenger beetles and earwigs. In this area, careful observation may reveal small dents in the sand surface made by beach hoppers or sand fleas. Where there is much dune vegetation there will probably be a few kinds of herbivores, such as maritime locusts, as well as ant lions and several species of flying insects; wolf spiders; small birds; and perhaps an occasional hawk, rabbit, deer, or nocturnal fox. Look for droppings or for tracks in the sand to help your search.

Intertidal Flats

The intertidal, or littoral, zone, as noted earlier in this chapter, is the breadth of the shore that stretches from the highest point reached by the tide to the lowest point exposed by the tide. The area between the extreme high and extreme low tide lines is known as the intertidal flats.

When intertidal flats are separated from the mainland by shallow pools of water, they become sandbars. On the Cape and Islands, they vary mostly from pure sand to sand and gravel mixtures; only a few are entirely mud or have a significant mud component, as in some flats off Cotuit and Sandwich. The most rewarding observations and satisfactory collecting in this habitat are found at the Barnstable Flats inside Sandy Neck; the flats of West Dennis, Brewster, Eastham, Wellfleet, Chatham, Waquoit Bay, and West Falmouth; and flats along Vineyard Sound and Nantucket Sound shores on the Islands.

Unlike the beaches, the intertidal flats are not as rigorous an environment for marine plants and animals because they are not affected as much by heat, exposure to storms, and by the drying action of air and wind. Since these flats are adjacent to many other habitats at sea and on shore, you will find not only typical intertidal organisms here but some animals from piers, pilings, groins, and marshes. A good rule of thumb is that the variety of plants and animals gradually increases seaward through the intertidal zone to the middle and sometimes outer edge of the subtidal zone.

Sandbars are free of any obvious vegetation although they may often be topped with clumps of seaweed torn from the bottom farther offshore and dropped by the ebbing tide. In late summer and early fall, on bars exposed to both Sounds and to Buzzards Bay, masses of gulfweed washed in on currents and eddies from the 700-mile distant Sargasso sea, south of Bermuda, may be mixed with the local seaweed. If you have a fresh collection of gulfweed, rinsing it carefully in a bucket of seawater may release a large community of exotic organisms including sea horses and curious indigenous crabs. The lagoons or shallow pools may have fairly extensive growths of eelgrass. Here, subtidally, eelgrass supports a varied seasonal population of microscopic animals and plants on which larger animals feed, such as carnivorous ribbon worms and flatworms, skeleton shrimp, jellyfish, sea anemones, chink shells, and small bivalves such as slipper shells, bay scallops, and crabs. On the sandbars, particularly those exposed to the open ocean, you will find hen or surf clams, the largest bivalve on the Cape, up to eight inches long by six inches wide.

Most animals living in a tidal flat use a very efficient burrowing technique. For this reason, when a tidal flat is first seen at low tide, it usually appears quite barren because the great majority of the organisms are living beneath the surface. Tidal flat inhabitants are for the most part filter feeders, living on the detritus—minute particles of organic matter produced by natural crushing and decay. Included in this group are several kinds of clams, such as quahogs, steamer clams, razor clams, and a great variety of worms.

Among animals that prowl and glide over the surface of the flats as well as prey on intertidal burrowers or feed on surface detritus are sand shrimp, grass shrimp, shore shrimp, hermit crabs, green crabs, spider crabs, and snails (including the ferocious moon snail, which feeds on bivalves and other snails by boring into their shells).

The naturally gregarious and populous fiddler crabs, discussed in the question and answer section following Chapter 4, merit special mention. They live on sand and on mud flats and are also found above the high-water line, between tide lines, in salt marshes, or where tall cord grass grows. Along the beach when the tide has ebbed, a horde of fiddlers— sometimes so large a group that their scurrying emits an audible rustle— will scuffle away when disturbed, retreating shoreward toward protective crevices or to the safety of their one- or two-foot-deep tunnels.

Although mud flats, as opposed to sand flats, are the least common intertidal flats on the Cape and Islands, they have the greatest variety of species living beneath their surfaces. Close examination will reveal signs of hidden life everywhere in the forms of differently shaped small holes, some with curiously sculptured castings; collections of individualistic tracks; and little mounds of fecal mud pellets. Here there are many kinds of bivalves, burrowing amphipods, and other crustaceans, as well as numerous worms. Occasionally you can see the mottled dog whelks or nassa mud snail, the New England dog whelk, or the eroded basket shell—all less than an inch long—making their way along the surface.

Two other kinds of snails seen in mud flats are the whelk or conch, represented by two species, the knobbed whelk and the channeled whelk. Both feed on quahogs and other clams and are found in the subtidal zone. The knobbed whelk is our largest snail, attaining a length of ten inches. The muscular foot of these snails is considered a delicacy in some quarters, and they are harvested accordingly.

If you see a whelk perambulating jerkily but determinedly over the tidal flat, its shell doubtlessly is occupied by a large, flat-clawed hermit crab. Sooner or later while prowling subtidally, you will come across a horseshoe crab, a large (up to twenty-four inches long) but harmless and splendid animal. Horseshoe crabs swim with a lurching motion along the bottom. Their shape is distinctive, and they cannot be confused with any other animal along our coast.

Subtidal Zone

Wading slowly seaward from the lowest part of the intertidal zone, you enter, imperceptibly, the subtidal zone, an area whose bottom closely resembles the zone you have just left, although it gradually slopes off to deeper waters. For the most part, you will find the same community of organisms here. Nearly all the worms, snails, clams, crustaceans, and other burrowers and wanderers of the intertidal flats are also found in the shallow waters of the subtidal zone. Exceptions are the fiddler crabs and the beach hoppers, which are ill-adapted to this kind of existence. Taking their places on the surface are the handsome swimming crabs, the lady crabs, and the blue crabs; and in the substratum live burrowing sea cucumbers, sand shrimp, sea anemones, and organisms that cannot stand exposure to sunlight.

We would like to draw special attention to a coarse, ropelike dark green seaweed called the oyster thief or dead man's fingers, or green fleece. This has only recently and accidentally found its way to the coast of Cape Cod. It is a serious pest because of its choking effect on bivalve mollusks. When it attaches to and grows on the shell of an oyster, for example, its weight may prevent the oyster from opening. One of the reasons green fleece is becoming a more dominant member of the subtidal flora is that it is not favored as a food source. When it washes up on the beach, often in ugly, heavy ropy masses, it drags along the living or dead object to which it was originally attached.

The carnivorous clam worm is the most common of the larger sea worms living in the subtidal zone. It is found under clumps of edible mussels, under stones, in burrows in the sand or mud, or in sand tubes whose cases are easy to spot.

The clam worm is now recognized as a secondary host for a parasitic fluke that lives in the intestinal tract of the common eel. But the clam worm is best known to fisherman, some claiming that it has no rival as bait for certain kinds of fish. Occasionally, worm watchers get a special treat when clam worms swarm, an activity that takes place in the summer during the dark of the moon. It is fascinating to see a large tangle of these long worms thrashing at the surface, flesh-colored iridescent males swimming spirally around the equally ripe reddish females and clouding the water with shed sperm and eggs. This seasonal reproductive scene is best seen by flashlight from the end of a pier or from a floating dock.

The water that covers the subtidal zone carries a variety of organisms from the open sea swept in by tides, winds, and waves. Probably the best known of these organisms are jellyfish. You should handle them with care; many of them sting. Some emit a nerve toxin that will stun their prey. Ordinarily, a jellyfish's stinging cells do not penetrate the thicker skinned parts of our bodies, but the nematocysts of the southern infamous sea nettle (which is starting to appear more and more in our waters), the lion's mane and sea wattle jellyfish, and the Portuguese man-of-war produce a stinging or burning sensation and inflammation in humans.

Approach large jellyfish with caution even if you find them washed up on the beach. The sea wattle is pink with a smooth surface, up to seven and a half inches wide, with as many as forty tentacles. The lion's mane is yellow or orange brown, up to eight inches across, and has a broad, flattish bell with numerous tentacles below. In the waters of the Gulf of Maine, it grows to be the largest jellyfish in the world, more than seven feet in diameter. The Portuguese man-of-war, which occasionally drifts to the Cape and Islands, is easily recognized by its balloonlike iridescent blue-to-pink-to-purple float below a deflatable foot-long sail, with which it sails before the wind, and its forty- to fifty-foot-long tentacles (that give off powerful but nonfatal stings).

These jellyfish, along with the translucent ten-inch moon jellyfish—with conspicuous white horseshoe-shaped gonads and numerous fingerlike tentacles—are late summer visitors along the Buzzards Bay and the Nantucket Sound coasts of the Cape; they favor the Atlantic coasts of the Islands. In addition, smaller jellyfish inhabit these waters during the warmer months. They are nearly transparent, simple in structure, and vary in size from less than three-sixteenths of an inch to (rarely) more than one inch across. To see these jellyfish properly, you need to scoop them into a large, clean glass jar and hold the jar up to the sun. You can observe them swimming gently, their transparent bells pulsating in the liquid.

Wading in the subtidal or intertidal zone barefoot, you may also be nipped by curious hermit crabs or by one of several species of small fish—the type depends on the season, location, and temperature of the water. Included among the attackers might be one of four species of mummichogs, killifish, or chogshead minnows; sheepshead minnows; the northern puffer; silversides, or the schooling young or juveniles of bluefish; sea robins; scup, or porgies; and possible needlefish. A characteristic shadowy ripple in the water surface often indicates a school of fish; an even surer sign is fish breaking the water while fleeing larger fish preying on them. The positions of these schools are also betrayed by individual or small flocks of bids—gulls, terns, cormorants, and ducks—diving on them at the surface.

The Joy of Collecting

Learning how to collect shells and marine organisms efficiently, enjoyably, and profitably is much like a neophyte learning how to clean and cook a fish. You can get a good start by reading a cookbook, but you must get a hands-on experience before satisfactory results are achieved. So it is with making nature collections along our shores. Without practice it is not easy to wend your way through the intertidal zone and recognize all of the objects commonly a part of the beach drift: egg case masses and ribbon-shaped egg case coils of the channeled and knobbed whelks; vertebrae of sharks; parts of fish skeletons; a snail's operculum (trapdoor used by a snail to close its shell after the animal withdraws inside); "mermaids' purses" (the egg cases of some skates); broken and whole shells of snails and mollusks; dried sponges; bits of wood riddled by the ubiquitous shipworm (actually a mollusk) or by the sea roach (related to terrestrial sow bugs); fragments of the hard parts of a host of invertebrates and vertebrates; and, of course, the artifacts of man's careless and untidy discards. The flotsam you may find may come from far beyond its usual range, washed in and deposited by disturbances of the environment, making it even more difficult to identify.

The objective in your quest for knowledge of our coastline should be to achieve the reverse of those who see a great deal but observe almost nothing. Patience and care should be your watchwords. Thoreau wrote, "The question is not what you look at, but what you see."

The most important collecting tools are your eyes, head, hands, and feet, probably in that order. Common sense dictates that they must all be protected: eyes with reflecting sunglasses; shortened fingernails and ordinary cotton gloves to save your hands from scrapes, splinters, and cuts from barnacles. Wear old tennis shoes or sneakers. Other safety measures include protection from sunburn; care in handling crabs that pinch, large jellyfish that sting, fish with well-developed spines, and rocks that are slippery from microscopic algae or are just wet. Always keep track of the tide when you are on sandbars or intertidal flats, and avoid or use special care in handling any dead fish or dead invertebrates that you suspect were poisoned by red tide. Pink or red discoloration of the tidal waters or the water in tidal flat depressions indicates a red tide condition.

Federal, state, and local agencies; coastal experts from the Cape's many institutions of science, natural resources, and conservation organizations; and media attention has centered on the disturbing and sad fact that our coastal environment is suffering increased damage daily. Our shores are attacked by population, development, and political pressures relentlessly applied. Among these encroachments are the construction of increasing numbers of docks, piers, marinas, and coastal condominiums, many of them trespassing on our wetlands and causing environmental alterations that often destroy shore habitat. They exert direct influence on the lives of the fauna and flora of the intertidal and subtidal waters. Sometimes their influence is more subtle—the effluent from sewage treatment plants; run-off from overfertilized lawns and golf club fairways; pollution from salted roads, power plants, and so on. Because the thin ribbon of sand, mud, rocks, and marsh that borders our region supports a larger number of species than any other ecosystem of the same size, and is affected so negatively by environment alteration and species loss, it is vital that all who visit our shores understand why this fragile environment should not be violated.

It is well to reflect on the bleak and sterile seashore that will remain if those of us who use it for recreation and relaxation needlessly turn over rocks, carelessly dig up sand and mud flats, pollute with artifactual wastes, and carry away every organism and every remnant of every organism on which we can lay our hands. Wise conservation of natural resources and proper environmental practices, acceptable outdoor manners, and truly civilized behavior suggest strongly that we and all coastal visitors observe these six rules:

1. Do not catch, dig, or pick up more than you really need; always leave behind some of the specimens in which you are interested.
2. If you must move rocks, seaweed, and flotsam, do it gently to avoid crushing animals under or beside the disturbed material.
3. Replace rocks, seaweed, and flotsam as nearly in place as they were, being careful of the organisms underneath.
4. For the safety of others, and to protect burrowers in the sand, fill in the holes you have dug for whatever purpose.
5. Avoid collecting in unusual or unique natural areas; plants or animals inhabiting them may seldom be seen elsewhere.
6. Always obey the fish and game laws as well as the beach and shoreline regulations (local, state, and federal) on collecting and scavenging the shore area you are visiting. This information should be readily available at town halls, local libraries, police stations, and conservation departments.

Q & A

Why is the water so much warmer in Nantucket Sound,
Q *Vineyard Sound, Pleasant Bay, and Cape Cod Bay than it is on the ocean beaches?*

Bays and sounds around the Cape and Islands are relatively shallow bodies of water that warm up much quicker than the deeper Atlantic, which reflects light and heat rather than absorbing it. Average peak summer temperatures of bays and sounds in the region are in the sixties and seventies, while average ocean temperatures usually hover in the mid- to high fifties, rising sometimes into the low sixties.

What are sea gulls? Do their feathers get wet?
Q *Why does it look like they stay in one place when they sit on the water?*

There isn't any species of bird called a sea gull. The two most common gulls on the Cape and Islands are the herring gull, which is the common, gray-and-white gull, and the great black-backed gull, which is larger and—as its name implies—is black and white.

Gull feathers are absolutely waterproof so no water ever touches a gull's skin. They apply oil with their beaks from an oil gland on their lower back, just above the tail. This makes them more buoyant. In a current, gulls paddle with their feet against the flow, making them appear to be staying in one place. Herring and great black-backed gulls are scavengers. They will eat anything from baby birds to fish to garbage at dumps that are many miles inland. Because gulls are seabirds it is easy for them to live as far as 50 to 100 miles offshore.

Q What is a sand dollar?

Sand dollars, shaped like large silver dollars, are related to the phylum of starfish, sea urchins, and sea cucumbers. On the top of their hard, flat dorsal surface they have a flowerlike, five-petaled pattern of tiny holes that are used for breathing. On the bottom they have a feltlike coating of fine spines by which they move and pass along food to the mouth in the center. Sand dollars are brown, purple, or red in color, but when washed up on the beach dead, they are quickly bleached by the sun. A favorite of shellfish collectors, sand dollars live in the sandy bottom of the Cape and Islands' many bays and sounds. They feed on microorganisms and are preyed upon by bottom-feeding fish. One of the best places to collect sand dollars is off Menemsha Bight on Martha's Vineyard.

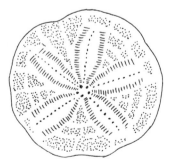

SAND DOLLAR

Q   What is a periwinkle? Where do you find it?

The periwinkle, one of the most common marine species on the Cape and Islands, is a small, dark marine snail, one of three or four species found on the New England coast. It inhabits the rocks, jetties, and break-waters just below the high-tide line, scraping a vegetarian living from the thin plant films on the surface of rocks using a unique filelike organ on its underside called a radula. Periwinkles, usually olive in color, grow to be about an inch wide and an inch in height. Their shells are cone shaped and ringed with spiral bands. Many periwinkles on the Cape and Islands, however, are yellowish white in color with tiny brown spots on their shells.

When the water is ankle deep you can wade out and watch these creatures migrating slowly, like miniature caravans, over and under rocks. Like their land cousins, periwinkles, also called pinkles, move at a snail's pace, but compared to the barnacles that share their habitat they are wonders of speed. You can also spot periwinkles in marsh grass at the edge of a wetland or on the mud flats of Cape Cod Bay.

In places like the British Isles, periwinkles are commonly gathered as seafood. Although they are equally abundant here, periwinkles seem to enjoy an immunity from American appetites. Periwinkle shells, however, are in great demand by both English and American hermit crabs.

Q   What are harbor seals? Where do you find them?

Harbor seals, also called common seals, are a species of marine mammal commonly seen in waters off the Cape and Islands from November to May. They breed along the coast of Maine and northward, then migrate south to our shores. They may be found off the Cape during the winter with large groups notable at Race Point in Provincetown, Great Island in Wellfleet, Coast Guard Beach in Eastham, Monomoy Island and adjacent shoals in Chatham, Great Island in Yarmouth, Woods Hole in Falmouth, and in waters surrounding Nantucket and Martha's Vineyard.

The brown and black seals have doglike heads, whiskers that resemble a cat's, torpedo-shaped bodies, a leathery fur, and four webbed flippers or feet. Harbor seals are playful and fun to watch. They enjoy swimming in cold, salty waters and feed on fish.

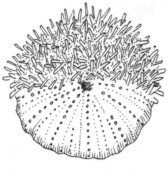

SEA URCHIN

Q What is a sea urchin?

Sea urchins are related to starfish, sand dollars, and sea cucumbers. They have hard calcium shells on which there are long, fine-to-coarse, movable spines of bright colors. They can grow to be the size of a rubber ball, slightly flattened. Like starfish, sea urchins move by tube feet that protrude through tiny pores in the shell. On the Cape and Islands, there are two kinds of sea urchins—purple sea urchins and green sea urchins.

Purple sea urchins live near pilings, piers, and oyster beds and on coarse sand to rocky bottoms well below the surface. They eat seaweeds and other invertebrates by scraping them from the undersurfaces of rocky substrates and scavenge on dead animals.

The larger, more common, green sea urchins are found on the deeper sand bottoms of Vineyard Sound and are the only sea urchin found north of Cape Cod. Their food is the same as that of the purple urchin, and they are eaten by cod and other fish, sea stars, and large shorebirds. Their eggs (roe) are a regular on restaurant menus along the coasts of Mediterranean countries, as well as in cities along our East Coast.

Q What are terns? Where do you find them? How do they protect their nests?

If Cape Cod had an official bird, it would be the tern. Terns, once called sea swallows, are truly native Cape birds, which numbered in the tens of thousands just a century ago but are much less abundant now. Terns have resided on the Cape for hundreds of years longer than even the herring gull, the most common sea gull.

TERN

Each summer four species of terns nest on Cape beaches. The dove-sized and swallow-sized species are the common tern, least tern, roseate tern, and arctic tern. Terns fish offshore and along beaches most everywhere on the Cape, but areas suitable for nesting are few. They prefer isolated areas, generally coastal dunes, away from disturbances—a rare commodity here. The largest tern colony in New England is on New Island in the Outer Cape's Nauset Marsh, where there are thousands of tern nests.

The dove-sized common tern has a red-orange-and-black-tipped bill and can be found in Nauset Marsh, on Monomoy Island, and on beaches in the Yarmouthport area. The swallow-sized least tern has a yellow bill and can be found in large numbers in Kalmus Park at the end of Ocean Street in Hyannis, the beaches of West Dennis, and the Popponesset Bay area of Mashpee. The rare, dove-sized roseate tern has a black bill with a red base and can be found in Nauset Marsh, on Cotuit beaches, and on beaches in Yarmouthport. Also rare, the dove-sized arctic tern has a dark red bill and can be found in Nauset Marsh, on Monomoy Island, and on Provincetown beaches.

Terns, particularly the common and least terns, go to great lengths to defend their nests. They will dive at intruders—man or animal—who venture into their nesting areas. This dive-bombing behavior is a defense mechanism to protect chicks and eggs from predators. Common terns have actually been known to peck humans on the head and draw blood. Least terns threaten intruders but rarely peck. Tern nesting areas inside the Cape Cod National Seashore and other sanctuaries are posted and roped off to keep the public out and protect the terns.

Q *What are lobsters? Where can you find them?*
Have they always been considered a delicacy?

Most people will agree that the lobster is the aristocrat of New England seafood. But did you know that in spite of its elegant scientific name— *Homarus americanus*—and its even more elegant price in local restaurants, the American lobster was once used primarily as fertilizer and as food for the poor? Historical records of the early days of Plymouth Colony tell us lobsters were found in almost unbelievable abundance in the offshore waters of Cape Cod Bay and Massachusetts Bay. Rows of lobsters eighteen inches deep were once thrown up on beaches after a storm. Such lobster beachings were regarded by the early colonists as nuisances; the lobsters were used to fertilize crops or as a cheap source of food.

In coastal parts of the South during the 1700s and 1800s, lobsters were regularly fed to servants and slaves. There is a record of a group of Virginia indentured servants who, in the early 1700s, petitioned the colonial government that they "should not be fed lobster more than twice a week." The petition was granted in mercy.

Perhaps people were put off by the grotesque appearance of this crustacean, with its horny armor plating, spindly legs, and menacing pincers. The lobster is as strange inside as it is out: most of its nervous system is along its stomach rather than its back; it has two brains, listens with feelers on its legs, smells with its feet, has teeth in its stomach, and kidneys behind its forehead.

Or perhaps our forefathers didn't like the idea of eating a scavenger. The lobster is more accurately a cannibal, eating not only its newly hatched young but other full-grown lobsters when they are in their "soft phase" just after molting (shedding a shell).

Whatever the source of the early prejudice against the lobster, once its taste caught on, its lowly beginnings and unsavory habits were quickly forgotten. Cape Codders seem to have been the first New Englanders to realize the intrinsic worth of the lobster, for it was primarily here that lobster fishing developed as a separate industry in the late 1700s. Maine, which now boasts by far the largest U.S. lobster catch, did not develop a lobster fleet until the 1840s. Today, this onetime fertilizer is a multi-million-dollar industry.

Although once abundant off our sandy shores, the lobster now resides primarily on rocky ledges and in crevices along the bottoms of ocean canyons from Maine to Connecticut. Generally, the smaller lobsters live in shallow waters nearer the shore while the giant ones, growing up to fifty pounds, are found in depths of 200 fathoms (a fathom is six feet) or more. The lobster's main diet consists of bits of dead seaweed and fish, which it rips into edible-sized bits with its two enormous front claws—one used for crushing and the other for tearing.

The lobster is ordinarily a slow-moving creature, walking sedately along the ocean bottom on four pairs of legs. However, when alarmed, the lobster shows its unusual swimming stroke—it flips its tail violently forward, which hurls the animal suddenly backwards and away from danger.

No doubt, the lobster has come a long way. Restaurant patrons pay from $6.95 to nearly $40.00 (depending on its weight, how it is prepared, and where you eat) to sample the sweet white meat of the lobster.

Q *What are starfish? How do they move?*
Where do you find them?

Have you ever picked up a live starfish, perhaps seen the mass of wiggling little feet underneath it? Have you ever taken the time to watch a starfish move on one of its crutchlike tube feet or one of its many arms? Such movement requires one of the most complicated hydraulic systems designed to produce movement in any animal.

A starfish is an echinoderm, a class of marine animals with spiny skin. Other common echinoderms are sea urchins and sand dollars. On the top center of a starfish's body you'll find an organ that looks like an eye. It allows starfish to take in water necessary for movement. The water is carried along a tube (called a stone canal) to a ringlike tube (called the ring canal) that circles the center of the animal's body. Five tubes extend from the ring of each of the starfish's five arms. When a starfish wishes to move, it pumps water down into its tube feet. The water's pressure forces suction cups at the end of each foot to work. The animal uses its muscles to pump water out of these tube feet and to pull itself along in the direction the suction cups were applied. The suction cups, however, will not work in soft sand. In this case, the tube feet act as hundreds of small legs operating together to help the animal move.

From a strictly economic point of view, starfish cause more harm than good. They destroy millions of dollars' worth of shellfish yearly, prying the shellfish open with their many suction cups. Lacking true arms or claws, the starfish cannot move food to its stomach, so it moves its stomach to the food by sliding it into the exposed shellfish. With the secretion of digestive juices, the shellfish is devoured in place.

Starfish, on the other hand, are an important part of the ecology of the sea, and like all links in the food chain, they help maintain the balance of the whole marine ecosystem.

Starfish, more properly called sea stars, have always inspired humans with a sense of awe and are one of nature's most intriguing animals. Worldwide there are 1,600 distinct species of starfish, although only four or five are found on the Cape and Islands. Starfish intrigue medical researchers with their ability to regenerate parts of their bodies. All creatures have some capacity for repair and replacement of broken parts, but nothing compares with the starfish. For years, oyster farmers tried to destroy starfish by ripping or chopping them into several pieces. To their dismay, they ended up, after the regeneration process, with three or four times as many starfish. Imagine the implications of surgical healing if doctors could invoke damaged cells to heal themselves.

A local cousin of the sand dollar and a distant cousin of the sea urchin, starfish are frequently found along beaches on Cape Cod Bay, Nantucket Sound, and Martha's Vineyard Sound.

Pick up a starfish the next time you see one, study it closely, but just remember to put it back where you found it. Mussel beds are usually a good place to spot them.

Q What is a sunfish?

The giant ocean sunfish, an animal of the open sea, is a remarkable fish. Known also as a head fish, mola, and pez luna, it ranges as far north as England, Cape Cod, and San Francisco. As one of the largest of all known fish, it reaches a length of about eight and a half feet and a weight of nearly a ton. Ocean sunfish may be seen offshore on a calm summer day off the east coast of the Cape, floating lazily on one of their bright sides, just breaking the surface, heavy pectoral fins moving slowly to and fro through the air. They move so slowly that they are attacked both internally and externally by many kinds of parasites and are a parasitologist's delight. Unusual anatomical features include

SUNFISH

its suborbicular shape (like a thick elongated manhole cover), the lack of an air bladder, ventral fins, spinous dorsal fins, and teeth completely united in each jaw forming a bony beak.

Q What are sea gooseberries?

Sea gooseberries—also called comb jellies and sea walnuts—can be found scattered across the surface of the sand near the tide line. At first glance, the two-inch shimmering little mound appears to be nothing more than a pile of Jell-O dropped by a child playing in the sand. The transparent, gelatinous-bodied animal floats on the surface of the ocean bay and sounds near the shoreline. The prismlike colors you see in a comb jelly are caused by the waving of eight bands of cilia (tiny hairs) arranged in rows for movement. The animal can move all of the cilia at once or one row at a time. But it is a poor swimmer and at the mercy of strong sea currents.

Comb jellies feed on small organisms that are caught and swept into their mouths by minicurrents when the cilia move. Young comb jellies may glow briefly when swirled by an oar dipping into the water or by the arm of a swimmer out for night exercise. There is no agreement as to why this happens. One theory holds that the light confuses predators. Another suggests a nervous response on the part of the comb jelly.

Comb jellies reproduce frequently, shedding both eggs and sperm from their mouths. Growth occurs while the larvae are drifting in ocean currents.

Q What is a ghost shrimp? What is a mud shrimp? What is a sand shrimp?

Pale yellow ghost shrimps, commonly mistaken for mud shrimps, are two- to four-inch crustaceans (invertebrates with a hard outer shell) that burrow in the sand or mud of protected beaches and bays, pumping water through these burrows with pistonlike abdominal appendages. Ghost shrimps, which resemble miniature lobsters, are thought to be more closely related to hermit crabs than to shrimp. They have a smooth rostrum (head) and two claws (in the male) unequal in size. Ghost shrimps are able to move rapidly through their burrows and are seldom seen, which accounts for their name. Their small brown fecal pellets are eaten by hermit crabs and other animals, while small pea crabs often cohabit the ghost shrimps' burrows, taking advantage of the flowing oxygenated plankton-rich water.

The mud shrimp, a close relative of the ghost shrimp in both size and appearance, can be found in shallow depths on the Cape's south shore. The specific species found here is called the Naushon mud shrimp, named after one of the islands in the Elizabeth chain where mud shrimps are common.

Sand shrimps are common to the shallow waters and tidal pools of Cape Cod Bay, Nantucket Sound, and Vineyard Sound. They are transparent miniature shrimps about an inch and a half long, and they appear to be sculptured from sand. You can feel sand shrimp at low tide tickling up against your toes.

Q What is a gribble?

Gribbles function as sea termites. They are a species of small isopod (flat dorso-ventral oval bodies) crustaceans, up to five millimeters long, that bore holes in pilings and driftwood. In some cases, gribbles are even more destructive than shipworms (a wood boring mollusk). They burrow into wood and can reduce it to a spongy consistency. But unlike shipworms, which feed on the wood itself, gribbles are thought to feed on wood-dwelling fungi.

The surface of a piling infested with gribbles is usually peppered with small holes less than two millimeters in diameter. When such a piling is eventually eaten through by gribbles at the sand or mud level—giving it an hourglass shape—the structure will fall.

Q What is a barnacle?

"The barnacle is an animal that lives by standing on its head and waving its feet in the air," the great naturalist Louis Agassiz once noted.

Barnacles are crustaceans (hard-shelled class of invertebrates related to crabs and lobsters). The most common type found here is the stalkless acorn barnacles that live, often in tremendous numbers, attached to firm surfaces that include boulders, rocks, pilings, boat bottoms, seaweed, oysters, turtles, and even whales. Acorn barnacles are cemented directly to their small, dark oval shells and are covered by a set of six tiny plates made of calcium, two of which act as doors that permit featherlike legs to emerge and collect food, in the form of microscopic plants, by waving back and forth in the water. Barnacles attach themselves to surfaces through a special adhesive they produce.

Also found in the area are goose barnacles or goose-necked barnacles, which have flexible extended stalks. Goose barnacles usually attach themselves to flotsam (marine debris) and feed on jellyfish, small fish, and plankton. They wash ashore on the Cape and Islands on boards, bottles, and floating objects.

Q What shellfish are you likely to find on the beach?

An integral part of the overall flavor of the Cape Cod experience is its bountiful harvest of edible bivalve mollusks. There are seven species which dominate recipe books of Cape Cod cuisine. The heart-shaped, thick-shelled quahog, whose shell provided wampum for the original native Cape Codders, are burrowers that inhabit the upper six inches of a variety of muddy to sandy subtidal and low intertidal substrates. The quahog may be more commonly known by its marketing names (based on size) of cherrystone, little neck, and chowder clams.

Sea clams, or surf clams, are the sandy subtidal producers of those large ashtray shells often acquired at the beach. Most commercial clam chowder is made from their meat. In the lower portion of tidal flats and the shallow subtidal, approximately dime-sized holes usually indicate the presence of either steamer clams or razor clams. Steamer clams have shells that are thin, oval, and white, with long, only partially retractable siphons or necks (useful for dipping into melted butter). Razor clams

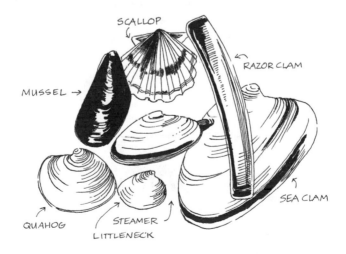

SCALLOP

RAZOR CLAM

MUSSEL →

QUAHOG

STEAMER
LITTLENECK

SEA CLAM

have short siphons, with long, dark shells the shape of an old-fashioned straight razor. Razor clam burrows are deep and the animal is quick; those caught usually end up in chowder.

The shell of a bay scallop is recognizable as the symbol of the Shell Oil Company. This remarkable, jet-propelled, multiple-eyed creature inhabits the subtidal, especially where eelgrass is found. Oysters have thick, variably shaped shells that are found attached to rocks, shells, and shell clutch at or below the tideline. Wellfleet oysters are especially renowned for their flavor. Finally there are blue mussels, which have just recently become popular to the American palate. These mussels are found intertidally and subtidally in often large colonies, attached to each other by special byssus threads (their "beards") that they produce. They have handsome blue-black, elongated, slightly triangular shells.

Q *What is a hermit crab?*

Hermits are small, common sand- and mud-bottom-dwelling, primarily scavenging, soft-bodied crabs that have become adapted to living in snail shells. Their well-developed, soft, and somewhat coiled abdomen is inserted into empty snail shells that they carry around on their backs and into which they retreat when attacked. Special appendages enable them to attach securely to the spiral central support of the shell, and they can be released when growth induces them to move into a larger shell. Males are generally larger than females; both sexes are amazingly feisty and spend a great part of their lives fighting.

Hermits can usually be found by the hundreds in tidal pools or shallow waters of the Cape and Islands' coves, sounds, and bays. A good place to look for them at low tide is in the islands of eelgrass on the flats of Cape Cod Bay.

HERMIT CRAB

Q   What is a sea hare?

Sea hares, a large (250 millimeters) species of snail or sea slug, are rare visitors to the Cape and Islands. Their sporadic appearances depend on gulf stream currents, which guide their paths. Unique wing-like folds that extend along their back on each side are used for swimming. This gives them a rabbit-like appearance when viewed head on. These massive snails, with weakly calcified internal shells, are brown in color with a fine black network of lines and light silvery blotches and specks. When handled, they emit a richly colored but harmless purple dye. Sea hares graze on seaweed attached to rock jetties, pilings, and eelgrass beds on the backside of the Cape.

Q   What is a sea mouse, a sea potato, and a sea cucumber?

A sea mouse is a bristled sea worm, a marine relative of the earthworm. The sea mouse is the Cape and Islands' bulkiest worm—it averages seven inches long, three inches wide, and two inches deep. The sea mouse gets its "mouse-like" appearance from green and gold "hairs" along its flank. It is usually found in the muddy sand of deep water, using its bristled feet to push it along in search of small prey.

A sea potato is not a marine vegetable, but one of the most advanced (in an evolutionary sense) of all the marine invertebrates. Its body—reddish and wrinkled—is enclosed in a sack or tunic, which is rooted in the ocean bottom by a long slender stalk. For food, the sea potato filters plankton from surrounding waters. The only hint of life is a slight contraction of its bulbous body when it is touched.

A sea cucumber is closely related to the starfish family but lacks the starfish's hard, spiny body, although it has the same tube-like feet. Resembling a gray-colored, small deflated football, the "sea cuke" is the most coastal of this trio of organisms. Its suction-tube feet are usually capable of holding it in place during storm surges, but often sea cucumbers are cast upon the beach. Two of the best beaches to find sea cucumbers several days after a bad storm are Coast Guard Beach in Eastham and Race Point Beach in Provincetown, both within the Cape Cod National Seashore. On the islands, you can find sea cucumbers along South Beach on Martha's Vineyard and on Nantucket's Surfside Beach.

Q   What is milt and roe?

Milt is another word for fish sperm; roe, a delicacy, is another word for fish eggs.

Q   What is Red Tide?

Red Tide is a natural algae that breeds regularly in local waters; outbreaks can be traced back as far as the time when the explorer Samuel de Champlain, visited the coast of Chatham and Eastham. Red Tide can discolor tidal waters to a pink or red. The algae thrives in a narrow temperature zone and will bloom only if salinity, nutrients, and summer sunlight conditions are correct. Areas such as Eastham's Salt Pond are ideal for the survival of this algae, which can be spread quickly by tidal flows through adjoining Nauset Marsh, according to the Eastham Natural Resources Department.

Shellfish consume the organism, breaking down its cells and releasing a toxic substance that can affect animals and humans eating the shellfish. The toxins cause Paralytic Shellfish Poisoning, which disrupts breathing and other central nervous system functions. Regular testing and the closing of affected shellfish beds protects the public against Red Tide.

Q   What is a sand dune?

A sand dune, simply put, is a hill of sand piled up by the wind. According to information provided by the Cape Cod National Seashore, the most extensive example of dunes on the Cape is found in an area known as the Provincetown Spit. The height of the dunes here varies from a few dozen feet to more than 100 feet in several locations, such as the Province Lands Visitor Center area off Race Point Road in Provincetown.

There are two types of dunes—linear and parabolic. Linear dunes, known as foredunes, are located just behind the beach, and are formed by onshore winds that carry beach sand inland, where it is caught by beach grass. The larger interior dunes are parabolic, or horseshoe shaped, and are geologic structures unique to the Cape. U-shaped dunes develop as the dune center is literally blown out by powerful northwest winter winds that lift sand up and over the peak of the dune. An example of this can be found on Route 6 near the Truro-

Provincetown line, where dunes are spilling onto the highway. The state has struggled to keep this stretch of road open by removing tons of sand every winter. We suggest that you take in this splendid barren landscape—cottages line Beach Point on the bayside; to the east, Pilgrim Lake and large parabolic dunes provide a breathtaking contrast. The lake was once known as "East Harbor," and served as Provincetown's inner harbor. Ships weathered storms by anchoring here. The arrival of the railroad led to the filling in of the East Harbor entrance by 1873. With an average depth of three feet, today's Pilgrim Lake is a brackish lake ruled by white perch and huge carp.

Chapter 4

The Wetlands

by Richard LeBlond

Of all the magnificent ecosystems of the Cape and Islands, it is the wetland that is most difficult to define.

"What is a wetland?" visitors often ask. The somewhat working definition is any perpetually saturated or periodically flooded land where you can ruin a good pair of sneakers. Wetlands, on the Cape and Islands, can be classified into two distinct groups: coastal saltwater wetlands, namely salt marshes; and freshwater wetlands that form in isolated depressions and along the borders of lakes, ponds, and rivers—freshwater marshes, wet meadows, swamps, bogs, and pond shores.

Biologically, wetlands are the most productive natural ecosystems on the earth, rivaling even our most fertile agricultural lands. All wetlands offer food, nesting sites, and protective cover to hundreds of species of plant and animal life, from the white-tailed deer to rare migratory birds. Salt marshes function as prolific fish and shellfish nurseries and filter harmful wastes out of the water. It is estimated that two-thirds of our commercial fish and shellfish spend at least part of their lives in a salt marsh. Wetlands also buffer and absorb floodwaters and storm energy; they prevent erosion of adjacent uplands by holding soil sediments in place, by dampening wave energy, and by reducing the velocity of water currents.

Wetlands are essential to water quality. They remove phosphorus and harmful nitrogen from septic wastes and provide valuable storage sheds for groundwater needed by plants and animals that inhabit these sanctuaries. Wetlands also act as a natural pipe, funneling surface waters into the subsoil.

On a global scale, wetlands contribute to our climate and to the maintenance of the sensitive ozone layer, helping to keep carbon dioxide and methane gasses in balance—critical to efforts aimed at slowing down a worldwide warming trend, as we note in Chapter 7. Lose a sufficient acreage of these wetlands and the plants and animals that inhabit them will not survive, and rainwater will lose a critical point of entry into the groundwater. More than half of the salt-marsh acreage from Maine to New York was lost between 1886 and 1976, primarily by the dumping of fill to build homes, shops, and businesses. Laws now discourage and in many cases prevent the filling of wetlands, but the threat is far from over. Scientists estimate that we will lose up to 90 percent of our remaining coastal wetlands in the next 100 years because of a worldwide accelerated rise in sea level and the subsequent construction of levees, bulkheads, and seawalls to protect coastal development. This fatal combination will prevent marshes from migrating shoreward, as they do naturally. Simply put, these wetlands will drown in place.

So enjoy them, learn about them, and explore them now; the Cape and Islands offer world-class wetlands.

The Salt Marsh

The beauty of our coast is all horizontal—a thin, sleek shoreline that runs virtually uninterrupted for thirty miles from Chatham to Provincetown where land meets the Atlantic on the backside of Outer Cape Cod; the sandy south shore of Martha's Vineyard from Wequobsque Cliffs to South Beach; the straight shot of shoreline from Nantucket's Great Point to Sankaty Head Light. The sea sprawls endlessly and on hazy days melts into the sky before reaching the horizon. It is a landscape that evokes serenity and invites participation and discovery.

Nowhere is this more apparent than in our coastal salt marshes, where a seemingly monotonous expanse of meadow sways in the wind, then in the water. But a closer look—the beginning of participation—reveals that a salt marsh is more than dominant swaths of grass. Threading and charging through these marshes are tidal creeks and their tributaries, some of them carrying greater volumes of water than any of our brooks and streams. Pockets of pooling water collect in and around the acres of grass, and thick strips of brown mud contour the edges. Each season brings new colors, peaking with lavender and yellow wildflowers in late summer. There are distinctions even in the grasses, as different species grow in different parts of the marsh.

The essence of the Cape and Islands brims in its salt marshes where most of the basic shoreline elements are present and interact; salt and fresh water; sand and tides; marine and terrestrial plants and animals. But land and sea do not merely meet here, they are in constant conflict. Beneath the visual serenity is a pitched battle of life and death, of destruction and creation, riding in and out with every tide. The salt marsh is a product of that battle and a prolific example of the ability of life not only to exist but to thrive in such a harsh habitat.

Imagine yourself as one of the countless salt marsh inhabitants meandering the tidal creeks or climbing the stem of a lanky cord grass plant. Twice a day your home is inundated by the incoming tide and by groundfish in search of food. Then there is the outgoing tide. Twice a day you are exposed to the air—hot in summer, cold in winter. You have to avoid drying out or freezing, and you have to worry about predators—the gulls, sandpipers, ducks, and fiddler crabs.

Yet, despite these harsh conditions, the salt marsh is exceedingly productive. How can such a hostile environment produce so much life? The answer is found by looking at the dynamic processes that form and maintain a salt marsh, but it can be summed up in one word: adaptation.

HOW SALT MARSHES ARE FORMED

Salt marshes form in quiet coastal waters protected from erosive wave action. The typical protector is a barrier sand spit, and the typical quiet water body is an estuary: a bay, harbor, or river mouth behind the sand spit. Take Sandy Neck as an example. The large barrier spit facing Cape Cod Bay on the East Sandwich-Barnstable line blocks waves from the bay, allowing the Great Marsh—the largest salt marsh on Cape Cod—to from behind its protective arm. Likewise, Nauset Marsh on the Orleans-Eastham line has built up behind the Nauset Spit barrier. Other good examples are the marshland that has formed along the shore of the Martha's Vineyard Felix Neck Sanctuary behind State Beach on the coastal road from Oak Bluffs to Edgartown and the salt marsh behind Eel Point at the west end of Nantucket. Even small barrier spits will produce pockets of salt marsh as long as the waves are kept out and the tide is let in.

But wave protection and tidal influence alone will not create a salt marsh. A suitable floor of sand is needed, one that is fairly flat and shallow to permit the growth of grasses that dominate, define, and nurture the marsh. The sand floor, known as substrate, is built up by a peculiarity of the tides. The rate of tidal flow into the estuary where a marsh is forming is greater during the incoming tide than during the receding tide. In other words, the incoming tide has an ocean pushing it, while the outgoing tide is propelled only by gravity. The incoming flow is strong enough to carry sediment (mostly sand and silt) into the estuary, but the outgoing flow is not strong enough to carry the sediment back out. This slow rise in the floor does two important things. First, it creates a habitat for the forming marsh. Second, this continuous addition of sand allows the marsh to keep pace with a worldwide rise in sea levels. The stability that results from these massive processes is formidable. The marsh deposits in the Great Marsh lying behind Sandy Neck reach a depth of at least thirty feet and represent 4,000 years of steady rise with the sea. It seems something of a miracle that one of the most dynamic and hostile environments in the world has created one of the most stable and uniform habitats.

Storm wash-overs—less frequent but more dramatic than tidal sedimentation—also supply sand to salt-marsh floors, as high-energy waves break through barrier spits and spew sand into the estuary. The marsh behind the breakwater at the west end of Provincetown Harbor near the Provincetown Inn is an example of a marsh that has benefited from this source. A great storm in the winter of 1978 broke through the protective Long Point barrier, pouring tons of sand into the flats adjacent to the marsh. Since then, the break has healed and the marsh has expanded over this new floor space.

PLANTS AND GRASSES OF THE SALT MARSH

From a distance, all salt marshes appear vastly uniform—broad, flat meadows of grasses alternately undulating in the wind and tidal flow. As first impressions go, this one is fairly accurate. The marsh appears uniform because it is dominated by two closely related plants—cord grass (*Spartina alterniflora*) and salt meadow grass (*Spartina patens*). The two grasses differ in their tolerance of tidal flow and consequntly occupy separate areas of the marsh called zones.

Cord grass, more tolerant of salt water than salt meadow grass, dominates the area washed twice a day by the tides—the low marsh zone. It is a major food producer. Each fall cord grass stems die and break off at the base. Much of this organic matter is distributed within the marsh system, but nearly half of its nutrients is exported by the tides to other

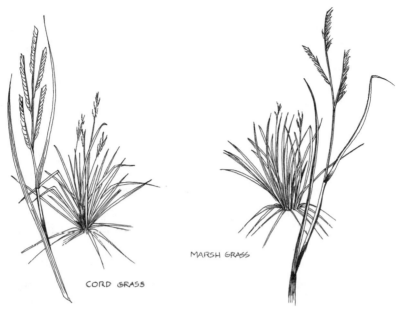

MARSH GRASS

CORD GRASS

coastal habitats. These nutrients, however, are not immediately available as food and must be processed by bacteria in the marsh muds before they can be eaten by other creatures.

Salt meadow grass (marsh grass) occupies the area washed only by the higher tides of the two-week tidal cycle—the high marsh zone. There was a time when salt meadow grass was a critical natural resource for humans and helped shape population distribution during the early years of European colonization. Salt meadow grass and a habitat associate, black rush, were harvested as "salt hay" for cows and horses; the high marshes were held in common by towns that sprang up around them. Cows were often pastured in the high marsh and were fitted with special shoes to give them stability on the soft soils.

Under the scrutiny of a discriminating second impression, these two grasses are strikingly different in appearance, as well as location. Cord grass, with inch-thick stems, stoutly rises three to six feet above the marsh floor. The wispy salt meadow grass, with stems barely a millimeter thick, reclines in a tumbled mass of tufts and cowlicks.

Now that you know what to look for, you can see that cord grass dominates the seaward or forward edge of the marsh, where the floor is lower. A closer look reveals what appears to be "rivers" of cord grass extending well up into the high marsh zone. The word river is appropriate here because cord grass straddles the low edges of the important tidal creeks meandering through the marsh. These creeks supply the marsh with seaborne nutrients on the incoming tide and transport the marsh's own magnificent production of nutrients to other coastal habitats on the outgoing tide.

The majority of our marshes, like the Great Marsh in Barnstable, have been sliced and diced by a grid of tidal creek replicas: the mosquito control ditches. These ditches are intended to drain the high marsh zone of pockets of standing water and thus eliminate breeding pools for the salt-marsh mosquito and dreaded green-head fly, whose bite is annoying to hikers and sunbathers. (Notice the blue and green boxes erected in many salt marshes to trap and control this pest.) Much controversy swirls around this means of reducing a nuisance at the expense of a natural ecosystem, but the mosquito ditch is just another tidal creek to cord grass, which grows along it, too.

Many of our larger marshes are dominated by the high marsh zone and its salt meadow grass. This is due to their age and centuries of sediment deposits. This slow accumulation has elevated their floors above the average high tide; they are washed by seawater only during the higher tides associated with a full moon or new moon, the so-called spring tides.

How salt meadow grass and cord grass, two freshwater-loving plants, have come to thrive in their respective zones is a remarkable story of adaptation. Of the two, cord grass has had to make the more radical change. Like man, cord grass gets its oxygen from the air, not the water. Because of this, cord grass is stressed by a reduced supply of oxygen during its high tide submergence. It can tolerate this deprivation for about half the tidal cycle, which is to say it can spend an equal amount of time inundated and exposed.

The marsh grasses, as well as other freshwater plants that have adapted to salt marshes, have two critical water problems to overcome: the need for a supply of fresh water and protection from the caustic properties of salt water.

Saltmarsh plants get a majority of fresh water from two sources—rainwater and groundwater. Because rainwater is unpredictable, groundwater provides the most reliable supply. This groundwater source is the seaward edge of an underground lens of fresh water beneath the Cape and Islands that flows slowly outward toward the sea. It is our drinking water supply.The rivulets you see running down the sandy beach into the waves are not leftover water from high tide but fresh water seeping out from the edge of the underground water lens. This phenomenon occurs in a salt marsh as well. Sometimes you can see fresh water welling up from vents in the floors of tidal creeks.

Even more stressful to plants than the availability of a freshwater supply in a salt marsh are the problems posed by the salt itself. In addition to the caustic effects to plant tissue from too much salt, salt marsh plants must also prevent a loss of vital freshwater "sap" during high tides. Salt water is more dense than fresh water and tends to pull fresh water out of marsh plants through osmosis. Through adaptive ingenuity, salt-marsh plants have overcome this threat. Using specialized cells, the plants produce chemical compounds that thwart this osmotic process and prevent the loss of fresh water. Cord grass is so good at this that it is actually able to extract fresh water from salt water, although it primarily relies on groundwater absorbed through its roots.

RESIDENTS OF THE SALT MARSH

Now that the war zones have been identified, it is time to turn our attention to the army of animals that maraud and seek shelter in these various habitats. These animals struggle in a bizarre world; half the time land, the other half sea. They eat during one part of the tide cycle and are hunted as food during the other. For sheer intensity and frequency of physical change, there is no more dramatic habitat in all of nature than a salt marsh.

Snails are abundant in the marsh, feeding on algae and organic waste on the bottom and on the lower part of the cord grass stems. The most common are periwinkles, salt-marsh snails, and mud snails. Ribbed mussels are found throughout the low marsh, and small shrimp can be seen in the tidal creeks.

There are several species of crabs in the marsh, but one—a midget with the forearm of Popeye—is particularly easy to spot, fun to watch, and important to the health of the marsh. This is the fiddler crab, which is discussed in more detail in the question and answer section.

All of the invertebrates that inhabit the marsh—the crabs, snails, shrimp, worms, and whatnot—add tremendously to the habitat's productivity. These small creatures only digest about 10 percent of what they consume. The rest is passed out as waste: ground-up organic matter infused with microbes from the animal's digestive tract and rapidly being processed by the microbes as food for someone else.

Certainly from our perspective, fish are among the most important inhabitants of the salt marsh. Some fish spend most or all of their lives in the marsh. These include small silversides, mummichogs, and minnows that can be seen schooling in the tidal creeks. For several species of oceanic fish, the marsh serves as a nursery. These include important commercial and recreational fish such as winter flounder, sea bass, striped bass, and bluefish. The sand launce, an important food fish for terns and whales, also gets its start in the salt marsh.

When the fish and planktonic animals depart on the outgoing tide, the exposed marsh grasses come alive with insects, particularly in the high marsh. Grasshoppers and crickets chew on the *Spartina* grasses, while plant hoppers and aphids suck the sap. Midges and the notorious green-head fly also live in the marsh muds as larvae. The salt-marsh mosquito breeds in the panne pools of the high marsh where fish predators are scarce. In the low marsh, insects are easy pickings for fish and shorebirds.

Several species of birds nest as well as feed in the marsh. These include rails, blue-winged teals, seaside sparrows, northern harriers (marsh hawks), and the short-eared owl. The last two species are officially recognized as rare in Massachusetts.

Rodents are the most abundant mammals in the marsh. While walking through the high marsh, tunnels can be seen running through the salt meadow grass at ground level. These are the runs of the marsh mice and voles. Voles are similar to mice but larger and darker. Of particular interest is the Muskeget meadow vole, a subspecies found on Muskeget Island off the west end of Nantucket and nowhere else in the world. These small rodents make their mark in the salt marsh, chewing away the bases of grass stems and individually consuming as much as thirty pounds of vegetation a year. The rodents in turn attract the predatory birds and mammals. Raccoons, weasels, otters, and foxes search for prey in the marsh during low tide, and deer, rabbits, and muskrats occasionally pick at the vegetation. The larger mammals are rarely seen in the marsh because of their nocturnal feeding habits.

Seaweed, and plenty of it, can also be found in the salt marsh. Knotted wrack, rockweed, and sea lettuce are very productive in the low marsh muds in spring and early summer before the habitat is shaded out by cord grass. Seaweed is a significant contributor to production in the low marsh but is nearly absent from the high marsh, most likely due to the persistent and dense growth of salt meadow grass and the longer periods of exposure.

The high marsh, with its smaller doses of salt water, is host to several flowering plants. Of particular interest are glassworts—fleshy plants that look like club mosses or tiny, spineless cacti. They are made up of bright green to deep red stems that resemble plump sausage links. Glassworts are all stems and braches; their leaves, the size of small scales, enclose the even smaller flower buds. Glassworts are also known as sea pickles. A nibbling of these salty, succulent, and quite edible plants will reveal why.

Another member of the high marsh community you should become familiar with is the sea lavender. It blooms from mid- to late summer, turning patches and swaths of the marsh mosaic a hazy violet. The individual flowers are only an eighth of an inch long, but each sea lavender plant produces so many of them that they collectively make a broad stroke on the marsh canvas. The tiny but abundant sea lavender flowers retain their color and shape after drying on the plant. This has made them a favorite of florists and decorator-minded visitors, who collect them for floral arrangements. Some Outer Cape salt marshes have been almost stripped clean of their annual sea lavender production. Some towns in response have passed a bylaw prohibiting the picking of sea lavender on town-owned land. We suggest the following antidote to fight off the temptation to collect wildflowers of the marsh. If you take them home with you, you can enjoy them only briefly. If you leave them in the marsh, you and others can enjoy them for a lifetime.

Freshwater Wetlands

The warm night rain pounds long and hard, settling into the soft soil and calling forth a deeply buried, seldom seen resident of our lands— the rare spade-footed toad. Following an ancient urge, the spade-foot leaves its place of concealment and heads down slope to the puddled landscape below. Once there, it finds a pool of water— a freshwater wetland—no wider than a bread truck and only six inches deep. It is the perfect amphibian nursery, and our spade-foot pilgrim—a male— grabs some rushes in the water and wails his mournful love song.

A female responds. Several days after the mating the fertilized eggs become tadpoles. Two weeks later the tadpoles are fully toaded except for a remnant tail. These new toads hop uphill to where their parents have retreated, and with the help of a hard toe on each hind foot (the spade foot), they entomb themselves two feet into the sandy upland soil where they will sleep until the next warm rain.

Soon after the toads leave their nursery, this wet patch of land disappears; some of the water has sunk into the ground, some has evaporated. The pool has become dry again, though the peat is still damp to the touch. This curious parcel—now standing water, now damp soil— is like a salt marsh in that it blends and fluctuates between aquatic and terrestrial extremes. But the "tides" are much slower in an inland, freshwater wetland. They pulsate to seasonal and annual clocks, not to the diurnal tuggings of the sun and moon. The tide of a freshwater wetland is groundwater, swelling upward in the rainfall and sinking in a dry spell. But because surface water is not always present, water alone cannot define a freshwater wetland. Another indicator—as in a salt marsh—is vegetation: particular rushes, sedges, grasses, wildflowers, shrubs, and trees that grow only where the soil is wet for all or most of the year.

Freshwater wetlands on the Cape and Islands form where the ground dips below the water table: in hollows, along stream banks, and around ponds. The streams and ponds themselves, however, are not classified as wetlands (though they are most certainly wet). These water bodies are defined as aquatic habitats. The distinction again is based on vegetation: what kind and how it grows.

PLANTS OF A FRESHWATER WETLAND

The plants of a freshwater wetland, like those of a salt marsh, are essentially land plants. They root in the soil and breathe, flower, and fruit in the air. By comparison, pond and stream plants—some rooted and some free floating—spend their lives completely submerged or lying on the surface of the water. True aquatic plants will not grow where the habitat is not always underwater.

There is also a distinction between wetland "land" plants and upland "land" plants. Water tolerance is the quick answer, but the more complete explanation is the old salt marsh bugaboo: suffocation. Most land plants get the majority of their oxygen through their roots from gaseous oxygen in the soil. When the soil becomes saturated with water, gaseous oxygen is no longer available. To survive, plants either have to wait out these periods of saturation or develop other means of obtaining oxygen. Wetland plants obviously can do this while the upland plants of grasslands, heaths, and forests cannot.

Fluctuating or shallow water levels are the major influence in a wetland, but there are many other factors at work to determine what kind of freshwater wetland will form: How deep is the water? When, and for how long, is water at the surface? Does it flow or is it standing? Is the water acidic? How long has the wetland been there?

Although we are familiar with the common names attached to various wetland types, most of us would be hard-pressed to define the distinction between a marsh and a bog and a swamp. These distinctions have challenged science as well. Every wetland is a product of complex conditions and interactions, and no two wetlands are exactly alike. Because conditions vary even within the same wetland, more than one wetland type is usually present at each site, and frequently they blend together.

Nonetheless, science has attempted to disentangle these complexities and develop uniform terms to describe the various wetland communities. As complex as these terms are (every third word, it seems, must be looked up in a dictionary), they elaborate on, rather than replace, the common terms we use. To the scientist, a marsh technically may be a palustrine emergent wetland, but it's still home to a duck.

Fortunately, science uses the same criterion the rest of us have used over the centuries to define a wetland: the dominant vegetation. Ahead is a description of each of the major freshwater wetland types found on the Cape and Islands. We will look at the specific vegetation that defines these wetland types and at the animal life these wetlands support.

FRESHWATER MARSHES

Freshwater marshes are found where groundwater is either at or above the surface for much of the growing season. They are dominated by grasses and grasslike sedges and rushes that can grow quickly and tall. These plants are able to emerge above the water and assimilate oxygen from the air. Trees and shrubs, which get their oxygen primarily through their roots, suffocate if standing water is present during the growing season. You won't find them in a freshwater marsh unless there are islands or mounds of elevated ground. Typical of the marsh plants are the cattail, reed bent grass, and military rush (so named because its uppermost, long-pointed leaf resembles the bayonet of a rifle slung over the shoulder). Some of these plants—the cattail in particular—can grow six feet or higher. Consequently, standing bodies of water six feet or shallower are likely marsh candidates.

Marshes are found in low areas around ponds and adjacent to just about every freshwater stream. To mention just a few, you will find well-developed freshwater marshes along the Mashpee River, which runs from Mashpee Pond to Popponesset Bay on the Upper Cape; along the Herring River in West Harwich; along the Pamet River east of Route 6 in Truro; at the headwaters of Mill Brook on Martha's Vineyard; and on Nantucket along the north end of ponds on the island's south shore. A good example of a shallow pond on its way to becoming a marsh is Lamson Pond in Barnstable near the Yarmouth line.

Some marsh plants live for several years (perennials), and some die after one (annuals). But whether they live through the winter hunkered down in their roots or as seeds in the muck, all of the growth aboveground dies in autumn. Their buff-to-tan stems, however, remain upright in the off-season, and the marsh retains its reedy character throughout the year.

ANIMALS OF A FRESHWATER MARSH

Freshwater marshes teem with small shrimp, snails, tadpoles, and insect larvae—dragonflies and damselflies, midges, pesky mosquitoes, and biting deerflies (also called horseflies). While mosquitoes and deerflies may be pests to us, they are food for other creatures in the marsh and are important pollinators of the marsh plant life.

For animals, life in the freshwater marsh differs radically from life in the salt marsh. First of all, there is no salt problem to deal with and the tides are seasonal, not twice daily. Resident animals remain for weeks and months, unlike so many salt-marsh animals, who have to abandon the marsh after every six-hour shift.

Whether a marsh is connected to or isolated from a stream or pond influences the type of animal life that will be found there. Generally speaking, when fish are present, frogs and salamanders are not. The eggs and tadpoles of amphibians are easy prey for fish, and thus frogs and salamanders seek out the smaller, isolated wetlands to breed in. Freshwater marshes typically are flooded in spring but frequently dry out in the fall. That, of course, is deadly to fish.

Marshes are an important habitat for birds. Marsh nesters include red-winged blackbirds, yellowthroat warblers, and several kinds of ducks. Ducklings feed on the insect larvae, snails, shrimp, and tadpoles in the marsh water. They themselves are prey to water snakes, snapping turtles, and hawks. Four turtle species are also found in local marshes—painted, musk, spotted, and box turtles.

The quintessential marsh birds are the members of the heron family, the bitterns, herons, and egrets. All of them are expert at standing perfectly still. This provides protection, especially for the bittern and green heron as they blend in with, and are nearly indistinguishable from, the marsh grasses. It is also a great hunting tool. Few scenes are as stunning as watching a great blue heron, frozen still, suddenly plunge its dagger beak into the water to retrieve a frog, snake, or fish. Its perfect patience punctuated by bursts of movement reminds one of the poise and economy of a t´ai chi warrior.

Muskrats are the premier mammals of the marsh. Look for their mounded dens built with reedy marsh plants. Related to beavers, muskrats feed on grasses, sedges, and rushes. The muskrats play an important role in the recycling of marsh nutrients through their consumption and processing of vegetation. Bacteria and insect larvae also are critical to this process as they digest organic matter in the water, muds, and peats. However, the marsh produces more nutrients than its creatures can consume. Some of these nutrients are exported to other habitats if the marsh borders a stream or pond, but much of the excess stays put, accumulating as peat and muck on the marsh floor. Given enought time, this accumulation may raise the ground level (thus lowering the water level), and the marsh may evolve into a wet meadow or swamp.

WET MEADOWS AND CRANBERRY BOGS

While it is hard to mistake a freshwater marsh for a bog, the differences between a swamp and a wet meadow are more subtle. A wetland that typically has standing water in winter and exposed damp soils in summer will most likely become a swamp, but these soil conditions also favor the herbaceous (nonwoody) plants of the wet meadow community, as well as the trees and shrubs found in swamps. The wet meadow community, however, needs plenty of sunlight and concedes the habitat battle to the shading canopy of swamp shrubs and trees.

Nonetheless, there are a lot of wet meadow habitats on the Cape and Islands. They are found primarily where someone has cut back the shrub and tree growth. Much of our wet meadow habitat is known by other names (cranberry bog and dune bog), and some of it is found in a habitat so peculiar and locally common (pond shores) that the habitat is treated separately here.

Like the marshes, wet meadows are dominated by grasses, sedges, and rushes. But these are mostly shorter species than those of the marsh because meadow plants don't have to sprout up through standing water. Wet meadows also host populations of richly hued wildflowers like the magenta meadow beauties and hot pink orchids.

Cranberry bogs—whether natural, cultivated, or abandoned—are more akin to wet meadows than to true bogs, which are dominated by sphagnum moss. This contradiction is forced upon us by water conditions and the resultant plant community. In a sphagnum bog (discussed more fully later in this chapter), the ground is saturated with water year-round. In a cranberry bog, the water level drops during the growing season and the soil is damp but not saturated—in other words, conditions favorable to a wet meadow or swamp. It is no coincidence that most commercial cranberry bogs were carved out of swamps.

The "meadowness" of active and abandoned cranberry bogs is evident in the plants they support. Take the cranberry itself. It can tolerate submergence in winter but needs to be fully exposed in summer to flower and fruit. While the cranberry grows in the saturated soils of sphagnum bogs, it is not early as productive there as it is in the drier soils of the wet meadow habitat.

The weeds of a cranberry bog are also wet meadow plants: the shorter sedges and rushes, lance-leaved violets, and even orchids (though it would take a ruthless gardner to call orchids weeds). The one exception is poison ivy, but this plant is every habitat's exception. Poison ivy has a wide range of water, soil, and sun-shade tolerances and grows in marshes, meadows, swamps, fields, woodlands, and dunes. It behooves the would-be hiker or naturalist to brush up on the identification of this reddish green, shiny-leaved plant before brushing up against the plant itself.

Abandoned cranberry bogs are found in virtually every town and are good places to see the meadow habitat. For one thing, they are no longer weeded. But remember, abandoned applies to use, not the property itself. Make sure you obtain the owner's permission first.

Natural cranberry bogs are mostly restricted to active dune systems, where they are called dune bogs. These bogs form where the wind has eroded the sand down to the water table. Many of these depressions are elliptically shaped and lie lengthwise along the direction of the wind that has formed them. In most cases, this is the winter-dominant northwest wind, and many dune bogs point toward the southeast.

Like the cultivated cranberry bogs, dune bogs are typically submerged in winter when groundwater is higher and are exposed in summer. This condition favors the cranberry and other meadow plants, including orchids. You should try to visit a dune system in June to witness an orchid Eden springing forth from powdered stone. On the Cape, dune bogs are best developed on Sandy Neck in Barnstable, Monomoy Island off Chatham, and in the Province Lands of Provincetown where the Cape Cod National Seashore offers guided walks.

SWAMPS

Swamps are wetlands dominated by shrubs and trees, or both. They are the most common freshwater wetland habitat on the Cape and Islands. Swamps mark the wet end of the slow transit from marsh to dry soil upland. The cycle works like this: dead organic matter in a wetland raises the ground level and, relatively speaking, lowers the water level. Hence, a shallow pond becomes a marsh, a marsh becomes a swamp (unless man intervenes to create a wet meadow), and a swamp becomes a dry soil woodland. You will not witness these transformations, however, because they will take hundreds, even thousands, of years.

Although wetland shrubs and trees obviously must be tolerant of wet soils and periods of standing water, they are less tolerant of these conditions than marsh plants. In most swamps, surface water is not present during the growing season, although the soil remains moist. Standing water is usually present in winter, but the trees and shrubs are dormant then and less bothered by the absence of gaseous oxygen in the soppy soils.

Because of the intense shading by shrubs and trees, grasses, sedges, and wildflowers are not as abundant in our swamps as in the marshes. Nonetheless, the swamp ground cover is one of the most beautiful of our botanical communities. Mosses and ferns luxuriate on the damp, dark floor along with jack-in-the-pulpit, violets, skunk cabbage, cardinal flower, and jewelweed.

More than forty species of birds nest in Massachusetts's swamps. Among these are the yellowthroat and Canada warblers, catbirds, black ducks, and wood ducks. Also, chickadees, blue jays, woodpeckers, and owls feed and seek cover in swamps during the winter, as do deer, which are fond of chewing on white cedar. Amphibians, like spring peepers and spotted salamanders, breed in spring pools in swamps.

SPHAGNUM BOGS

The sphagnum bog is our most fragile and potentially most dangerous habitat. Like other wetland communities, sphagnum bogs are most easily identified by their dominant vegetation. The eminent bog plant is (as you might have guessed) sphagnum moss, also known as peat moss. Frequently, almost the entire surface of a bog is covered with sphagnum; other plants rise out of it. Some of these plants, rare orchids among them, are almost exclusively restricted to sphagnum bogs.

Most sphagnum bogs can be characterized as a living mat of sphagnum and other plants over a saturated bed of peat that can be several feet deep. In some places this living mat grows out over the surface of a pond. This is what is called a quaking bog (there is one off Shank Painter Road in Provincetown), and walking on it is like walking on a water bed or in a rowboat. The liquid land undulates beneath every footstep. The buoyancy of the sphagnum and the horizontal root network of the shrubs and dwarf trees give enough strength to the mat to suppport the collective weight of the plant and animal community.

The most fascinating members of this unusual community are the carnivorous plants—the pitcher plants, the sundews, and the bladderworts. Following separate evolutionary lines, these plants have developed mechanisms for trapping and digesting small animals— mostly insects but also small shrimp, tiny fish, tadpoles, and mosquito larvae.

Lucky for those of us interested in the gory details of plants that eat animals, the sundews are the most common and easily found of our carnivorous plants. Sundews also grow around pond shores and in wet meadows, including cranberry and dune bogs. The sundew is a close relative of the Venus's-flytrap. There are three species of sundews on the Cape and Islands: the thread-leaved, the spatula-leaved, and the round-leaved. The amazing sundew is discussed in greater detail in our question and answer section.

In addition to the sundew species, several orchids are native to the sphagnum bog. These include the rose pogonia, grass pink, and the arethusa or dragon's mouth—one of the rarest and most attractive wildflowers.

One thing to remember about sphagnum bogs—they are fragile and unstable, particularly quaking bogs. A bog walker is at risk. Weak zones on the soft mat are common and not always visible. A bog adventure could be a one-way ticket to the slurpy peat beds below.

POND SHORES

With the exception of always-saturated sphagnum bogs, seasonal water level fluctuation is a key ingredient in all of the freshwater wetland communities we have discussed so far. This phenomenon is most easily seen on the shores of the majority of our ponds. During most summers, a white, sandy beach or peaty meadow appears at the margin of a pond, only to be submerged by winter's rising water table. But those of us who have watched these ponds over the years also know that sometimes water levels remain high throughout the summer, and consequently we have to cart our beach belongings to the more reliable ocean shore.

These conditions have produced one of the most unusual and rarest of wetland communities, known as the coastal plain pond shore.

The coastal plain pond and its shore are almost exclusively restricted to southeastern Massachusetts, New York's Long Island, and New Jersey.

The pond habitat itself is discussed in detail in Chapter 5, but our interest here is with the shoreline. Basically, there are two types of coastal plain ponds: those with outlets (streams) and those without. Ponds on the Cape and Islands rise and fall with the groundwater because they are, in fact, part of the groundwater. If a pond has an outlet stream, periodic rises in groundwater from rainfall will exit through the outlet. In these ponds, the water level remains fairly constant, except during periods of extreme drought. Ponds with outlets typically have shorelines that are characterized by a narrow band of wetland shrubs and trees on the lip of the surrounding uplands. If the pond with an outlet is shallow enough, a marsh community may emerge near the shore. Ponds of this type include Upper Mill and Lower Mill ponds of Brewster and the Gull Pond complex in Wellfleet.

A very different community develops around shores of ponds without outlets, and this condition characterizes the majority of ponds on the Cape and Islands. The water level in these ponds fluctuates with the groundwater. As in other isolated wetland basins (without inlet or outlet), pond levels tend to rise in winter and drop in summer and fall (this can be accelerated by evaporation).

These pond-level fluctuations are often dramatic and, biologically speaking, traumatic. As with so many of our wetlands, we have to keep in mind not only the seasonal fluctuations but also the year-to-year trends. During periods of extended above-average rainfall, pond levels may remain high for several years in a row and, during times of extended droughts, the levels remain low. And so we have a shoreline that alternately is submerged and exposed from season to season and from year to year. Because of periodic exposure, aquatic plants die back. Because of periodic submergence, shrubs and trees cannot grow. Complicating this problem is the erosion of the shoreline by waves generated by the movement of wind across the pond surface.

To grow in this habitat, a plant has to overcome the stresses produced by submergence, exposure, and erosion—often in a relatively short period of time. Plants best adapted to these conditions are grasses, sedges, rushes, and wildflowers that can grow quickly during short periods of exposure and then survive the rigors of submergence and erosion as seeds in sandy pond shore soils. As a community, a pond shore most closely resembles a wet meadow.

Of great significance from a naturalist's point of view is the presence in a pond shore of a handful of species that are either restricted to this habitat or are rarely found elsewhere. These very special natives include some of our most beautiful wildflowers: the Plymouth gentian, rose coreopsis, and slender arrowhead.

Pond shores on the Cape and Islands are as interesting as the ponds themselves. Next time you find yourself walking along the shore of a pond, pause for a minute or two to look above the waterline.

Q & A

Where the largest and most interesting saltwater
Q *marshes on the Cape and Islands? What can I expect to*
find there?

The Great Marsh on the Cape Cod Bay side of Barnstable, measuring about 4,000 acres and visible from Route 6A, is the largest salt marsh in our region. Its peat deposits are thirty feet deep and date back 3,000 to 4,000 years. It is likely this is the oldest living salt marsh on the Cape and Islands. The Great Marsh is primarily a high marsh (washed only by the higher tides) and is dominated by salt meadow grass (described in Chapter 4).

Nauset Marsh in Eastham on the ocean side south of Coast Guard Beach is also quite expansive and has a much different appearance. It is a low marsh (an area closer to the sea that is washed twice a day by tides) and is dominated by islands of cord grass, separated by wide channels of salt water during high tide.

On the islands of Martha's Vineyard and Nantucket, well-developed salt marshes can be found at Felix Neck Sanctuary near Edgartown and behind Eel Point at the west end of Nantucket.

Salt marshes are one of nature's most productive biological laboratories; they teem with birds, fish, crabs, snails, mussels, and, at the upper edges of the marsh, acres of wildflowers, particularly in late summer.

Q *Where are the largest and most interesting freshwater marshes on the Cape and Islands? What can I expect to find there?*

The largest freshwater marshes are found along our rivers, streams, and brooks. Extensive marshes occur along Bumps River in Centerville, along the Herring River in West Harwich, and along the Pamet River in Truro. On Martha's Vineyard, freshwater marshes can be visited at Ross Woodlands at the head of Mill Brook. On Nantucket, freshwater marshes are best developed at the northern ends of the narrow ponds along the south side of the island.

Like their saltwater counterparts, freshwater marshes are rich with animal life and are excellent places for viewing our region's bird life. In a freshwater marsh, you can expect to find fish, frogs, snakes, muskrats, and turtles, as well as magnificent marsh birds such as herons, egrets, bitterns, and warblers.

Q *What are pannes?*

Pannes are naked pockets, shallow basins, or swaths of exposed mud or pooled water in a salt marsh. It is not known for certain what causes this phenomenon, but there are a few likely suspects. Pannes may be areas of poor drainage where standing water or accumulated high salt levels have prevented vegetated growth. Pannes may also be caused by tidal deposits of massive rafts of dead cord grass stems, which kill off underlying vegetation. It is also possible pannes are caused by ice. During winter cold snaps, thick ice sheets form on the surface of a marsh. The ice grips the vegetation, and incoming tides often tear away loose slabs of ice and its trapped vegetation and peat, creating denuded patches.

Q *What are cattails? Some look short and fat; others long and thin. Why?*

Cattails are common plants not only on the Cape and Islands marshes but on marhses around the world. These large plants, growing to a height of six feet or more, get their name from the velvety brown, sausage-shaped fruiting structure at the top of the stem (a tail fit for a stubby, fat cat). The cattail grows new stems from thick runners that thrive in the soft marsh muds, creating large colonies that are often several acres in size.

Two kinds of cattail are widespread on the Cape and Islands—the broad-leaved cattail and the narrow-leaved cattail. The narrow-leaved cattail is one to two feet shorter than the broad-leaved. Everything about the narrow-leaved cattail is narrower, including its slender cattail fruiting structure. Broad-leaved cattail is the common cattail of our freshwater marshes. The narrow-leaved cattail is tolerant of low levels of salt water and grows where fresh and salt water mix, such as near river mouths and in coastal ponds that are occasionally washed by spring or storm tides.

Q *What are the very tall, feathery reeds that grow along the borders of many marshes?*

Even taller than the cattails are the feathery plumes of the common reed (*Phragmites*), a member of the grass family. The reed also grows by runners and produces very large colonies often adjacent to the cattails. Common reed is an aggressive colonizer of former salt marshes that have been diked off from the sea. This has fueled a common misperception that the reed is not native to salt marshes. Although found worldwide, the common reed grows best in North America, commonly on disturbed areas and on sand spoils. Its appearance in former salt marshes is a symptom, not a cause, of an altered habitat.

Q *What is a fiddler crab?*

The trademark of the fiddler is the cartoonishly huge claw found on all males. When the claw is waved back and forth, it resembles someone bowing the violin, thus earning the crab its appropriate moni-

FIDDLER CRAB

ker. The big claw is used primarily for display. During the mating season, the male proudly flaunts his oversized claw to attract the female. At other times, the big claw is used to ward off other males. A male fiddler climbs out of his burrow in local marshes and on mud flats claw first and crawls back into the hole flaunting his claw until he is well hidden. At the slightest provocation, the fiddler is ready for a good fight. Although these crabs live in dense colonies, they will go to great extremes to defend their tiny territories.

All male crabs are born with right-handed fiddles, but if the claw is lost in battle or has been plucked by a predator, a new oversized claw will grow back on the left side. This conserves energy in that the injured side only has to produce a small claw. Close observation of any fiddler crab colony reveals there is a pretty good mix of righties and lefties.

If a fiddler crab is seized by one of its ten legs, an automatic reflex will separate the leg from the body. This self-amputation enables the crab to escape quickly. The leg will grow back during the next molt. Often tidal creeks, marshes, and mud flats are littered with legs and claws lost in battle. Look for them.

Lacking the big claw, the female fiddler crab is more docile. After mating, she carries her eggs on the undersides of her abdomen, constantly fanning it back and forth to aerate the eggs. Just before birth, she transports her eggs to the edge of the water, releasing her young with each forward thrust of the abdomen.

The young fiddler crabs begin their lives as part of the free-swimming plankton community, completely at the mercy of the currents and a wide range of predators. Each fiddler crab larva, called a zoea, is no bigger than a grain of sand but is fully developed with a head, abdomen, and four legs; in a few months, it grows to be a full-sized crab.

Like most crabs, the fiddler has gills for breathing in water. But it is also equipped with a primitive lung, enabling it to live on land for several days at a time. During each flood tide and throughout the cold season, the fiddler retires to its burrow, often three feet deep into the mud. The crabs dig with their walking legs, packing small particles into pellets and removing them from their burrows. The openings of these burrows are often plugged with some of these pellets to hold in moist air and keep out water. The burrowing stirs up surface sediments and increases soil productivity. One study found that fiddler crabs annually turn over as much as 18 percent of marsh deposits buried six inches into the ground.

Much can be learned from fiddler crabs. The next time you see a throng of fiddlers hustling across the marsh, take a moment to stop and observe their curious behavior. They are among the unique and colorful residents of the Cape and Islands.

Q What is a marsh hawk?

The marsh hawk, now officially called the northern harrier, is no stranger to the Cape and Islands. You can watch this majestic bird soaring over river valleys, dunes, and local wetlands. Its white rump patch and slender shape stand out, making it easy to distinguish a marsh hawk from other birds of prey. Like the turkey vulture, the marsh hawk flies with its wings slanting upward. Usually it cruises only a few feet above the ground, leisurely beating its wings or gracefully gliding in the wind.

Few creatures delight in the power of wind as the marsh hawk does. When gale winds surge across the salt marshes, the marsh hawk seems most in its natural element. It glides and tilts with the wind, while systematically searching for its prey.

In early spring when warm winds set the natural world in motion, the marsh hawk engages in spectacular courtship display. There is nothing that matches the dexterity and precision of the marsh hawk's nuptial flight. The performance includes magnificent nose dives, hairpin turns, and an occasional loop-the-loop. The male ascends to a great height and plunges downwards as much as 200 feet. In the words of Edward H. Forbush, "As he bounds up and down in the air, he seems more like a rubber ball than a bird."

Many have observed the male, in his efforts to entice the female, dropping his prey in the air and the female catching it with her talons as it falls. These romantic overtures are often repeated again and again. This display is accompanied by the hawk's exceptional calls, ranging from a shrill plaintive cry, to a loud raucous "ke-ke-ke-ke," to an ear-piercing shriek.

The male and female stay together for most of the season. Both assist in preparing the nest, which consists of sticks and grass loosely arranged on the ground. Both also share the job of incubating the eggs.

Despite its reputation for eating poultry and songbirds, the marsh hawk feeds on mice and other rodents and will dine on a bird when the opportunity arises.

SUNDEW

Q Are there plants on the Cape that capture and eat insects?

Sundews are the most common and easily found of our carnivorous (insect-eating, in this case) plants. They grow in sphagnum bogs, around pond shores, and in wet meadows, including cranberry bogs and dune bogs.

The sundew is a close relative of the Venus's-flytrap. We have three species of sundews on the Cape and Islands: the thread-leaved, the spatulate-leaved, and the round-leaved. The thread-leaved is rarely found here. The other two species are similar-looking small plants that measure no more than three inches in diameter. They are bright red and often grow in large colonies, making them easy to find in sparsely vegetated damp sand or peat. The small leaves look like spoons radiating out from the center of the plant. Look closely at the plant and you will notice that sundews glisten; in fact, they are covered with "dew drops." These droplets are sweet and sticky globules at the ends of tiny hairlike structures that protrude from the handles and rounded ends of the plant's "spoons." The sweetness of these droplets attracts insects; the stickiness captures them.

These hairlike structures are called tentacles because they move. Through chemical messages, they are able to determine if the sundew's prey is insect, vegetable, or mineral. Only when an insect is captured does the digestion process begin. Within twenty minutes, every tentacle in the immediate vicinity begins to arch toward the struggling insect. As small as sundews are they can catch insects as large as a damselfly. When contact is made, the tentacles inject an anesthetic into the insect to keep it from struggling free. The tentacles then inject digestive fluids into the victim that are capable of breaking down proteins, fats, and carbohydrates, which are consumed by the plant along with minerals and vitamins from the insect. Nothing is left behind but the insect's external skeleton.

Q *What is the first flower on the Cape to bloom?*
What is the last flower to bloom?

Though it may not fit the popular notion of wildflower, the skunk cabbage quietly flowers within the hidden recesses of its pointed spathe (or colored bract) as early as late January or early February.

Because of its ability to produce warmth through its cells, skunk cabbage can actually melt the winter snow around its cowled spathe, making it one of the earliest and most eagerly awaited signs of spring.

The tiny, greenish flowers are arranged along a club-shaped growth called the spadix within the spathe. The fetid odor that gives the plant its name is designed to attract its main pollinator, flies.

A good place to look for skunk cabbage is a red maple swamp. The spathes are easily found and come in a variety of attractive designs, some with dark crimson striping.

Long after the last goldenrods and asters of autumn have passed, witch hazel is sprouting its spidery, yellow flowers in rocky woods.

A tall shrub, witch hazel's flowers are fresh sometimes into mid-December in a mild fall. The blossoms somewhat resemble the cultivated forsythia, with the long, crepe-paper petals reaching two inches in length.

Witch hazel is much more common in the rocky moraine of the Upper Cape and is rare east of Barnstable. Its qualities as an astringent and styptic agent are well known, and it is still used today for medicinal purposes.

Q *What is the long green moss that grows on the branches*
of trees in swamps? Is it harmful?

The green moss is actually a lichen called old-man's beard. Resembling the Spanish moss of the Deep South, old-man's beard is common on the dead or living branches of hardwoods like oaks and maples, and softwoods like the Atlantic white cedar. With its pendulous branches hanging from a dead or dying limb, it may look as if damage to the tree was resulting. This is not the case.

Emitting a weak acid that helps break down organic matter such as dead wood and inorganic material such as rocks, lichens play a role as decomposers and builders of soil. There is no evidence that lichens harm healthy living trees.

Lichens were once thought to be a single primitive plant. They are actually two plants microscopically intertwined; an alga that provides food through chlorophyll and a colorless fungus that serves to protect the plant from drying out. Scientists now believe this partnership to be a mild form of parasitism, with the alga acting as the host and the fungus deriving nutrients from the alga's photosynthetic properties. The name old-man's beard may be derived from the beardlike appearance of the lichen or by the ancient belief, first described by the Greek naturalist Theophrastus in 300 B.C., that the plant was useful in stimulating hair growth.

Q *What are the brilliant red trees found around pond shores in the fall?*

In early autumn the red, or swamp, maple garlands our swamps and wetlands with a blaze of fiery red, orange, and gold.

One of the commonest trees in eastern North America, the red maple owes its bright fall colors to orange and red pigments in the leaf. The combination of decreasing sunlight and cool nights triggers the formation of a wall of corky cells across the leaf petiole, or stem. With this blockage of nutrients from the branch, the green chlorophyll in the dying leaf is used up and breaks down, leaving the hitherto hidden pigments to display their colors.

Red maples are rapid growers for the first twenty to thirty years. They may live up to a century and attain heights of 90 to 100 feet, though in most cases the red maple is a medium-sized tree. The wood has been used in making cheap furniture, gunstocks, flooring, and carved objects.

Another tree that grows near pond shores and displays a vivid bronze red in fall is the tupelo, or black gum.

Chapter 5

The Ponds

by John Portnoy

Cape Cod is not just land surrounded by water. There's a lot of water surrounded by land as well; by one count almost 500 freshwater and saltwater ponds of various sizes—as large as the 743 acres of Long Pond shared by Harwich and Brewster and as small as your backyard. On the islands of Nantucket, Martha's Vineyard, and the Elizabeth chain, you'll find scores more.

From the air, the Cape and Islands appear to be a flooded land-scape; the level brightness of the ocean, bay, and pond surfaces overwhelms the gray green hills of oak and pitch pine and the miles of sandy shoreline. This is no illusion. Since the glacier began receding thousands of years ago, land has literally given way to the rising sea. And fresh waters from rains and snowmelt, buoyed upward by the seepage of seawater under the ground, have flooded previously dry lowlands.

Most of these ponds are shaped alike—perfectly circular, the loose irregular edges having been worn away. They are geological fossils of those late-melting blocks of ice that remained after the final Laurentide sheet retreated to the north and formed our kettle ponds.

What Is a Pond?

While it is difficult to mistake Squibnocket Pond on Martha's Vineyard, Tom Nevers Pond on Nantucket, and the large Wakeby-Mashpee complex on the Sandwich-Mashpee line for anything other than ponds, scientists have stumbled with a textbook definition. It is impossible to define a pond by a single characteristic—size, depth, temperature, or vegetation. And on paper, it can be equally challenging distinguishing a pond from a freshwater marsh, a bog, and even a wet meadow.

In the most general of terms, a pond is a body of standing water that fills a depression in the earth's surface. While there is no scientific distinction between a pond and a lake, the term pond usually refers to a body of standing water shallow enough for plants—rooted on the pond bottom—to reach the surface. On the Cape and Islands, however, local usage dictates that most of these standing water bodies are to be called ponds, although these kettle depressions are more like lakes by virtue of their clear and open waters unbroken by vegetation and by their depths of up to sixty-five feet.

Legally, the Commonwealth of Massachusetts distinguishes between small and large ponds by designating any standing body of water with a surface area greater than ten acres as a "great pond." To guarantee protection and public access, state law prohibits the private ownership of any great pond. But to confuse matters even more, the words pond and lake are used interchangeably to identify great ponds on the Cape and Islands. For instance, the largest standing body of fresh water in Wellfleet is Gull Pond off Gull Pond Road, while down the road in Orleans the largest standing body of water is Pilgrim Lake off Monument Road.

While most ponds look the same to the naked eye, there are subtle and not-so-subtle differences: the distinction, for instance, between a freshwater and a saltwater pond and the definition of a brackish pond—a pond with a mixture of both fresh and salt water. Then there are streams; think of them as flowing ponds. The Cape's few small streams occur only in deep valleys that were scoured out by glacial meltwater, where the land surface dips (like kettle ponds) to the depth of groundwater. An excellent example of this geological feature, called a pamet, is Truro's Pamet River, which begins just west of Ballston Beach on the ocean side and meanders the width of the Outer Cape to Pamet Harbor and Cape Cod Bay.

Type of Ponds

FRESHWATER POND

As its name implies, a freshwater pond is filled with fresh water. Most ponds on the Cape and Islands fall into this category—kettle depressions that are flooded by our existing groundwater table, where a lens of fresh water as thick as 300 feet sits atop the salt water that underlies all of the Cape and Islands. This lens of fresh water is fed, as we noted, by rain and melting snow that trickles down between the sand and gravel beneath the earth's surface, filling pockets of air between rock particles. The trickling continues until it reaches an existing pool of water that sits between rock particles anywhere from several feet to more than 200 feet below the surface. This pool of water is called the freshwater lens—its surface is called the water table. The simplest definition of a freshwater pond is the point where a kettle depression meets the water table. The height of this water table is controlled by the level of the sea. As the sea rises, so does the water table, pushing its freshwater lens closer to the surface. All groundwater flows from the center of the water table at its highest point downhill toward the sea, pulled along by the forces of gravity. The water table (and hence the surface of freshwater ponds on the Cape and Islands) is generally six to thirty-two feet above sea level.

Other examples of freshwater ponds with relatively easy public access are Gibbs Pond on Nantucket, off Barnard Valley Road on Nantucket Conservation Foundation land (the pond is next to the world's largest natural cranberry bog); Sasachacha Pond off Polpis Road on the east end of Nantucket; Duarte Pond on Martha's Vineyard, off Lambert's Cove Road in Tisbury; Fresh Pond in East Falmouth on the Cape, off Fresh Pond Road; Hoxie Pond in East Sandwich, off Old County Road; Mill Pond in West Barnstable, off Cedar Street; adjoining Upper Mill and Lower Mill ponds in Brewster, off Stony Brook Road at the town's herring run; and Brewster's Cliff Pond, off Route 6A inside Nickerson State Park.

SALTWATER PONDS

Saltwater ponds introduce a whole different dynamic. They are, for the most part, tidal ponds—ponds with outlets to the sea, which provides their primary source of water. Good examples of saltwater ponds are Sengekontacket Pond on Martha's Vineyard, off Beach Road between Oak Bluffs and Edgartown; Lagoon Pond on the Vineyard, also off Beach Road between Vineyard Haven and Oak Bluffs; and Salt Pond at the Cape Cod National Seashore Visitor Center off Route 6 in Eastham.

Many of our salt ponds were once freshwater ponds that were transformed by the intrusion of seawater across a barrier beach or through a tidal inlet. Eastham's Salt Pond, Town Cove in Orleans, and Ryder Cove in Chatham are examples. As the sea continues to rise and erode the shoreline, most of our fresh ponds will be turned into salt ponds. In the process many of these ponds will contain brackish water, a mixture of fresh and salt water—fresh water from the water table, salt water from the sea. Some examples of brackish ponds or former salt ponds are the lagoons off Waquoit Bay in Falmouth, Hamblin Pond and Jehu Pond; Mill Pond in Orleans; Menemsha Pond off Menemsha Harbor on Martha's Vineyard; and Pilgrim Lake on the Truro-Provincetown line, off Route 6.

Provincetown is also a good place to view dune ponds—ponds that were formed by wind and wave-washed sediment that piled up in sand spits along the shoreline long after the ice sheets receded. These water bodies were formerly saltwater bays and coves.

A Year in the Life of a Pond

While there may be a geological sameness to ponds on the Cape and Islands, there is nothing static about them. They shift and change with the seasons, and as each month is torn from the calendar a new natural picture appears. Gull Pond in Wellfleet, off Gull Pond Road about a half mile west of Newcomb Hollow Beach, is the pond we will follow through the seasons. By Wellfleet standards it is large, but Gull Pond is of average size for a kettle, about ninety acres and up to sixty-five feet in depth. In many ways it fits the profile of a typical pond.

SPRING

We begin our year in the life of a Cape Cod pond most fittingly in the spring when all of nature begins to waken from the winter's dormancy. It is early April, and while the thermometer may be registering only in the fifties, the warmth of the sun gives promise of the season ahead. The wind is blowing, but for the first time in months, it does not bring a chill to the marrow. The warmth of the sun and the force of the wind are the two most important forces in a pond ecosystem. The sun provides the light energy essential for photosynthetic oxygen and carbohydrate production by algae and larger plants; the wind induces the physical mixing of pond water. Every pond process, from basic water chemistry to complex animal life cycles, follows from the admixture of sun and wind. (Photosynthesis, as you probably recall from high school biology, is an essential process by which plant cells make carbohydrates from carbon dioxide and water in the presence of chlorophyll and light and release oxygen as a by-product.)

Gull Pond, our prototype, is connected by an outlet to Higgins Pond and Williams Pond; then by stream its waters reach the sea. The pond water is quite clear and slightly acidic (containing natural acids from surrounding pine and oak woods that contribute to the normal clarity of ponds). Most ponds on the Cape and Islands are naturally acidic.

Warm water achieves greatest density at forty-one degrees Fahrenheit. So, when the surface water of a pond first begins to warm with the new season and its temperature begins to rise, it becomes denser than the cold water beneath and sinks through these cold waters to the bottom. That leaves the lighter colder waters to rise to the surface to be warmed, in turn, and then sink back down to the bottom. It's sort of like tossing a salad to make sure the dressing is evenly distributed. Brisk spring winds step in once the pond has reached maximum density to thoroughly mix the entire water mass. This process continues until all the pond waters are about the same temperature from surface to bottom (usually in the seventies during summer).

As a result of this spring overturn, nutrients trapped near the bottom of a pond in winter are fairly rapidly mixed into the surface waters. By early April, algal cells, the simplest of green plant forms, bathe in these newly available nutrients and benefiting, as well, from the longer periods of sunlight reproduce explosively. At no other time during the year will there be as many algal cells, or algae, crowding the water. Algal cells have no roots, stems, or leaves but contain chlorophyll that converts energy from sunlight into food.

As in most aquatic and marine ecosystems, these drifting algae (also known as phytoplankton) are the primary producers of what is called the pond food web—the organisms responsible for converting solar energy and then making it available as food for a long line of consumers, from tiny crustacean zooplankton (microscopic or near microscopic animals that drift in the open waters of a pond) to large fish and birds. (Phytoplankton are microscopic and near microscopic plants that drift in the open water of a pond.)

The Cape and Islands are famous for their reluctant spring seasons because the surrounding seawater is slow to warm. The surface of the ponds, however, warms much faster, and this difference sets the stage for some dramatic animal migrations.

As pond water temperature reaches the midforties in late March and early April, the gulls, which for months have loitered about the frozen ponds or rafted on the water, suddenly take renewed interest is the pond outlet. They are attracted by the migrating herring or alewives and other anadromous fish that swim upstream to spawn in the pond but mature in the sea.

SUMMER

As summer approaches, the herring fry begin to hatch and school up to feed on zooplankton in the shallows. They are joined by resident adult pumpkinseed sunfish who, like the herring's parents, also are intent on reproduction. Adult male sunfish spend most of their time in June and July preparing and protecting their redds, or spawning beds. The redds are cleared of all organic debris by the fastidious males—perhaps to ensure abundant oxygen—and thus stand out as immaculate depressions along the otherwise weedy pond shallows.

The sunfish males attract females to deposit eggs in these redds and then fertilize and subsequently defend the spawn against all invaders. These fish are almost without fear and will rush forth aggressively even against such a formidable threat as a man in bulky rubber hip-waders. This parental protection doesn't last very long, however. Males abandon their young as soon as the fry are free swimming.

Fish reproduce by the many thousands for a very good reason. As soon as the eggs are laid, they join the menu of a host of pond predators, including snails and painted turtles as well as other varieties of fish. Those that survive to larval and juvenile stages become prey to such as white suckers, chain pickerel, turtles, water birds, and raccoons, as well as fishermen who use them effectively as bait.

By midsummer, juvenile sunfish have left the spawning redd and they're on their own. They have schooled up to feed on zooplankton and other small invertebrates in weedy shallows, dodging when possible large schools of predatory yellow perch and bass. Stocked trout are less of a danger at this time because these salmon-like predators cannot tolerate the warm water of the surface and prefer a cooler refuge in the deep.

Just as winter cold and the ice cover inhibit the mixing of water in a pond, summer heat creates a similar stagnation, particularly since mild summer breezes do little to stir the waters from without. Stratification of warm over cold layers of water can develop, and this is true to some degree in all of the deep kettle ponds. You can often feel this effect when swimming near the center of a pond; the water on your chest is warm, but your legs are cold.

The cold dense waters on the bottom differ sharply both physically and chemically from the warm surface waters, and this contrast further inhibits mixing, which keeps oxygen received from the atmosphere near the surface. In the more nutrient-rich ponds, algal growth at the surface can block out the light and slow or inhibit photosynthesis below the surface. If this stratification is prolonged, a thick layer of oxygen-depleted water accumulates at the pond bottom to create a lethal condition for cold-water fish. This is less of a problem in naturally clear kettle ponds.

While the summer pond represents an arena fraught with danger for aquatic animals, the pond shoreline can provide many diversions for human visitors. Freshwater mussels are common in ponds like Gull Pond that are not predominately acidic and are connected by streams to the sea. These shellfish leave deep, three-quarter-inch trails in the shoreline sands as they move about filtering algae from the water.

Smaller furrows are left by burrowing dragonfly nymphs, which are voracious predators of other aquatic insects, tadpoles, and small fish. These lurk just under the sand bottom and can be found by gently probing with the fingers along their narrow plowed trails.

Dragonfly nymphs are just one of the myriad, and diverse, aquatic insects that spend their immature stages either on, or in, the pond sediment. After the first year of life on the pond bottom, they climb up plant stems in early summer and shed their nymphal coverings, emerging as winged adults. Damselflies, mayflies, and midges also abound in the pond. If you are walking along the edge of a pond, check plant stems that rise above the surface for the discarded nymphal coverings—called exoskeletons—of dragonflies and damselflies.

In the weeds below the water surface, look for water tigers, or predatory water beetle larvae, as they stalk the tadpoles of green frogs, bullfrogs, and Fowler's toads. During still summer evenings, many ponds echo with the bullfrog's deep monotone "moo" (also sounds like the "thrums" of a bass fiddle) and the sonorous, buzzing call of the Fowler. Many confuse this toad's young—called toadlets, a half inch long—with insects as they scurry around the margins of the pond by the hundreds in July. In midsummer, the surface of many ponds is textured, not just by the wind but by rafts of spidery water striders, who are true bugs. Whirligig beetles also mass on pond surfaces by the hundreds of thousands.

Gull Pond is only moderately productive and therefore not a great turtle pond. However, a few painted turtles and an occasional snapper eke out an existence subsidized by the annual herring bonanza. The water snake and garter snake stalk tadpoles in the shallows, but none of the few snakes to be found here are venomous.

Perhaps the most bizarre among the pond's animals are the brainlike masses of colonial ectroproct or bryozoan (mosslike animals). Their rounded colonies resemble sponges and are attached to submerged sticks and vegetation in the weedy pond shallows. The full-sized adults resemble in size a human skull. Completely harmless, ectoprocts filter algae and other fine material from the water and, actually, serve as indicators that the pond is not polluted.

As autumn approaches, migrant water birds, including many fish eaters, pause to dine on the kettle pond. Besides a regular flock of herring gulls and great black-backed gulls whose numbers peak in autumn, the common, roseate, and least terns often gather to bathe and drink just before their southward migration. Double-crested cormorants, red-breasted mergansers, pied-billed grebes, red-throated loons, and ring-billed gulls frequently fish the massive schools of juvenile herring in spawning ponds. By mid-October, migrating ospreys frequently hover over the pond, periodically diving from heights up to 200 feet to attack fish feeding on the surface or in shallow water.

AUTUMN

With autumn's longer and colder nights, surface water is cooling and sinking, eventually equalizing the water temperature, destroying summer stratification, and setting the stage for a fall overturn that completes another full cycle of the water column. As with the spring overturn, the wind plays a major role. Cape Cod's brisk fall breezes from the northwest, combined with the passage of a cold front, can complete this turnover in just a few days Nutrients, released by the sediments but held in the oxygen-poor bottom water all summer, suddenly circulate through the pond to stimulate a last hurrah for the algae before extreme cold and shortened days slow their growth.

WINTER

Gull Pond in January and February provides a peaceful if bleak refuge for resident gulls and occasional waterfowl and eagles. The nights belong to the night herons, great blue herons, and great horned owls. On calm winter evenings their eerie croaks and monotone hoots echo across the frozen slopes of the watershed.

Although the nearby North Atlantic provides a moderating influence, ponds on the Cape and Islands may experience a three-week period of ice cover any time from mid-December to late March. The ice can reach a foot in thickness, and with low light levels and cold water temperatures, biological activity is nearly at a standstill. The ice also keeps the winds from stirring the surface water. Nevertheless, drifting planktonic algae continue to harness even the dimmest beams of sunlight to slowly build organic molecules from dissolved carbon dioxide and water.

Under clear sections of the ice one may observe zooplankton continuing to migrate through the water as they feed on algae and each other. Immature forms of aquatic insects like the phantom midge and dragonfly also are active throughout the winter in pond sediments, and fish—like yellow perch and bass—continue their pursuit under the ice of both smaller fish and insect larvae. In deepest water, the temperature may remain near fifty degrees Fahrenheit.

Other animals continue to visit the frozen pond. These include gulls, who appreciate an open expanse on which to rest, and wintering eagles, almost always immature balds. Humans come as well, whether to ice-skate or to fish. Ice fishermen often will feed undersized yellow perch from their catch to the eagles.

Meanwhile, most resident stream organisms that haven't fled to deeper (and warmer) water—either upstream into the ponds or downstream into the estuary—are dormant in the frigid water and sediment as all await the first warming spring breeze to begin the cycle anew.

How Ponds Were Formed

Not as famous as our ocean beaches, ponds on the Cape and Islands are often taken for granted, but concern now is growing about their preservation. The more we know about the origin of these ponds, the more we can appreciate their beauty and, one hopes, dedicate ourselves to maintaining them in their original natural state.

When the glaciers receded, large chunks of ice were left behind embedded in outwashed sand for thousands of years. During this period, soil washed from the retreating ice masses accumulated around these giant ice cubes. Pine taiga forests similar to those that today can be seen in the northern reaches of Russia and North America took root. The trees were basically spruce, fir, and arctic willow.

About 10,000 to 12,000 years ago, these ice blocks completely melted leaving holes as deep as 100 feet. We call them kettle holes because of their rounded kettle-bottom shape; many of them flooded. As we can see from the dates, this was a gradual process that did not proceed at a steady rate. To understand how they flooded requires both a knowledge of sea level, which we've already discussed, and an understanding of pond sediments.

FOSSIL REVELATIONS

A diver swimming along the bottom of a clear Cape Cod kettle pond from shoreline to deepest point might be surprised to find that white bathing beach sand is only a shoreline phenomenon. A gooey, easily roiled mud fills the thirty- to sixty-foot depths of many of the clearest kettles. These accumulations of organic mud range from thirteen to twenty feet thick, and they represent 10,000 to 12,000 years of pond and watershed life that has died and funneled to the bottom. The scarcity of oxygen and constant temperatures about fifty degrees Fahrenheit slow the decomposition process of these plants and animal remains. (However, as the pond ages it becomes shallower by the buildup of this accumulation; the process, called pond succession, is described toward the end of this chapter.)

Until recently, scientists assumed that the deepest kettles, such as Gull and Duck ponds in Wellfleet and Long Pond in Brewster and Harwich, were first flooded by rising groundwater about 7,000 years ago when the sea level rose to the kettle-bottom elevations. However, careful collection and examination of core samples from the very deepest pond sediments disclosed irrefutably that the ponds actually were flooded 12,000 years ago when the sea level and groundwater should have been well below their basins. How could this have happened? Scientists aren't quite sure. One theory holds that silt and forest litter acted to seal in the melting ice.

Analysis of this sedimentary material also reveals a detailed record of pond biology over many millennia. Layer by layer and year by year, this sediment not only tells the story of the pond but its whole watershed. The sediment record is so complete and undisturbed that scientists have been able to reconstruct prehistoric vegetation (from pollen grains and plant fragments), the frequency of fires (from charcoal flakes), sedimentation rate (by carbon-14 dating), and even water quality (from sensitive algae called diatoms). They have done this for the entire Outer Cape.

One researcher, analyzing sediment seven meters thick from Great Pond in Truro, discovered at the bottom of her core the twigs of an arctic willow, a relic of the forest that had taken root upon the melting ice block. On the twigs, still tenaciously gripping the bark, were 11,000-year-old scale insects that had been preserved along with their host plant.

From these core analyses it is also known that the present high acidity of many ponds on the Cape and Islands has been a common condition of kettle pond water for the past 12,000 years (challenging theories that acid rain has increased pond acidity, inhibiting fish and plant life—see question and answer section to follow). Given Cape soils and vegetation, this should come as no surprise. In sandy soils, natural minerals that buffer or neutralize acidity are scarce. Also, the Cape's vegetation almost always has been predominantly coniferous, which is another contributing factor. The pitch pines that dominate most pond watersheds today have been doing so for 9,000 years. When their needles break down, they release organic acids that leach through the soil into poorly buffered, or unprotected, pond waters.

Given this background, it is easy to see why these waters—nutrient poor, highly transparent, and naturally acidic—are so sensitive to change. Consider a man who through his entire life has existed on a strict subsistence diet. The sudden addition of fat, for example, is certain to trigger dramatic physiological reactions. It's the same with the kettle ponds, evolving as they have for 10,000 years in basins of barely soluble quartzite sand. Human additions of nutrients to these systems can produce major digestive problems for these ponds.

POND ZONES

Like the seashore, wetlands, woodlands, and the earth's atmosphere, ponds can be divided into zones. There are two major pond zones that run vertically from the pond surface to the pond bottom: the littoral zone, which is near the shore and in shallow water; and the limnetic zone, which is in deeper water and closer to the pond center.

The littoral zone is the most active zone. Here you'll find a variety of plant and animal life. Common plants found in a littoral zone include cattails, reed grass, spike rush, bulrushes, and sedges. The shallow water makes it easier for light to reach the pond bottom and encourage growth. In the littoral zone you are also likely to find tadpoles, frogs, small turtles, water snakes, insects, and shellfish.

In the limnetic zone, little if any vegetation grows on the surface and pond bottom. The water is too deep for sunlight to penetrate. However, you will find large turtles, like the snapping turtle, some crayfish, and larger fish, like the pickerel.

The Ponds Today

Peer over the gunwales of your canoe into the depths of Gull Pond on a bright May morning and you can watch yellow perch foraging along the bottom up to thirty feet below. The water of these ponds is so transparent that drifting on their surface on a windless day is almost like floating on air.

This clarity is due less to the dearth of silt than to the scarcity of plant nutrients (or fertilizers) in the native sandy soils. Pond vegetation also is limited by the scarcity of nutrients in local surface waters, just as adjacent forests are kept small because the poor sandy soil is unable to provide a hospitable base that will help overcome the rigors of high winds and salt spray. Therefore, if you come upon a deep kettle pond that is unnaturally clouded with algae, there's a good chance that human activities (swimming, seepage from septic systems, and runoff) have played a role.

On our same May morning, you may just barely discern a dense area of dark green on the otherwise white, sandy bottom of any kettle pond found on the Cape or Islands. This is not primarily algal growth but the lush mossy vegetation, including sphagnum, one might normally expect to find in a shallow bog. But it survives in the clearest kettle ponds because their very transparency allows sufficient light penetration to support plants even below forty-five feet.

POND SUCCESSION

In all living things, change is inevitable. And so it is with ponds. There is a natural process, a succession of stages if you will, by which ponds are born, develop, and then die. Unlike the erosion of an island or the disappearance of a mountain range that take thousands of years, the cradle-to-the-grave cycle of a pond can be witnessed in generations, as one form of plant follows another, leaving sediment behind on the pond bottom that builds up until the pond literally fills in, becoming a marsh, then a swamp, and finally upland. Although your favorite pond may seem unchanged from year to year, this cycle is progressing.

As the pond basin begins to fill with this organic muck, nutrients become more available to the well-lit and biologically active pond surface. More nutrients means more algae and denser aquatic plants, which in turn contribute to pond filling.

A good example of the marshy stage of pond succession is Williams Pond in Wellfleet, which is joined by an outlet to Higgins and Gull ponds. Surrounded by dense shrubs and invading water willow and lilies, this ten-foot-deep marshy kettle someday may become a damp and fertile red maple swamp, like Red Maple Swamp in Eastham.

One can understand, and even accept, how these originally clear and deep sandy-bottomed basins naturally age over thousands of years. But now a disturbing trend is becoming apparent. This process of succession—also known as eutrophication—is speeding up. Tight nutrient budgets responsible for clear water only a few decades ago have been upset. Large quantities of nutrients, a diet foreign to the ecology of kettle ponds, are imported every year by humans. This process has been dubbed cultural eutrophication and is responsible for much of the cloudiness and weed proliferation of certain ponds today. In the long term, cultural eutrophication may doom all the naturally clear ponds that today are enjoyed by anglers, swimmers, boaters, and naturalists of all ages.

The problem began when European settlers first cleared the forest 200 to 300 years ago, allowing the erosion of forest soils and their nutrients into the ponds. Shoreline erosion remains an increasingly serious problem today as more and more people discover these ponds and then clear out a right-of-way to get them down steep slopes.

Additionally, more and more homes are being built very close to the shorelines. Like all rural dwellings, sewage is not piped away but deposited by one method or another into the ground nearby. Much of this nutrient-rich material finds its way into the groundwater and seeps ultimately into adjacent ponds. Sewage is rich in nitrogen and phosphorous, two essential plant nutrients, the scarcity of which normally limits the growth of algae in fresh kettle ponds, streams, and coastal lagoons. The introduction of these man-produced nutrients removes this governor and allows algae and shoreline plants to proliferate. Thus man, through his inattention to the delicate ecosystem's limits, ends up destroying the pristine clear-water environment that originally attracted him.

Even the solid waste disposal practices of more urban landfills add to the nutrient loading of ponds on the Cape and Islands. At the turn of the century, large gulls were rare in this region. But, from the 1940s through the 1960s, their populations in the northeastern United States increased rapidly. The creation of large garbage dumps provided a significant food subsidy for inexperienced young gulls, and so more and more of these birds survived to breed. Presently over 40,000 gulls breed in this region, and many more show up during fall migration.

These birds are very much attracted to the larger kettle ponds, not to feed but to rest, drink, and bathe. More than 2,000 have been counted at one sitting resting on appropriately named Gull Pond. While in attendance, they excrete their phosphorous-rich guano that further degrades the water quality. Waterfowl, especially Canada geese who are lured to certain ponds by well-meaning residents or visitors, who feed them, also contribute to eutrophication in this manner.

Of course, for those simply interested in what they can get out of the pond (more algae leads to more little fish and in turn to more big fish), nutrient loading may be considered a plus; at least over the very short term. But rampant algal blooms will block sunlight and seriously deplete oxygen in pond depths, eventually causing major fish kills.

Q & A

Q Why are some ponds fresh water and some salt water?

The salinity of a pond is dependent on its proximity to the sea. All ponds isolated from the sea for at least a few years become increasingly fresh, due to fresh rain, snowfall, and inflowing groundwater. Although salty groundwater completely underlies Cape Cod, a lens of fresh groundwater (about 300 feet deep at its thickest) floats on its surface and thus fills and flows in and out of the ponds' basins. Salty ponds are almost always produced by the regular intrusion of seawater across barrier beaches or through relatively stable inlets. Of course, as sea level continues to rise and erode our ocean shorelines, more of our fresh ponds will be overwhelmed by the sea, and more will be created in depressions at higher elevations.

Q *Where does the fresh water come from that fills ponds on the Cape and Islands?*

A pond on the Cape and Islands is like an open well dug down into the water table—the surface of fresh groundwater that floats, as we noted, atop salty groundwater. Like an open well, the pond fills with this fresh groundwater that percolates through the permeable sandy soil here. Few ponds on the Cape and Islands are spring fed because groundwater seeps so easily through this porous material, rather than being funneled to the surface. Springs occur where groundwater, confined between rock and impermeable silt loam and clay, is abruptly released into the surface waters of a pond.

Q *What role do streams play in the life of a pond?*

Streams are the principal transportation routes from ponds and coastal marshes to the sea. Most streams begin as kettle pond outlets, then quickly gain volume from tributaries and seeping groundwater, and end as meandering tidal creeks that flow to the sea.

An essential migration route for herring and American eels, the stream also provides a nursery habitat for the young of many commercially valuable finfish that move up and down the estuary in search of both food and safety from predators. Migrating fish and animals are dependent on the quality of these flooded highways. However, human alterations have often made this water quality less than ideal.

With the best of intentions, our predecessors diked estuaries and channeled and straightened coastal streams in hopes of easing fish passage and draining mosquito-infested lowlands. Unfortunately, these practices caused stream water quality and fish habitats to deteriorate, and because fish populations were reduced, one of their major prey insects—the mosquito—ironically prospered.

Some relief is in sight for these estuaries that have been altered by man. Wellfleet's Herring River and Provincetown's Hatches Harbor are the subject of research and restoration programs. It is clear these wetlands can recover with the controlled return of tidal flow.

Q *Why is there fog over some ponds? How does it form?*

The air just above the pond is laden with moisture in the form of water vapor evaporated from the sun-heated surface waters throughout the day. During windless nights, cold air settles into each pond basin, chilling the water-vapor-laden air. The vapor then condenses into tiny water droplets, small and light enough to float in air as fog. Morning fog is usually dispersed by daytime winds or revaporized by the heat of the sun.

Q Why does ice form at the top and not at the bottom of ponds?

Since liquids become denser as they get colder, you might expect the coldest water to be at the bottom of a pond in winter. But water is truly an exceptional liquid. It reaches its maximum density at about forty-one degrees Fahrenheit (five degrees Celsius), at which point it is still liquid. As the water becomes colder at this point, it becomes less dense, eventually floating to the pond surface where it turns to ice.

Q In late summer, I sometimes see swarms of little fish swimming in circles near the shore. What are they?

If the pond is connected by an outlet stream to the bay or ocean, perhaps even indirectly through other downstream ponds, these fish are very likely young alewives or herring. They were spawned in the pond in the spring and by late summer form massive schools as they circle the pond shoreline, feeding on plankton and searching for the exit downstream and thence to the sea. Another possibility is the young of pumpkinseed sunfish. These have pale vertical bars, unlike herring, and group in less-organized schools, milling about in the shallows rather than determinedly coursing along the shore.

Q Can you catch lobsters in ponds on the Cape and Islands?

No, not unless the pond is salty and connected to a salt marsh or the sea. Unlike their freshwater relatives, lobsters cannot survive for long in low-salinity water. Lobsterlike crayfish inhabit some of our fresh ponds, feeding on organic debris in the shallows, but these grow to only four inches in length.

Q What are the "clams" I find on the bottom of some ponds?

These are freshwater mussels that plow through the pond sediment surface, filtering tiny algal cells from the water. They are abundant only in those ponds with enough calcium to allow shell development. Because the levels of calcium largely control pond acidity (the more calcium, the less acid), the presence of these mollusks indicates the pond is relatively low in acid with pH above 6.0. (Most Outer Cape ponds have pH between 5.0 and 6.0.)

Small freshwater clams can also be found in some Cape and Islands ponds.

Q *What forms of life other than fish are found in ponds?*

The real shakers and movers in a pond ecosystem are some of its smallest inhabitants: zooplankton, algae and bacteria, and invertebrate animals in the sediment. Although fish and water birds are most conspicuous to us, and do have important roles as predators in the pond system, the pond's basic chemistry is most affected by its smallest and most numerous residents, which are described in detail in the preceding chapter.

Q *What is the green scum on summer ponds? Is it safe to fish and swim in it?*

A thick green scum floating on a pond surface or drifting below it is a mass of filament-forming colonial algae. Their stringy growth form is easy to see if you cup pond water in your hands, then watch the strings trail down between your fingers. Although the presence of this algae may be natural in some ponds, large masses of it are not expected in clear kettle ponds unless human or animal activities somehow increase the supply of plant nutrients, a process called eutrophication, which is discussed in the preceding chapter. This algae is an indication the pond is aging; the accumulation of plant nutrients and organic matter will eventually cause the filling of a pond's basin.

In any case, these scums—though not particularly appealing—are not dangerous to swim or fish in.

Q *Why do gulls swim on some ponds and not on others? Do they eat fish in these ponds?*

No one really understands this, but gulls seem to choose large ponds near a dump or shore-feeding site. Almost every dump on the Cape and Islands has an adjacent "gull pond," where birds traditionally congregate. These flocks attract other shore-feeding birds and coastal migrants, who seem to enjoy the fresh water for drinking, bathing, and resting. To a gull, a large pond may represent relative safety from predators on the ground and in the air.

Most of these gulls, primarily herring gulls and black-backed gulls, are large birds that do most of their feeding along the ocean and bay shorelines, at dumps (sanitary landfills), and out at sea. They rarely catch fish while loafing on a pond.

Q *Why do aquatic plants like water lilies and rushes only grow around the edges of ponds?*

These plants must have abundant light to make food, and at the same time they must be rooted in sediment to obtain the nutrients that they cannot synthesize. In the deep ponds, these two requirements are met only along the shore. These plants are specially adapted to tolerate the constant flooding and low oxygen content of pond sediments.

Q *Are there any active beaver dams on Cape and Islands ponds?*

No. Although beavers were present historically, the destruction of the forests for agriculture, fuel, and building materials over the last two centuries has eliminated their habitats. The general scarcity of rivers and streams and bottomland hardwood trees for food (especially beech, maple birch, and aspen) suggests that these large rodents were never abundant here. Muskrats are common, however, and often build dome-shaped lodges out of aquatic plants in cattail marshes. Muskrats are much smaller than beavers and lack the flattened tail.

Q *What is acid rain? Where does it come from? Does it damage ponds on the Cape and Islands?*

There is much controversy over "acid rain" and its effect on ponds. Acid precipitation is pollution—primarily sulfur dioxide emissions from industrial plants—that is carried eastward by wind currents and returned to earth in the form of contaminated rain, sleet, and snow.

Many scientists and naturalists have charged that this rain has increased the acidity of ponds on the Cape and Islands, killing off certain plant and fish life that cannot survive in water that is highly acidic. Many believe limestone added to pond waters will neutralize this acid.

Some scientists make the point that ponds on the Cape and Islands are naturally acidic and have not increased substantially in acidity since they were formed during the Ice Age. Pond acidity, they say, is caused by native soil conditions. The ponds should be left alone, they insist. Liming will only alter the water chemistry, increasing the amount of algae, which cuts down light entering a pond and chokes off plant and animal life.

In recent years, this second—and most controversial—of the two theories has gained momentum. A study of Duck Pond in South Wellfleet indicates the pond has remained consistently acidic for its 12,000-year history—with a mean pH of 5.2, indicating slight increases and decreases in acidity. As you learned in high school, pH is a symbol for measuring both acidity and its opposite—alkalinity. Pure neutral drinking water, with no acidity or alkalinity, has a pH of 7. Any pH measurement below 7 indicates acidity; above 7 indicates alkalinity. For example, the pH of vinegar is 2.2, the pH of an apple is 3, and the pH of baking soda is 8.2.

While some argue Duck Pond is a special case, private and public studies indicate that the acidity of the average pond on the Cape and Islands hasn't changed appreciably in 150 years. Of greater threat to the ponds, these studies warn, is runoff from storms, unrestricted recreational use, and seepage from neighboring septic systems.

Chapter 6

The Woodlands, Heaths, and Grasslands

by Robert Finch

Most visitors to Cape Cod and the Islands dismiss our forests as, at best, something to be driven through on their way to the beaches or the ponds. Unlike the sequoias and redwoods of California or the spruce-fir rain forests of Washington or the live oaks of Georgia or the white pines of Maine, our trees are generally not considered one of our attractions. Our pitch pines, cutover oaks, red cedars, swamp maples, and other indigenous trees are small and scrubby by mainland standards and, though colorful enough in fall, are hardly serious competition for the blaze of northern New England's sugar maples and birches. Given their vulnerability to periodic gypsy moth infestations, when millions of crawling, leaf-gobbling caterpillars denude whole tracts of our forests, there are times when many visitors and residents alike think we might be better off without them entirely.

Yet as much as our more famous features—beaches, tidal flats, sand dunes, salt marshes, and kettle ponds—our trees are indigenous expressions of the landscape and the forces acting upon it. As much as any other local habitat, forests have played an important part in Cape Cod's history and, more than most, their present appearance and makeup is a living history book of the interaction of human beings with this land over the centuries. Modest and scrubby they may be, but our woodlands, heaths, and grasslands are marvels of adaptation and environmental toughness and contain some of our most critical wildlife habitat. To disdain our trees because they are scrubby is like disparaging desert vegetation because it is sparse or arctic plant life because it is low. If we can overcome our big woods bias and look at our native flora for what it is, rather than what it is not, we will discover a fascinating and at times mysterious story, not unlike a detective mystery that unravels through modest clues. It is a story that reveals the existence of an impressive, vanished forest never since equaled in size or extent and the making of the unique man-made forest we see today.

Hints of Change

Compared to, say, sand dunes or beaches, forests appear to us as something relatively stable in the environment—at least until the bulldozers begin to graze over them. Here on Cape Cod and the Islands our view of woodlands may be more limited than in other places, for most of us either visit the area for brief periods or have lived here for only a short time. We may, at first, see the widespread stands of pitch pine and scrub oak as permanent and original with the Cape. But we do not live here very long before we begin to sense that we are mistaken. Even within the lifetimes of some of the older local residents, dramatic and widespread changes have taken place in the Cape's forests, changes that hint at even older changes.

Pollen grain analyses of peat more than 5,000 years old, buried deep in Barnstable marshes, indicate that a boreal-type forest of northern spruces and firs, dwarf birches, and arctic willows existed on the Cape and Islands in the early postglacial era. No visible evidence of those prehistoric forests remains, however.

But what were the Cape's forests like fifty years ago? A hundred years ago? Two hundred years ago? What were they like before the white men came? Were they similar to the rest of New England's forests? Was it a forest primeval of great towering white pines, all mossy and hoary with age, such as we frequently read about? For that matter, what is a forest primeval anyway?

These and other speculations about the history of Cape Cod forests often lead to surprising discoveries. For instance, look at some of the old photographs taken at the turn of the century in any Cape Cod town and you will behold, for the most part, a treeless landscape. (Two good sources are the display of H.K. Cummings prints at the Snow Library on Main Street in Orleans and *Brewster: A Cape Cod Town Remembered,* a collection of historical photos pub-

lished by the Brewster Historical Society available in local bookstores.) A very graphic example of this change in the mid-Cape area
can be found at the Brewster Mill Sites on Stony Brook Road. There,
beside the herring run, in a verdant glacial valley shaded with tall
willows and maples, the surrounding hills thick with stands of pines
and oaks, you can examine a display of photographs of the area
taken in the 1860s showing a barren, boulder-strewn landscape that
looks as if it were taken in Labrador rather than where you stand.

Much of this treeless land, of course, was in farming, but records
of the time speak of a generally barren and unforested landscape.
Henry David Thoreau, for instance, riding along what is now Route
6A in a stagecoach in 1848, spoke of the towns of Barnstable,
Yarmouth, Dennis, and Brewster this way:

> The country was, for the most part, bare, or with only a little scrubby
> woods left on the hills . . . There is a thin layer of soil, gradually
> diminishing from Barnstable and Truro, where it ceases; but there
> are many holes and rents in this weather-beaten garment not likely
> to be stitched in time, which reveal the naked flesh of the Cape, and
> its extremity is completely bare.

An early Massachusetts geologist, Edward Hitchcock, writing of
the Lower Cape in 1847, said that he felt "he was in the depths of an
Arabian or Libyan desert." And in *Moby Dick*, Herman Melville's
deliberately exaggerated description of Nantucket Island at about
the same time nonetheless reflects what was a common sight to most
travelers and inhabitants in the nineteenth century: a bare, treeless
landscape. Were the Cape and Islands always treeless, then? We
have only to go a bit further back in time to find out that they were
not.

A Backward Look

Let us journey further back into the past, then, back before the
present stands of pitch pines had taken hold on an impoverished
soil, before the winds blew freely over unprotected terrain, before
the Puritan settlers, so frugal in other ways, had begun to hack down
the native forests for a multitude of purposes.

It is 1602, eighteen years before the landing of the *Mayflower* at
Plymouth. Bartholomew Gosnold, sailing from Falmouth, England,
in the ship *Concord*, has already reached the outer shore of Cape
Cod and, amazed by the schools of codfish that surround his vessel,

gives this peninsula the name by which it has been known ever since.

But we know of another natural resource that impressed members of his voyage. John Brereton, a sort of public relations man on Gosnold's ship, described the following sight as the *Concord* cruised off the Elizabeth Islands, a chain of seven glacial islands stretching southwest from Woods Hole:

> High timbered oaks, their leaves thrice so broad as ours in England; cedars, straight and tall; beech, elm, holly, walnut trees in abundance . . . hazelnut trees, cherry trees, sassafras trees in great plenty all the island over . . . also divers other fruit trees.

Four years later, in 1606, the young French explorer, Samuel de Champlain, entered Chatham Harbor and, except for some native American village clearings, saw a countryside covered with "walnuts, oak and cedar." His testimony was repeated some fifty years later when William Nickerson, Chatham's first white settler, reported finding the hillsides covered with great oak forests and the swamps filled with gigantic cedars.

Even at Provincetown, which must always have been the most barren and harsh region of the Cape, we have firsthand reports that a sizable and impressive forest once covered a good part of the area. William Bradford described the view that greeted the *Mayflower* passengers as they entered Provincetown Harbor in 1620:

> The whole countrie, full of woods and thickets, represented a wild and savage view.

When the Pilgrim party made their first venture ashore, they found the present sand hills of Provincetown

> much like the Downes of Holland, but much better, all wooded with oaks, pines, sassafras, juniper, birch, holly, some ash, walnut, the wood for the most part open and without underwood, fit to go or ride in.

Wood End, in fact, where the lighthouse of that name now sits on the barren back shore of Provincetown, may well refer to the end of the forest that once covered this area.

What kind of picture do all these accounts give of the early forests on the Cape and Islands? We might, after all, distrust one land-starved sailor or publicist's account as being somewhat exaggerated. But even if we discount these early descriptions somewhat, there is more tangible evidence to go on. During the eighteenth and even into the twentieth century, many Cape Cod towns supported thriving ship-building industries—such as Shiverick Boat Yard at Sesuit Harbor in East Dennis—ships whose keels, beams, ribbing, and planks required oak trees in a number, size, and quantity that no longer exist here. In early Cape Cod houses, constructed before the Cape needed to import its building material, it is common to find pine floorboards and wainscoting two and even three feet wide. In the West Parish Congregational Church on Route 6A in West Barnstable a visitor can see beams of native oak sixteen inches square and forty-eight feet long. And in many cases the very foundations of the houses were made from cedar rolls, the split trunks of the great Atlantic white cedars that once flourished in our local wetlands. By any present standards, then, a great forest once covered the Cape.

It was not, however, the "forest primeval" of Longfellow's poem. In fact, the concept of a primordial forest, composed of nothing but enormous ancient trees, has been largely discredited by contemporary forest historians. There were large trees, yes, but natural forces such as lightning fires, hurricanes, and species competition were constantly creating temporary grasslands, open clearings, and new generations of saplings, even where man's presence was not felt.

But, in fact, human alteration of the land had preceded European settlement. Archaeological evidence suggests that the local Pokanoket tribes practiced a type of slash-and-burn agriculture common to most southern New England Indians, clearing fields by girdling and burning the trees, growing maize and other crops for several years until the soil was exhausted, then moving their settlements to new areas.

In addition, these first Cape Codders seem to have practiced extensive woodland management, periodically burning the higher and drier slopes and ridges to clear land for game forage, hunting, and overland travel. Upland forests, then, were probably a mixture of undisturbed forest tracts, open fields, and second-growth forests in various stages of succession. Lower and wetter areas were generally left alone, producing the curiously split forest described in *Mourt's Relation*, an early (1623) account of Puritan explorations: on one hand, "areas of wood . . . for the most part open and without underwood, fit to go or ride in," and on the other hand the "valleys of boughs and bushes . . . which tore our very armor to pieces." These latter areas were no doubt the extensive thickets of catbrier and viburnum that still render the Cape's swampier areas virtually impassable today.

A Forest Disappears

In the early periods of human settlement on Cape Cod and the Islands, the fate of the original woodlands is part of the larger story of the great eastern American forest. But in its middle chapters and its current setting the unique character of this maritime environment, both natural and human, has played a significant part.

The first Pilgrim settlers who came to Cape Cod from Plymouth and Boston in the mid-seventeenth century were neither fishermen nor sailors but farmers, men of the land. As such, trees presented both a resource and a barrier. They provided lumber for homes and fuel for the hearth, not to mention a vast array of pioneer appliances, tools, and conveyances. On the other hand, farming meant clearing land, and vast areas of woodland were cut over, simply to be rid of the trees. In many cases, the woods were burnt off, a practice also used by the Indians, though it was never done completely or as extensively before the Europeans arrived.

In these practices of land clearing, the early Cape settlers were one with the pioneers of the inland wilderness. They may have had, in historian Eric Sloane's words, "a reverence for wood" that came from intimate contact with and knowledge of native building materials, but they demonstrated a wanton contempt for and ignorance of the forests themselves, which seemed to stretch, even here, in unending abundance. So frugal in many ways, the Pilgrim settlers from Plymouth differed little from others in their new freewheeling treatment of the land.

Evidence that the Cape's forests were not inexhaustible and, in fact, were particularly vulnerable, was not long in coming. These first, hard lessons in ecology took place in Eastham, originally called Nauset, whose soil was said to be the best in the Old Colony. In fact, its reported fertility was largely responsible for bringing a contingent down from Plymouth to settle the town in 1639. Immediately the settlers began cutting down the Eastham woods, farming, and grazing their herds of cattle and sheep. By 1660, only 20 years later, the "blackish and deep mold" of topsoil that William Bradford had originally found at Eastham was gone. What had happened to it?

No longer protected by the forests, the soil quickly dried out and blew away in the ever-prevalent winds. Any hardwood sprouts that began to grow back were soon grazed off by sheep, 10,000 of which were reported in Barnstable County in the late 1600s. In other words, the Eastham soil, once held and protected by the forests, was literally "gone with the wind." And without the forests, the soil could not re-form.

Similar experiences took place in other Cape Cod towns, and as early as 1676 Sandwich enacted bylaws exacting fines of twelve pounds against anyone found "peeling oak" or deliberately letting wood rot.

Woodland destruction happened even more quickly on Nantucket and Martha's Vineyard, where there were also once substantial forests. But these, too, were stripped, and by 1670 Nantucket had to import logs from the mainland to build their houses, and residents were fined if trees were cut for any other reason. Rents were already beginning to appear in the fabric of the original forests.

Curiously, the original forests might have lasted much longer if Cape Codders had not taken to the sea for a living. After three or four generations of farming and grazing, much of the soil had dried up and blown away, and some of the settlers began to fish in earnest for a living. Fishing, however, takes boats, and boats take wood.

Beginning in the late 1600s and continuing for almost a century and a half, shipbuilding was an extensive and profitable trade on the Cape. It also helped to demolish the forests. Though Cape shipyards produced only a few of the larger clipper ships, the native oak and pine provided wood for many schooners, barks, whalers, and packets, as well as numerous smaller fishing vessels.

Another sea-related industry that helped deplete the woodlands was salt making. Before John Sears of Dennis invented solar saltworks—a process of obtaining salt from seawater by solar evaporation in large, shallow trays—in 1776, Cape Codders made their salt by boiling seawater in great iron kettles and scraping off the thin film of salt left on the sides. It is estimated that it took one and a half cords (192 cubic feet) of wood to produce one bushel of salt. But wood was plentiful, while salt was not.

Whale blubber, too, was often tried out, or boiled down, on the shore, using wagon loads of wood hauled out of the neighboring forests. Even the cranberry bogs helped to contribute to the destruction of the Cape forests. Many present-day bogs grow on what were once extensive swamps filled with tremendous Atlantic white cedars. These trees provided not only moisture-proof foundations for early structures but the ubiquitous white cedar shingles that sheath most Cape Cod houses. Unlike most local forests, these cedar stands were managed and protected by the early settlers to create a sustained yield. However, once commercial cranberry cultivation began in the early 1800s, many of these swamps were drained and the cedars completely cut down for bogs. Cedar shingles, once a native building material, are today largely imported from western Canada.

The destruction of the Cape Cod forests did not take place overnight, but it happened relentlessly and irrevocably. As late as 1807, an early traveler by the name of Jonathan Kendell reported "lofty forests" in Truro, and in 1820 the Reverend Timothy Dwight, president of Yale, observed thirty ships taking lumber from Sandwich to Boston. Wellfleet shipyards continued to thrive on native lumber well into the nineteenth century.

Nature Forecloses

By the beginning of the nineteenth century, however, it was clear, even to the most shortsighted natives, that something was going wrong. Nature extends long credits but eventually forecloses on overdrawn accounts. Not every town on the Cape got as dramatic a notice as Provincetown or Chatham, but their examples served to warn others.

Provincetown probably always had thinner soils and poorer forests than most Cape Cod towns, yet the early settlers quickly stripped what there was and set their cows and sheep out to pasture on the hills in back of the town. Early in the 1700s some farsighted observers and legislators saw what was happening and passed laws against tree cutting and pasturing in the Province Lands—the publicly owned lands outside of the town, now part of the Cape Cod National Seashore. But law was hard to enforce in those early days, especially in a remote place like Provincetown, long notorious among Cape Cod towns for its less than law-abiding inhabitants. The townspeople largely ignored the law, and the cows continued to graze.

But they could not ignore the sand that was beginning to blow over their town. Although the forests of Provincetown were never lofty, they supported vital plant communities, developed over the centuries, that had held down the dunes. Now, laid bare by tree cutting and overgrazing, the sand hills began an assault on the town. At first they banked sand against the houses and then actually buried them. Sand removal became a constant town activity, and roads were frequently blocked.

By 1800 it was reported that the dune ridges themselves were advancing on the town and harbor at a rate of ninety feet a year. With their vital harbor threatened, the inhabitants finally took action. All grazing was stopped, and the planting of beach grass to hold down the dunes was begun.

Once let loose, however, a wild land like ours does not tame overnight. It was over half a century before the dunes had stabilized around the town, and even today the great dunes that hover over Route 6 near Pilgrim Lake threaten to bury the highway each winter.

For similar reasons the town of Chatham was also threatened by the bare sands of Great Hill in the early nineteenth century, and in 1821 Chatham initiated the first recorded reforestation project in the United States—albeit, under duress.

Not every town was so actively threatened. But by 1800 most of the original forests were long gone, and it was clear to most, if not all, Cape Codders that their forests had become mere shadows of their former grandeur. Local inhabitants had become dependent on outside sources of lumber and have remained so ever since. Native trees, which once supplied lumber for homes, ships, and a considerable export industry, were now used primarily for the production of mackerel barrels and nail kegs. Even the great solar saltworks industry was dependent on pine from Maine to build its extensive wooden sheds and troughs; native wood was fit to supply only posts and pilings to support the main structures.

Even with these depleted resources, however, the ingenious Cape Codders found new ways to use up what little was left. Iron foundries were a minor industry on the Cape in the early 1800s. Forges were operated in Sandwich, Yarmouth, and Dennis that produced considerable quantities of shipping gear. Before Pennsylvania coal was introduced about 1830, these forges used great quantities of charcoal, and though local trees were no longer suitable for lumber, they could still burn.

During the Civil War, lampblack, a component of explosives, was extensively produced on Cape Cod through partial burning of wood in large brick ovens called funns. Enormous amounts of pitch pines were consumed in this process, which not only left its name in such places as Funn Pond and Funn Road in Dennis but also left the local hills barer than ever.

Meanwhile, industrial centers began to develop in the larger towns and cities off-Cape. Since fuelwood was not available around these centers, they shipped it in from available sources. Cape Cod was available. With the decline of the farming and shipping industries in the late nineteenth century, the cutting of fuelwood for export became an important local industry. In fact, it was said to be the most important source of income for Falmouth residents from 1850 to 1890. But while Cape Codders may have benefited from these new markets, their forests did not. In many towns, in fact, even fuelwood began to get scarce. By 1800 peat dug from the bogs was a common home fuel in most Lower Cape towns and was used as far west as Yarmouth as late as 1870, when coal replaced it.

Because of their relative inaccessibility, the morainal hills of Sandwich escaped wholesale deforestation well into the 1800s, until about 1825 when the Sandwich glassworks was founded. Despite a popular misconception, the famous glass factory was not located in Sandwich because of its abundant sand, which was deemed impure and useless for glassmaking, but for the still vast pitch pine and red oak forests that fired the glass furnaces for more than sixty years and left the Sandwich hills as barren as the other towns.

Shifting sands and the lack of fuelwood were not the only results of forest destruction in the late nineteenth century. Forest fires, which were once a controlled means of eliminating undergrowth, became chronic disasters. These fires were the direct result of land use and land alteration. From continual cutting, much slash wood accumulated on the forest floor, drying out in the summer sun like so much tinder. Even more important was the change that had taken place in the vegetative cover of much of the forests. The original forests had been described by the early settlers as open and parklike in appearance and had been kept so in part by the light burning of underbrush by the Indians. With intensive and repeated clear-cutting of the trees, however, conditions became ripe for the spread of shrublike growth—scrub oaks, sheep laurel, bearberry, huckleberry, viburnum, and catbrier. This thick, dry, inflammable growth not only produced chronic forest fires but made the forested areas highly impenetrable, as you can realize if you've ever tried to make your way through a catbrier thicket. Thus, not only were fires more numerous, they were more difficult to fight. In fact, fire-fighting techniques often became a matter of heading off the fire with backfires and attempting to get it going in the direction of a neighboring town. If successful, the local fire fighters would head home and let the next town worry about putting it out. So demoralized and pessimistic had Cape Codders and Islanders become about their forests, if fact, that many fires in the interior sections were not fought at all, since there was little or no lumber or property of any value to save.

When the Old Colony Railroad first reached the Cape in 1848, it opened up one last industry for what was left of the native forests: track ties made from oak and pitch pine. But sparks from engine smokestacks became still another contributor to the worsening forest fire situation. Indeed, by the time of the Civil War, relations between Cape Codders and their woodlands had reached a moral and biological low point. Convinced that their forests never would and perhaps never had produced anything better, Cape Codders did little or nothing to protect and restore their native trees. And the more worthless they were considered to be, the more worthless they became. It seemed like a pretty hopeless situation on both sides.

A New Beginning

Left to its own devices, however, nature usually finds something to suit the situation. Ironically, when men finally abandoned the land as lost, natural repairs finally began. After the Civil War millions of acres of New England farmland were abandoned, including some 58,000 acres in Barnstable County. On the mainland most of these abandoned fields and pastures began to seed into stands of white pine. But on Cape Cod, where soil conditions were harsher, a different species became the pioneer tree.

Even in prehistoric times the pitch pine, *Pinus rigida*, had grown widely over the Cape—on the high dry hills burned by the Indians or out near the sea bluffs, battered by the wind and sea. It is a hardy tree, capable of taking much punishment, and so it was originally characteristic of the Cape's waste places, where few other trees could grow.

PITCH PINE

Now that much of the land had been turned into wasteland by chronic human abuse, the pitch pine's remarkable survival capacities made it the natural choice for the task of recolonizing a land that had all but been given up to the sand dunes.

Not only will pitch pine thrive in open, barren fields, but it is relatively resistant to wind and salt spray, and thus it was capable of re-colonizing the more seaward edges of the Cape as well as the interior.

But perhaps the single most important characteristic of the pitch pine, at least as far as Cape Cod and the Islands in the late nineteenth century was concerned, is its remarkable adaptation to chronic forest fires—despite the fact that the wood itself, as its name implies, is highly flammable. Crown fires that consume treetops will not ordinarily kill it, since pitch pine contains buds beneath its thick trunk bark that will sprout after such a blaze. Even if burned to the ground a pitch pine will ordinarily send up one or two more sprouts from the crook of its base. The ability to sprout from its base is possessed by only two other American conifers. Moreover, some of the pine's cones are seroti-nous—that is, they will remain tightly closed until touched by naked flame, after which they will open and spread their seed on the burned-over land. It is easy to see how these qualities made the pitch pine remarkably suited to survive and spread in a countryside that was riddled with chronic forest fires for over a century.

Men soon recognized the amazing vitality of the pitch pine and began to aid the natural process by deliberately planting it in large areas to hold down the land. In 1849, Thoreau, traveling by stagecoach to Orleans, noticed large tracts of pitch pine in Yarmouth and Dennis, planted, he says, "four or five years before":

> They were in rows, as they appeared when we were abreast of them, and excepting that they were extensive vacant places, seemed to be doing remarkably well.

This simple observation is a landmark in the environmental history of Cape Cod: for the first time in over 200 years of continuous exploitation, Cape Cod's inhabitants were planting forests instead of destroying them. Extensive plantings of pitch pine took place all over the Cape in the last half of the nineteenth century. A United States government forestry report for 1884 states that over 10,000 acres of pitch pine were planted in waste tracts in Orleans, Harwich, and Chatham. The present forested conditions of this and many other sections of this peninsula attest to the success of such programs.

Despite its success in recovering the barren landscape of the nineteenth century, the pitch pine is not generally regarded highly today. Often it is considered trash wood with no commercial or aesthetic value and is bulldozed off without compunction—to be replaced by exotic species. Looked at from a narrow point of view, it is, I suppose, of little commercial value—although the early colonists used it to extract tar and turpentine from its highly resinous sap—a fact that explains the presence of several Tar Kiln roads to be found in various Cape towns. But the tree is of poor lumber quality: it is brittle, grows crooked, and rarely attains saw-log size. It is even poor firewood, burning very smoky and often leaving highly inflammable deposits on flue linings that can cause chimney fires. Unless we happen to enjoy its scraggly, stark appearance for itself, most of us, I suspect, merely tolerate the pitch pine or, at best, take it for granted.

But on its own terms, the pitch pine deserves our admiration. It will withstand repeated injury and insult and yet continue to thrive. Although the individual trees may seem brittle and stiff, the species as a whole possesses surprising flexibility. In its denser stands, where the young trees have to compete for space, individual pines will twist and turn in corkscrew fashion in their search for light; one tree I found in Wellfleet had made a complete 360-degree loop in its younger years. Out on the windswept bluffs, the pines will hug the ground and creep out like a carpet toward the edge, growing perhaps no more than three feet high in sixty to seventy years. The results of this flexibility may often be grotesque in form, but they are survival itself.

Other groups of trees have also helped to restore our forests. The most conspicuous of these are the oaks. Cape Cod oaks are often, and mistakenly, referred to uniformly as scrub oaks, probably because of their relatively small size and scraggly appearance. But the true scrub, or bear, oak, *Quercus ilicifolia,* is only one of many oak species on the Cape. Scrub oak is even more salt tolerant than pitch pine and is commonly found in thick, impenetrable stands in the more barren areas, such as the edge of ocean bluffs in the Cape Cod National Seashore, where it rarely exceeds a person's height. It, too, is highly fire resistant, sending up new sprouts from its buried root balls after the tree has been burned to the ground.

But besides scrub oak, there are considerable black oak, white oak, red oak, scarlet oak, post oak, and a number of hybridized species that often make a definitive identification difficult even for experts. Look closely at our forest oaks, though, and you will notice that many

SCRUB OAK

of them grow in clumps of two or more from a single base. This is because all our native oaks are sprout hardwoods and, like the pitch pine, have survived repeated cutting and burning through their ability to send up new sprouts from old stumps.

Though most stands of old-growth oaks were cut down early by the Pilgrim settlers and their descendants, there remains in North Eastham at least one small stand that contains, if not virgin woodlands, trees that must have stood in lush contrast to the bleak plains of Nauset a century ago. It was preserved not by early conservationists but by religion. "Millenium Grove," as it came to be known, was famous in the years before the Civil War as the site for the annual Methodist camp meetings that took place there each summer. The ten-acre tract, located on the bay side of Route 6 at the intersection of Campground and Herring Brook roads, was purchased by the Camp Meeting Grove Corporation of Eastham in 1838. Though the camp meetings are long gone, the trees, mostly black oaks, still stand out in size and stature from the surrounding second-growth woodlands.

Eastern red cedar (*Juniperus virginiana*) is another pioneer species that helped to recolonize the Cape's abandoned farmland. Botanically not a true cedar at all but a juniper, these tall, handsome cone-shaped trees with tiny, flat dark-green needles and bright blue berrylike fruits are also known as pencil, or aromatic, cedars and were traditionally used in the making of graphite pencils and as linings in cedar closets and hope chests. Crush one of the berries between your fingers and you will recognize the common flavoring used in gin. Though not as salt tolerant as pitch pine, cedars can survive repeated mowings and grazings and often survive as plants only a few inches high for many years. For this reason cedars tended to colonize pastures, as opposed to plowed fields, after the former were abandoned and are thus an indicator of former land use. They are also common ornamental trees in older cemeteries. Red cedars are particularly abundant in the Orleans-Eastham area, and one of the largest pure stands of cedars can be found along the nature trail at the Fort Hill area of the Cape Cod National Seashore in Eastham.

Another pioneer recolonizer, though once associated with wetlands rather than uplands, is red maple (*Acer rubrum*). As more and more of the smaller and less economically feasible cranberry bogs have been abandoned in recent decades, many of them have reverted to red maple swamps. Red maple is probably the most common hardwood on Cape Cod after the oaks. Though generally associated with low-moisture areas, these trees will also grow on higher, drier sites. One of the largest and most mature red maple swamps can also be experienced along the nature trail at Fort Hill and is particularly lovely with bright red colors in autumn.

Atlantic white cedars (*Chamaecyparis thyoides*), on the other hand, do not recolonize abandoned bogs nearly as rapidly or as widely, and white cedar swamps remain generally rare on the Cape and Islands. They are, however, a special and arresting environment and well worth seeking out. Their tall, tapered pencil-straight trunks rise up from raised mounds called hummocks and branch out at their tops in dense, opaque foliage creating a dark, hushed atmosphere in the tea-colored swamp waters below. The lower branches are frequently hung with old-man's beard, a lichen that may remind visitors of Spanish moss in the southern live oaks. This lichen is used by one of the Cape's rarer breeding birds—the parula warbler—to build its nest, and in summer you may hear his buzzy trill rising through the dark canopy above. Two extensive white cedar swamps equipped with boardwalks can be found at the Marconi Station in South Wellfleet and the Flax Pond Conservation Area in South Dennis.

Another wetland-associated tree common to the Cape and Islands is the black gum (*Nyssa sylvatica*), also known as tupelo, and is usually found around the margins of ponds and maple swamps, though it, too, will grow on upland sites. Recognized by its dark, deeply furrowed trunk and horizontal zigzag branches, it is one of the first trees to turn color in the fall. Its blood red leaves, ringing our ponds and wetlands in September, probably exhibit the most intense color produced by any of our native trees. Tupelos can be observed along the marsh edge on the South Trail at the Cape Cod Museum of Natural History. On Martha's Vineyard, the tree is still referred to as the beetlebung, an interesting etymological derivation that comes from its tough wood that was once used extensively for the heads of wooden mallets, called beetles, used to pound stoppers, or bungs, into casks of whale oil. There is a large stand of these trees in the town of Chilmark on the Vineyard at an intersection of roads known as Beetlebung Corners.

One other common tree species deserves mention here for its role in recolonizing the deforested landscape on the Cape and Islands, even though it is not a native. The black locust (*Robinia pseudoacacia*) is a tree of the southern Appalachians, but it was introduced as a reforesting species for several reasons. It grows rapidly, even in barren, dry soil; it spreads rapidly as well, sprouting from underground runners in the manner of blackberries and catbrier; and it is a legume, or nitrogen-fixing plant, like beans and peas, its botanical cousins. Thus, it adds nitrogen and helps enrich the soil in which it grows. Because of this, locust stands often have lush green carpets of grass growing beneath them. Though we may be most aware of this tree today in June when its sweet clusters of white blossoms droop from its crooked branches, the locust is an immigrant tree that has naturalized itself and more than earns its place among our forest trees throughout the year. Since locusts are also pioneer trees and not shade tolerant, they tend to be replaced by oaks and other hardwoods after a few decades. The most sizable stands of locusts on the Cape today can be found in recently abandoned fields, old cemeteries, and in such places as Locust Road in Orleans.

Survivors, Comebacks, Remnants, and Exotics

White pine (*Pinus strobus*), while never as common or as large here as on the mainland, can still be found in significant stands, especially on the Upper Cape. An impressive grove, containing trees over two feet in diameter, can be seen at the Beebe Woods, a 400-acre forest preserve at the end of Depot Avenue just west of Falmouth center. Here one can still see dozens of large moss-covered fallen trunks, all laid out in a northeast-southwest direction, silent testimony to the destruction caused by the memorable 1938 hurricane. One of the largest stands of white pine in the Lower Cape area is in Brewster's Nickerson State Park. Most of these trees were planted in the 1930s as a Works Progress Administration (WPA) project, as can be seen by the straight rows that many of the trunks grow in.

Another hardwood that is locally common on the Upper Cape is the American holly (*Ilex opaca*), with its characteristic bright, shiny evergreen leaves ending in sharp prickles and deep red winter berries on the female trees. An extensive variety of holly trees, native and exotic, can be enjoyed at the Ashumet Holly Reservation in North Falmouth, which sells holly sprigs at Christmastime.

Cape Cod lacks numbers of species associated with richer, maturer forest soils—trees like walnuts, yellow poplar, sycamore, and sugar maples. It does, however, possess a number of stands of American beech (*Fagus grandifolia*), generally in the hillier, rockier areas of the glacial moraine. A mature stand of beech can be observed along the Museum of Natural History's South Trail.

At the Lowell Holly Reservation on Wakeby Pond in Mashpee a mature forest of towering beeches shades a rich understory of hollies, dogwoods, and other uncommon trees. Beeches are not generally found on the more exposed soils of the Outer Cape, with the singular exception of the Provincetown Beech Forest on Race Point Road. This dune forest is likely a remnant of the original forest cover of the Cape's tip and indicates what may have existed across most of the Province Lands when the Pilgrims arrived there. Today one can walk the half-mile trail and behold the extraordinary sight of a cool, shaded, mature beech forest whose edges are being buried by twenty-five foot moving walls of sand.

In addition to the Provincetown Beech Forest, two other unusual woodlands deserve a look by the visitor to the Cape and Islands. One is the maritime forests of Sandy Neck in Barnstable. Sandy Neck, a seven-mile barrier beach on Cape Cod Bay, is unusual in its stability. Unlike most barrier systems of the Cape and Islands, Sandy Neck has retreated little over its long history. Because of this there exist, behind a protective line of high dunes, several stands of hardwood forests that have remained virtually undisturbed for centuries. The soil of these oak-maple stands is richer than in most places on the mainland and contains such uncharacteristic understory plants as trillium and columbine.

But perhaps the most extraordinary forests of all on the Cape and Islands are the famous Hidden Forests of the Polpis region of Nantucket. What look like typical low scrubby trees from the surrounding plains are actually the tops of stands of massive beech, swamp maple, oak, tupelo, holly, and sassafras that grow in the peaty bottoms of former kettle ponds. One walks down the slopes of these kettle holes into a world of sudden, still darkness, as into a hidden gorge. Cardinal flowers, cinnamon fern, and jewelweed grow in the rich soil of these unexpected groves, which have been used as trysting places for young Nantucketers for generations.

Of course, a large number of exotic species have been planted as ornamental trees along our roads, in parks, and in private yards. But occasionally the careful observer will notice unusual stands or species whose origins are something of a mystery. One such unexplained presence is an extensive stand of European black alder (*Alnus glutinosa*) growing in the wetlands on both sides of Route 6A at the intersection with Airline Road in East Dennis. Another is a solitary European linden (*Tilia europaea*) growing on the backside of Hog Island in the middle of Pleasant Bay. Imported trees, like imported birds and insects, do not always stay where we put them.

There are even some reported examples of surviving virgin woodlands on the Cape and Islands. One such tract, a climax oak-beech forest, is reported on Naushon Island, the largest of the Elizabeth chain and a private preserve not open to the public. Other sources mention similar tree coverings on Half Way Pond Island in Half Way Pond, Plymouth, and on some small islands in Mashpee's Wakeby Pond. A few years ago I did a survey of the Wakeby Pond islands and, in fact, on two of them I found evidence of a forest that at least approximates an undisturbed southern New England hardwood forest. Like forests primeval, however, virgin woods tends to call up images not appropriate to the reality. What I found were not giant oaks or white pines but rather a community of species uncommon to most of our forests, most noticeably black birch, yellow birch, scarlet oak, hemlock, and witch hazel. Because of their isolation, these tiny island forests may indeed have escaped the fate of ax and fire that claimed nearly all of our original woodlands.

Much more could be said about other present-day forest species on Cape Cod and the Islands, each with its own reason for being here. One of the most interesting accounts of our local forest history is a ninety-page monograph entitled "The Forests of Cape Cod," written in 1938 by H. Stanford Altpeter, a copy of which is in the Clarence L. Hay Library at the Cape Cod Museum of Natural History. Another useful guide is Donald Schall's *The Evergreens of Cape Cod*, part of the natural history series published by and available at the museum.

A Forest in Transition

What we have seen is that, to a large degree, our present-day forests are a result of a centuries-old struggle between man and the land, with the land usually being the loser. Equally important to remember, however, is that the way our woodlands look today is only another passing stage of change. Already, for instance, we can see how the oaks, being more tolerant of shade than pitch pines, are crowding out the pines in older stands. For the first time in centuries, oaks rather than pitch pines are the most common trees on Cape Cod.

A more important change in the wind is the tendency of our forests toward diversification. When nature intends to reclaim barren ground, it usually chooses a few hardy species for the job as the quickest means. In the case of our local forests this has led, in a very short time, to the establishment of a great many trees but relatively few species, primarily pitch pine and oak. Such an arrangement is called monoculture and is, generally speaking, not very stable over the long run; hence, once established, nature strives to diversify itself. Monocultures tend to be very vulnerable to diseases and infestations, and one of the most familiar and notorious is the periodic gypsy moth infestations that sweep through and often completely defoliate our oak woods.

Human beings tend to regard the gypsy moth epidemics as destructive and undesirable, and until recently local communities have spent hundreds of thousands of dollars in pesticide-spraying programs in a dubious attempt to eradicate the pest. The moth larvae are destructive, in a short-term sense, to the oak forests, and they are certainly undesirable when thousands of tiny black larvae are crawling all over the sides of your house or attack your favorite yard tree. But in a larger context they are one of nature's primary agents of diversification. For when the weakened and repeatedly defoliated oaks die, other trees, less susceptible to moth predation—such as red maple, pignut hickory, beech, alder, and white pine—take the place of the oaks. If left to themselves, these processes would in time produce not only a more varied but a healthier, more stable forest. Man's attempts to "save the forests" through the use of pesticides reflect his own short-term, cosmetic interests rather than nature's long-term purposes. Ironically, by attempting to maintain these monocultures in their present form, we not only thwart a natural tendency but may actually prolong such invasions by interrupting the course of natural population cycles in these and other forest insects.

Of course, having infested our woods so thoroughly ourselves, it is not so easy to simply say let the bugs have them. Yet we should realize that in a place like Cape Cod, where frequent and continual change is the rule rather than the exception, whenever we try artificially to maintain or freeze a particular state of the land, we do so at our own peril. Whether it is a forest, a line of elms along our boulevards, an eroding barrier beach, or a pond beginning to fill up with weeds, our attempts to halt or slow natural processes may not only be futile but may in fact turn out to aggravate and hasten those processes.

The return of much of Cape Cod's original forest cover since the turn of the century is impressive. It cannot, however, be regarded as an unmitigated environmental success story. For one thing, although our tree cover is probably greater today than at any time since the seventeenth century, we are once again in the process of destroying it at a rate comparable to the initial destruction. Instead of wood for fuel, homes, farm fields, salt making, boat building, or glassworks, however, today's forests are being removed to make way for commercial development, homesites, and subdivision roads. From 1951 to 1971, forested acreage decreased by 12 percent while urban development increased 247 percent. Ironically, because of the present thick forest cover, much of this development is not as obvious as it might have been 100 years ago. Tree buffers and green belts are commonly left as token aesthetic gestures to the environment, but any aerial flight over Cape Cod or the Islands reveals an increasing encroachment of winding, branched roads and house sites, like an immense pattern of chip circuitry, into the green hearts of our forests. While salt marshes and freshwater wetlands have received ever-increasing federal, state, and local protection in recent years, our uplands are still up for grabs, reflecting a mentality that still divides a landscape into compartmentalized, separate units rather than seeing it as a seamless, interdependent whole.

The ecological effects of this encroachment far exceed the actual amount of acreage cut down, though this is substantial enough. Many animal species are intolerant of human presence and require large uninterrupted areas of forest to survive. On Cape Cod these include ruffed grouse, whippoorwills, ovenbirds, and blue-winged warblers. Deer, which may happily roam through your garden in search of tender shoots of corn, need isolated areas of woods in order to drop their fawns. Even a few roads or houses effectively break up a forest into biological islands, reducing the number of species that a forest can support and introducing dogs, cats, and such human-associated bird species as house sparrows and starlings into an area. Substantial undisturbed areas of forest on Cape Cod are becoming increasingly rare. It is telling that when a recent attempt to restock wild turkeys into Barnstable County was undertaken, the only area deemed large enough to support them was the Otis Air National Guard Base in Sandwich—a bombing range.

Nor has the recovery of our forests since the turn of the century been advantageous to all wildlife species. Combined with the decline of local agriculture, the return of woodlands has greatly reduced the amount of grasslands, heaths, orchards, and pastures. The result, noticeable to anyone living here over the last few decades, has been a concurrent decline in the numbers of such open-habitat bird species as bluebirds, meadowlarks, short-eared owls, prairie warblers, and woodcocks. Birds of the pine barrens, such as whippoorwills and saw-whet owls, have also been declining as a result of the succession of oak stands due to fire suppression.

Grasslands and Heath Lands: Endangered Habitats

Even more important perhaps from an ecological point of view is the continuing loss of two nationally important upland habitats found on Cape Cod: grasslands and heath lands.

Sand-plain grasslands are in a sense coastal prairies—dry, sandy open land typically vegetated with native bunchgrasses, such as the little bluestem, a common prairie grass on the Great Plains. They are restricted almost entirely to such glacial outwash areas as Cape Cod, Nantucket, Martha's Vineyard, and Long Island. As such they contain several plants that are rare, not only within the state but globally.

Two of the most significant of these are the sand-plain gerardia, a delicate, sparsely branched, light green annual with pink and purple bell-shaped flowers; and bushy rockrose, a low-branching shrublike plant with bright yellow flowers that blossom at the end of its long thin branches. Only some seventy sites of the bushy rockrose are known worldwide;

over sixty of those sites are found on the Cape and Islands, with the largest populations on Nantucket.[1] Sand-plain gerardia is even more rare. Only seven sites of this plant are known on earth, two of them on Cape Cod— in nineteenth-century cemeteries in Falmouth and Sandwich. Other threatened species of our native grasslands include the sand-plain flax, narrow-leaved bush clover, and grass-leaved lady tresses orchid.

What was once a widespread, common habitat on Cape Cod is now, with the dual encroachment of development and reforestation, restricted to remnant patches such as power line rights-of-way, roadsides, and the scruffy edges of golf course fairways, old cemeteries, and in a few places, the median on the Mid-Cape Highway. Most of the surviving grassland habitats are found in the Upper and Mid-Cape areas. Three of the largest remaining examples of native sand-plain grasslands can be found at the Hewlett-Packard field in East Sandwich, the Crane Wildlife Management Area in North Falmouth, and the Danforth Property at the junction of Route 149 and Race Lane in Marstons Mills. The first two properties are still being managed as open habitat.

Heath lands, more commonly called moors, were also once common and widespread on the Cape and Islands but are now restricted to increasingly smaller areas, primarily on the Outer Cape and Nantucket. They tend to be characterized by such low-growing woody plants as low-bush blueberry, huckleberry, and bearberry but include sixteen rare plants, such as the broom crowberry. The best examples of Cape Cod heath lands can probably be seen in Truro, on the hogback hills north of the Pamet River and in the Corn Hill area. But the largest remaining areas of heath lands are to be found in the central sections of Nantucket, where they have for generations been referred to as the Nantucket Moors. With their brilliant burning colors in the fall like a prairie on fire, it is the moors that, in most people's minds, define the characteristic landscape of that island.

Like the Provincetown dunes, however, Nantucket's moorland is primarily a man-made habitat, though no doubt heaths always existed to some degree in such a salt-sprayed windy environment. Sheep grazing and periodic fires maintained the moor habitat for centuries, but within the last forty years much of Nantucket's moorland has disappeared, some of it to development but even more to scrub oak, so that today much of

---

[1]Please note: for conservation reasons, specific locations of rare and endangered plant species are generally not made public. Further information on local state-listed plants can be obtained by writing to the Massachusetts Natural Heritage and Endangered Species Program, 100 Cambridge Street, Boston, MA 02202.

the island is an impenetrable tangle of waist-high oak and viburnum. Some 2,000 acres of moorland remain on Nantucket, about half of it on land protected by the Nantucket Conservation Foundation and other conservation organizations, the rest in private hands with increasing development pressures on it.[2] Recently the Massachusetts Audubon Society has undertaken experiments in controlled burning and other management techniques to see if the process can be halted or even reduced in favor of the moors, but it seems a formidable task with insufficient funds and manpower to make much of an impact. It may be that, within a few more decades, the Nantucket moorland, and with it our traditional image of that island, may be all but gone.

An Uncertain Future

Whatever the future may hold for our woodlands, grasslands, and heaths, however, we need to remember that today's upland vegetation is the product of a number of shifting forces, whose outcome we cannot entirely predict, and which we should not try to control recklessly. Cape Cod and the Islands are constantly changing, constantly fluctuating entities, highly resourceful and highly resilient, yet also highly vulnerable to human activity. They are also lands that remain highly dependent upon their forests, regardless of the fact that we now import nearly all our lumber and firewood.

The value of trees in the conservation of water, the replenishment of soil and air, the regulation of temperature, the development of wildlife habitat, and numerous other areas is a relatively recent realization. It is still only a partial realization, for we still find it easier to bulldoze than to build around them, to chop up and pave over fields and meadows than design and limit development for environmental values. As Americans we criticize and mourn the wholesale destruction of global rain forests and worry over possible dire effects, yet we continue to diminish our own forests as if they had no value beyond being a commodity. In this sense we have not progressed very far or learned very much from our predecessors.

Like so many things in nature, our present-day woodlands, heaths, and grasslands are a direct result of our dealings with them in the past. It is a past that has been full of mistakes, mistakes we can continue to

[2] A guidebook to the foundation's extensive holdings can be obtained by writing to the Nantucket Conservation Foundation, Inc., P.O. Box 13, Nantucket, MA 02554

ignore or try to understand more fully in order to better guide the future.

Q & A

Q   Why are the trees on the Cape so small?

Accepting the premise that size is always relative, the smallness of Cape trees can be attributed to nutrient-poor soils and the salt-spray horizon.

Almost from the moment European colonists settled the Cape in the mid-1600s, the impressive forests that had stood for centuries guarding the rich soil against the onslaught of wind and wave erosion were, as mentioned earlier, cut down to build dwellings and ships, provide fuel for hearth and salt making, and to clear the land for agriculture and grazing. As early as the 1670s, inhabitants of Sandwich and Nantucket were faced with criminal penalties for needlessly cutting down trees.

By the early nineteenth century, the once deep and fertile loam of the Outer Cape had literally blown away with the wind. During this period, inhabitants of Provincetown wondered if their town would not be completely buried by the huge sand dunes migrating, not anchored by vegetation, toward the village.

Without the protective barrier of the forest, the salt-laden ocean winds desiccated (removed water from) the delicate leaves and new growth of the remaining trees and shrubs, burning or shearing off the tops of trees entering the salt-spray horizon. This shearing effect is most evident in species such as tupelo and Eastern red cedar, both of which grow close to coastal windswept areas.

To say that all Cape trees are stunted and gnarled by soil and wind conditions is not true. Many areas of the Upper Cape in Bourne, Falmouth, Woods Hole, and Mashpee still retain good-sized stands of white pine, black and red oak, American holly, American beech, and Atlantic white cedar. Even sheltered areas on the Outer Cape, such as the Beech Forest of the Cape Cod National Seashore in Provincetown, contain impressive specimens of forest trees.

Q   Why are there so many white pines in Brewster's Nickerson State Park?

During the height of the Great Depression in the 1930s, President

Franklin Roosevelt created the Works Progress Administration (WPA) to provide work for America's unemployed millions.

As part of the WPA, the Civilian Conservation Corps (CCC) was charged with constructing trails and ancillary structures such as bridges, roads, stairs, lookouts, and cabins in the country's state and national parks. It also planted thousands of white, red, and Scotch pines, row after row, in an attempt to provide a commercial timber harvest.

In 1935, the CCC constructed the first roads, camping sites, and picnic areas in newly designated Nickerson State Park. It also planted 88,000 white pine, red pine, Eastern hemlock, and spruce trees.

These conifer plantations are still flourishing not only in Nickerson but also in other state parks like Shawme Crowell off Route 130 in Sandwich and Miles Standish in Plymouth.

Outside of a few red squirrels, blue jays, and chickadees, not many native plants or animals live in the sterile environment of a pine plantation.

White pine is a majestic conifer when found growing in more appropriate haunts on the Upper Cape and mainland. It becomes less common in the sandier soils of the Lower Cape where it is very sensitive to desiccation and needle burn from the salt-spray wind.

Q Do different trees grow on different parts of the Cape?

Generally, trees on the Upper Cape in the towns of Bourne, Falmouth, Sandwich, and Mashpee are more typical of the mainland than trees in the Mid- to Lower Cape in both size and diversity of species.

With a richer, less sandy soil and more inland shelter from wind-driven salt spray, such species as white pine, red oak, American beech, hickories, American holly, flowering dogwood, black birch, and eastern hemlock may be found in their native habitat.

Good places to look for these uncommon trees are Wakeby Pond and the Lowell Holly Reservation in Mashpee, the Ashumet Holly Reservation and Beebe Woods in Falmouth, and the Bournedale Hills in Bourne. Isolated enclaves of these mainland-type forests are found on Sandy Neck in Barnstable, Nickerson State Park in Brewster, and the Beech Forest in the Province Lands of the Cape Cod National Seashore.

These trees either disappear entirely or become much less common and smaller in size as the Cape attenuates eastward. Where the Cape becomes narrower, its soil becomes poorer and its vegetation becomes scrubbier, shorter, and more able to combat the rigors of storm, salt spray, and sand. Such stalwarts as pitch pine, black oak, bear oak, black cherry, and tupelo and red maple in the damper areas, make up the predominant forest of the Outer and Lower Cape.

Q What are the hidden forests of Nantucket?

In the northwest corner of Nantucket near Polpis Harbor are the famed hidden forests. What appear to be low-growing patches of scrub oak from the surrounding moors are actually the tops of full-grown hardwoods like American beech, oak, holly, and sassafras. They grow in deep depressions called kettles formed by Ice Age scouring 12,000–15,000 years ago.

Q What is a post oak?

Post oak is a small oak of the coastal plain that reaches the northern limit of its national range in Barnstable County. Common on Martha's Vineyard, this species is rare on Nantucket and on Cape Cod, and is found nowhere else in the state. It is officially listed on the Division of Fisheries and Wildlife's watch list as a species to monitor for any decline in populations.

Post oak, while superficially resembling a diminutive white oak, has distinctive leathery leaves arranged in patterns that resemble a Greek cross.

Named for its strong, durable wood, post oak is still used in the manufacture of fencing, posts, and pilings in the southern United States, where it grows to great heights.

Q Why do so many trees in the woods have multiple trunks?

Virtually all of the woods left on Cape Cod are second- or third-growth forests. The tall, mastlike tree trunks found in western and northern New England are almost nonexistent here.

Most deciduous trees and shrubs regenerate readily from cut stumps. Such common Cape trees as black oak, white oak, red maple, black cherry, and sassafras all send up sprouts that form new trunks off the old cut main stem, resulting in the multiple trunk form so familiar in Cape woods.

Coniferous trees such as white pine, hemlock, and spruce do not have the ability to sprout after the trunk has been cut. Pitch pine is a notable exception among conifers and will regenerate from dormant buds found at the base of the tree.

Q What causes trees to have large burls on their trunks?

Burls are large round to oblong growths or swellings in a tree's trunk or branch usually caused by a fungus attack or a virus. Despite their ominous appearance, burls are generally not fatal to the tree.

Certain fungi will only infect a certain tree species. The Atlantic white cedar forms oblong trunk burls in response to the fungus. A black knot on a cherry tree is another example of fungal injury.

Oak burls are known for their beautifully ornate wood grain patterns and for centuries have been cut and polished by carpenters and artisans to produce wooden objets d'art.

Q What are the large, flat mushrooms that protrude from the trunks of so many trees?

Commonly seen growing in dead or dying hardwood trees, the bracket or shelf fungi belong to the family of mushrooms called the polypores. Fan shaped with concentric growth rings that can be quite colorful in some species, the polypores are one of the most recognizable of the Cape's fungi.

Polypores are prolific in attacking unhealthy or deceased trees but can occasionally attack valuable timber trees, causing damaging heartwood rot. The shelf fungi is but a small portion of the total plant, with literally miles of thread-like mycelium growing out of sight within the heartwood of the host tree. The mycelium exudes an enzyme that breaks down wood fiber, eventually weakening and felling the infected tree.

Some polypores are delicious if harvested when still young. The beefsteak polypore tastes like rare steak. And the artist conk has a smooth, white underside that provides a ready-made canvas often used in rustic folk art.

Q Why do I sometimes find wild black cherry trees growing in a straight line in old fields?

Surveyors in search of old property lines will often look for rows of black or choke cherry trees. This linear, unnatural growth pattern often outlines the location of a long gone fencerow or barbed wire line built originally to mark the property boundary.

Birds, after gorging on the wild cherries, would leave lines of seeds in their droppings beneath these convenient fence perches. The result—long lines of an otherwise wild, noncultivated tree species—acts as a sort of blueprint detailing human use of the land long after man-made structures have passed from the scene.

This ability to "read" the landscape is the hallmark of any good surveyor, naturalist, engineer, or archaeologist.

Q *What is the bright orange, jellylike growth I often see on cedar trees?*

After a heavy spring rain, the curious orange, jellylike tendrils of the cedar apple or apple rust often decorate red cedars everywhere there are apple or crab apple trees in the vicinity.

This grotesque growth is actually a type of gall produced not by an insect, as in other galls, but by a fungus.

Beginning as a hard, purplish growth on red cedar leaves, the characteristic bright orange tendrils form after the first spring rains in April and May. Spores produced by these strange appendages are carried by the wind on dry days to any nearby apple or flowering crab apple tree. They then germinate into yellow spots that penetrate and infect the leaves.

If untreated, these spots grow and eventually produce another type of spore that travels via the wind back to the nearby red cedars, where the cycle begins anew next spring.

Interestingly, the spores cannot travel from cedar to cedar or from apple to apple but must have both species as alternate co-hosts in order to reproduce.

Apple growers will typically destroy any red cedars that attempt to colonize near an orchard because of the potential damage caused by the cedar apple fungus.

Q *Many trees near the beach look burned or mostly dead. What causes this?*

The sand- and salt-laden wind that blows off our ocean waters is the most stressful element afflicting coastal plants. Salt is a desiccant, meaning it drives water out of a plant's cells, killing the tissue and creating the burned effect so prevalent in seashore woods and dune areas.

As the wind blows salt and sand over the primary dunes, a "salt spray horizon" kills any living plant material that attempts to grow above the dune crest into this salt zone. Most trees and shrubs found near coastal areas have adapted to this periodic pruning of their upper branches without succumbing completely. This sculpted effect can be quite attractive in some species such as tupelos and red cedars, found near coastal swamps.

Sometimes the salt spray horizon extends much farther inland than normal, such as during hurricanes and tropical storms. This can cause great damage to Cape trees more sensitive to salt drying such as white pine and American beech.

Reports of salt spray damage 20 to 50 miles inland are not uncommon following major storms.

Q   Do dead trees serve any purpose?

Dead trees serve as important providers of food, shelter, and breeding habitat for a variety of wildlife. These den trees, or snags, as they are called—unsightly as they may appear—act as high-rise apartments for many animals that benefit man.

Large dead trees, exceeding fourteen inches in diameter, provide homes for opossum, raccoons, gray foxes, and wood ducks. Trees with a diameter of twelve inches or more can provide homes for flying squirrels, screech owls, kestrels, woodpeckers, and nuthatches. Smaller den trees are used by chickadees, titmice, swallows, and bats.

Most, if not all, of these animals eat insects or rodents that cause crop damage and pose public health hazards.

Q   What will the forests look like 100 years from now?

Assuming there will be any forests left after a century more of development, our upland woodlands will undoubtedly be predominantly oak species with American beech and holly on the north-facing, moister slopes.

The oaks, including black, white, scarlet, and occasionally red and post, are even today shading out large tracts of pitch pine. Oak tree species are also encroaching on open fields and sand plains, eliminating these critically important habitats for state-listed rare plants and animals. Thus, in a century's time there will actually be more oak forest on Cape Cod than exists today, though ecological diversity may suffer because of it.

Q *What tree has a fruit used as a flavoring for gin?*

The eastern red cedar, with its aromatic wood, needles, and fruit has long been used in the production of perfume, art supplies, cedar chests, and pencils. By crushing and sniffing its distinctive blue female berry, another use comes readily to mind—as a flavoring agent for gin.

This common conifer of old agricultural fields has been flavoring a variety of drinks for many centuries. The French word for juniper (this tree's actual botanic name) is *genevrier*, the French word for gin is *genìevre*. The berries are still used by commercial distilleries to give gin its pungent taste and aroma.

For those teetotalers among us, red cedar berries and needles can be brewed into a tea good for soothing sore throats and gums. Don't drink too much, however, as it does have the effect of a diuretic.

Q *What are Indian pipes?*

Indian pipes are small herbs of the pyrola (wintergreen) family usually found growing in the shade of pine or oak woods in mid-summer. It is a plant that lacks the green pigment called chlorophyll and so must derive its nutrients from the rotting humus of the forest floor. This is accomplished by an intricate arrangement between the plant's roots and a soil fungus, much like that found in wild orchids.

INDIAN
PIPE

The white waxy countenance of the Indian pipe gives it an eerie appearance as it pokes its single nodding flower head up out of the leaf litter. Its spectral air once gave it the names corpse plant and ghost pipes.

Despite the ominous labels, Cape Indians made a lotion from the stems and flowers to soothe inflammations of the eyes.

Q *Lady's slippers are so beautiful. Can I transplant them?*

As the largest and perhaps loveliest of all our wild orchids, the pink lady's slipper, or moccasin flower, is a constant temptation and target for transplantation. But wild orchids and specifically lady's slippers are notoriously poor transplants.

Orchids are extremely site specific in their ecological requirements. Amount of sun or shade, soil, moisture, and the presence of pollinators are all critical elements in the seed germination and general vigor of these plants.

Most important is the presence of mycorrhiza, a root fungus that enables the orchid to better absorb nutrients from the soil. Transplanting a lady's slipper to an area lacking this vital fungus will result in almost certain failure.

Keeping in mind the considerable failure rate of orchid transplantation, it sometimes becomes necessary to rescue lady's slippers in danger of being destroyed by the encroaching bulldozer. Good points to remember in the transplant endeavor:

1. Obtain the property owner's permission to remove the threatened plants.
2. The transplant site should be as close to the removal site as possible. If not possible, the new area should have the same plant species, including other lady's slippers, as the removal site.

LADY'S SLIPPER

3. Take a large root ball, insuring a healthy supply of mycorrhiza. A root hormone solution, available at most nurseries, can be used to stimulate root regeneration.

4. According to the New England Wild Flower Society, the best time to transport lady's slippers is when the plant is flowering. *Be sure to remove the floral pouch before digging.* Transplantation is a traumatic experience for any plant, and the lady's slipper must redirect considerable energy into surviving the operation.

If the plants continue to flower for three growing seasons, then congratulations are in order.

Q *Are wildflowers on the Cape and Islands different from those on the mainland?*

Cape Cod's sandy, acidic soils, glacial kettle ponds, and maritime influence have created the unusual conditions to support a very different plant community than found on much of the Massachusetts mainland.

The Concord naturalist Henry D. Thoreau always knew he was approaching Cape Cod by the presence of poverty grass, or beach heath, a denizen of Barnstable County's dry heaths and sand plains.

Many rare plant species are found on the Cape and Islands and nowhere else in the state. The warming ocean currents that keep Cape winters mild creates a climate similar to that of the coastal plain of Virginia. Wildflowers found more commonly in the southern United States reach the northern limit of their range on the Cape and Islands. These include redroot, Maryland meadow beauty, thread-leaved sundew, and creeping Saint-John's-wort. A few northern species, such as oyster leaf, reach the southern limit of their range on Cape Cod and Nantucket.

Conversely, wildflowers commonly found on the mainland, such as trillium, columbine, hepatica, and bloodroot, are either missing or rare on the Cape due to their preference for more neutral, less-acidic soils.

How abundant is poison ivy on the Cape and Islands?
Q *What does it look like? How can you protect against it?*
Are there any similar plants here to avoid?

Poison ivy is one of the most abundant and adaptable plants on the Cape and Islands. This protean species that causes skin to bubble and

POISON IVY

itch incessantly can grow as a woody vine, as a shrub, or as a diminutive forest-floor herb.

Poison ivy can be found in almost any habitat, from dry sand dunes to swamps, marshes, and deep woods. The old saying, "Leaves of three, let it be," is a good reminder that poison ivy has three somewhat triangular leaflets, glossy green in summer and turning a deep, red bronze in fall. Branches of the plant are also adorned with clusters of dingy white, dry berries that provide food for birds, such as robins, flickers, and yellow-rumped warblers, which are not affected by the plant's resinous sap.

Poison ivy's infamous reputation is only partly deserved. The plant is one of the most effective erosion control agents; its long-running root system anchors shifting sand dunes, and its leaves ward off foot traffic that could further destabilize them.

Contrary to popular belief, you cannot get ivy poisoning by merely being near or downwind from the plant. The poisonous sap must be present through a break in the leaf, stem, or roots before exposed skin can be affected—unless the plant is being burned, when the oil can be airborne.

Once the itchy rash is noticed, some forty-eight hours after exposure, it is too late for the recommended brown soap scrub and it's time for the calamine lotion, a poison ivy ointment, or a doctor's appointment. One purported natural remedy for ivy poisoning is the juice of the spotted jewelweed, a common wildflower found along streams and wetlands.

The only other Cape plant poisonous to the touch is the closely related poison sumac, a much less common shrub that grows only in freshwater marshes, swamps, and bogs.

INSECT GALLS

Q *What are insect galls?*

Galls are growths or tumorlike structures produced by the depositing of
insect eggs or larvae within the tissue of a plant. By either mechanical
or chemical irritation, the adult insects or larvae induce the host plant to
build the abnormal structure, apparently in an attempt to isolate the
source of irritation. An obvious analogy to gall growth in plants is the
formation of pearls within oysters and other shellfish in response to a
sandy irritant within the soft tissues of the mollusk.

The most familiar gall to casual observers is the spherical oak apple.
This gall is produced by a tiny wasp, which deposits an egg inside the
branch bark (near developing leaves) of most oak trees. The result is a
golf-ball-sized gall that houses a single wormlike larva. The gall provides a perfect incubator for the developing wasp, which emerges in
midsummer, leaving an empty apartment for other insects to use. Tan
oak apples usually have a single exit hole, indicating the escape of the
original tenant.

There are many hundreds of gall types, most notably found on
goldenrods, oaks, hickories, red cedars, and Canada rush.

Q *Are there deer on the Cape and Islands?*
Are they endangered by development?

The eastern white-tailed deer is the only big-game mammal presently
found on Cape Cod and the Islands. A full grown buck grows to 400
pounds and three and a half feet at shoulder height. The record antler
spread for a whitetail is nearly three and a half feet across, though Cape
bucks rarely display racks over two feet in diameter.

While actual population figures are unknown for Barnstable County, the Division of Fisheries and Wildlife hunting figures show more than a 50 percent increase in harvested deer—from 98 in 1982 to 157 in 1987 according to data from the division's deer-checking stations. It would appear that the Cape's deer herd is at least holding its own and may even be increasing in numbers.

Deer tend to become acclimated to their natal breeding area and will stay in the general vicinity even if starvation threatens. This limited home range, along with a healthy reproduction rate (a doe can breed as early as six months in age), can and does cause local overpopulations of deer.

With the many inroads made by human development in the past five years, the deer habitat is fast disappearing on the Cape. This inevitably will lead to overbrowsing and potential damage to crops, orchards, and gardens where deer numbers exceed the carrying capacity of the land. Starvation and disease within the herd and the potential spread of Lyme disease to area residents from the deer tick are also problems resulting from habitat loss.

The best times to watch for deer are early morning and late dusk, when they may commonly be seen in open fields and even road edges and backyards. Extremely wary, a deer will bound off if even slightly alarmed, flashing the white banner of its tail to warn off other members of the group.

Q *Are certain animals associated with certain kinds of woodlands?*

The presence of certain animal species in a particular area is directly related to the plant community's ability to provide the vital ingredients for the animal's survival—food, shelter, breeding grounds, and room to move. For example, a walk through a recently cutover area dominated by young aspens growing amid fallen logs is ideal breeding habitat for the ruffed grouse but is hardly suitable for the bobwhite quail, which needs open pastures and fields edged with brushy shrub growth.

Matching or manipulating woodland habitats for certain forms of wildlife is a basic tenet of game management. The recent reintroduction of the wild turkey in the Otis Air National Guard Base in Sandwich is a good example.

TICK

Q *Are there ticks on the Cape and Islands? Where do you encounter them? How do you protect yourself against them?*

There are two species of ticks found on Cape Cod—the dog, or wood, tick and the deer tick. Both are, unfortunately, abundant on Cape Cod and the Islands from May to September.

The dog tick is found in grassy areas, fields, and dunes. After feeding on the blood of a warm-blooded host, a fully engorged female extends from three-sixteenths of an inch to over half an inch long. At this point she falls off, never to feed again as her mouthparts are left behind in the victim.

The deer tick is common in shrubby and wooded areas, being most partial to deer runs through scrub oak country. The size of a pinhead, this tiny relative of the spider and scorpion is the focus of increasing public concern due to its role in the spread of Lyme disease.

Lyme disease is caused by a spirochetal bacteria introduced through the bite of the nymphal deer tick. The nymph stage and hence the main infectious period runs from May to July, though infection can occur at any time of the year.

Early symptoms include joint aches, fever, and a rash around the bite. Long-term health implications can be serious if the disease is untreated.

Anyone walking through tick country should wear light-colored clothing to aid detection. Pant cuffs and shirts should be tucked in and the entire body checked thoroughly after an outing. There are commercial tick repellents that do work.

Removal of an embedded tick should be done with tweezers and the bite mark swabbed with a disinfectant such as hydrogen peroxide.

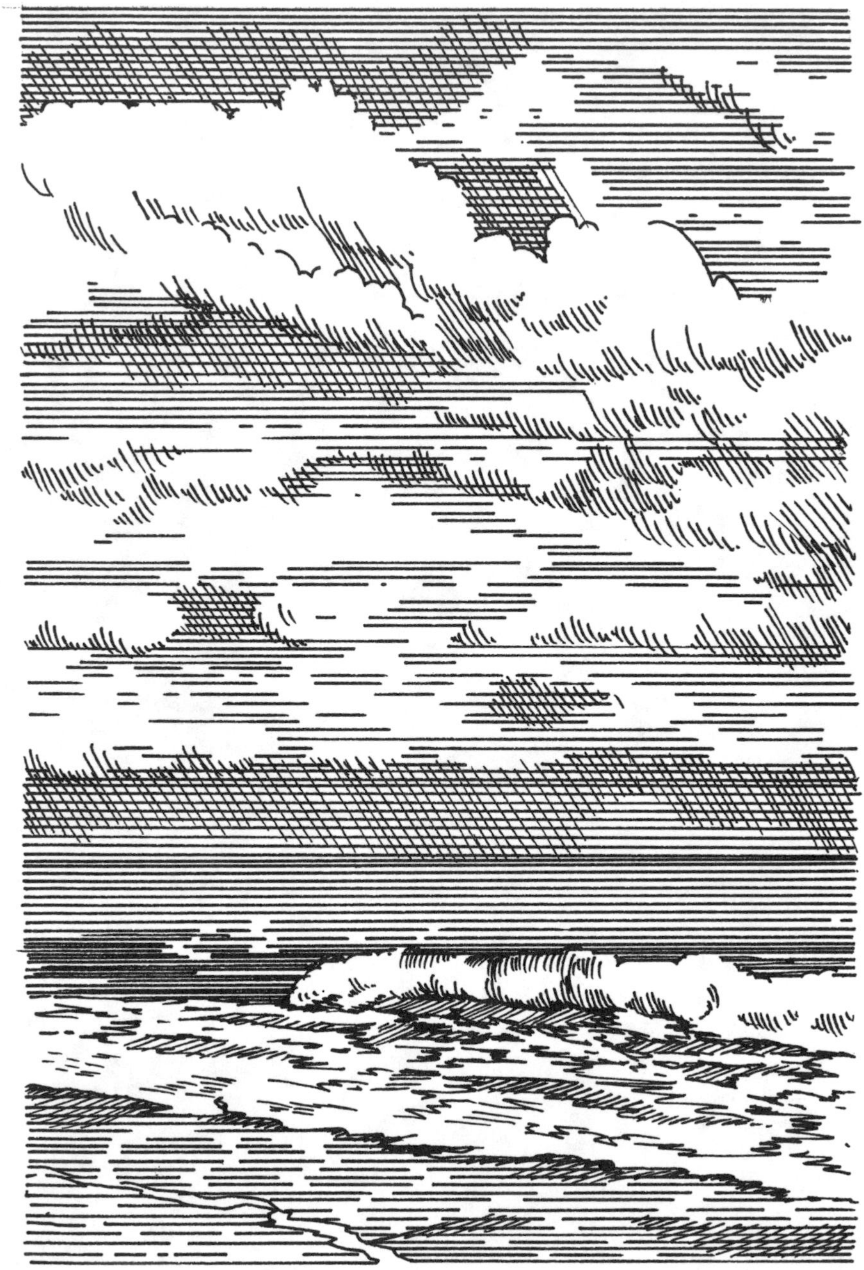

Chapter 7

Cape and Islands' Weather

by Robert Barlow

First-time visitors to the Cape and Islands often base their planning and packing on weather information generated in the greater Boston area. But once they arrive, many discover to their dismay and often discomfort that they might as well have collected forecasts from downtown Cleveland.

When visitors first tune in Boston weather reports they hear not only current and predicted weather for the city and suburbs but a separate report for the Cape and Islands—one that usually varies greatly from that of the Hub, just fifty miles up the Pilgrim Highway from the Cape Cod Canal. Cape and Island reports can vary so dramatically that casual listeners might be excused for thinking their dials have picked up vagrant transmissions from distant areas.

The reason is simple. Cradled by large bodies of water on all sides, the Cape and Islands are effectively insulated against the extremes of weather that are a part of year-round life in the rest of Massachusetts.

Not only is there a significant difference between Boston and Cape weather, the weather on the Cape and Islands often differs from one town to another. It baffles visitors that on a particular summer day, it can be delightful in Provincetown, foggy in Chatham, muggy in Hyannis, and stormy in Sandwich. At Menemsha on Martha's Vineyard the sky can be gray for days, while Oak Bluffs—about twelve miles away—is basking in the sun. In a word, the weather here is unpredictable, in spite of the best efforts of our local forecasters, who mean well but who have the batting average of a ball player in a July slump. This unpredictability is both the region's curse and part of its charm.

The seas that surround the Cape and Islands contribute most to the slowing of local weather and climate clocks. Spring here often begins later and brings more clouds, coolness (five to ten degrees cooler), dampness, and rain than the mainland. Like spring, autumn also is late in arriving but well worth the wait. Autumn lingers two to three weeks longer on the Cape and Islands and, as a season, is much warmer than the rest of the state. The first frost arrives later, too, usually well into October or November. In fact, by New England standards, the weather on the Cape and Islands is pretty mild right up to Christmas. The coldest month of the year here, as you might have guessed, is January, our month of heaviest snowfall (an average of ten inches). December, however, has the coldest extreme temperature.

Yes, it does snow here—37.1 inches in the average winter. But times of heavy snow and acute cold on the Cape and Islands are shorter than in the rest of New England. Once the rush or spill of cold that has caused a winter weather disturbance passes, the relative warmth of the sea quickly moderates the temperature.

In summer, this enormous mass of water around us also provides a large evaporation pool and contributes to humidity that tends to hang around like an unwanted houseguest until a front pushes it along. Cloudiness, the result of condensation of this moisture, is more frequent in May through July, when the contrast in temperatures between land and deeper offshore waters is greatest.

Two major ocean currents—rushing by the Cape and Islands from opposite directions—combine to shape much of our weather: the Gulf Stream and the Labrador current.

The Gulf Stream, a fifty-mile-wide flow of warm water traveling north along the Atlantic coast (until it begins to curve east off New Jersey), brushes the Cape's elbow off Chatham on its serpentine route to Great Britain and Scandinavia. This massive flow of warm water, estimated at 1,000 times the average daily flow of the Mississippi River, warms the Islands and the southeastern part of the Cape from Bourne to Chatham. When this tremendous volume of warm water comes in contact with surrounding cooler lands and waters, the result creates those swirling fogs that are so much a part of summer in Chatham.

The Labrador current, on the other hand, is a river of cold, dense Arctic water flowing south from its origin in the polar ice caps and Greenland's Baffin Bay. As this current washes the backside ocean beaches of the Cape from Provincetown to Chatham, this naturally refrigerated water lowers the temperature of Outer Cape lands dramatically. The result: less extreme weather than the rest of the Cape in summer and more extreme weather in winter. In summer, a scorcher in Falmouth may be a pleasant beach day in Wellfleet; and in winter, a dusting of snow in Mashpee may drop seven inches of powder in Eastham.

The Cape and Islands owe much of their climate to the fact that water absorbs heat energy and releases it much slower than does land, almost like a solar heat panel on the side of a roof. In spring, land here warms long before adjacent deeper waters. Just look at a map. Is it any wonder cool offshore waters have a greater influence on shaping our weather than the narrow band of warmer lands? Our mild weather also allows plants and animals native to warmer southern climes to survive in a region that should, by all rights, be too far north and too cold. Autumn landscapes here are blessed with brilliant glossy red leaves of the southern sourgum (also known as tupelo). The cattle egret, best known as a bird of southern cow pastures, has successfully extended its territory northward to the Cape and Islands within the last ten years. In addition, the white dogwood, native from the central Atlantic states southward, can be found here. Wellfleet and Nantucket support stands of opuntia, a cactus with yellow blooms not found wild in inner Massachusetts or, for that matter, throughout most of northern New England.

The opportunities for playing golf virtually year-round, picking fresh roses well into the fall, walking along our fabled beaches and in our thick woodlands, and being able to follow a fisherman's impulse twelve months a year have been powerful magnets for people to move here or just visit. As a result, the traditional three-month tourist season has been extended to seven months—May through November. Each year more people are discovering the secret joys of September and October. Early September is considered by locals to be the most glorious time of year, warm enough for the beach but too late in the summer for crowds.

Weather Fronts

To understand weather, it is helpful to understand weather terms and patterns. Like a giant picture puzzle, how weather patterns fit together on a given day determines the kind of weather we're going to have. Is a high on the way? Should we batten down for a low? Or get the bathing suits out for a warm front? Here are the basic weather terms and patterns.

HIGH-PRESSURE ZONES

Great variances in temperatures around the globe create winds that run north and south. The earth's rotation, in turn, changes the direction of these winds from north–south to east–west and creates air circulation patterns—large masses of air in constant motion across the oceans and continents. These swirling masses of air are called highs (high-pressure zones) and lows (low-pressure zones), depending on their weight and temperature.

When such a mass of air collects above frigid parts of the Northern Hemisphere (Canada, Alaska, and Iceland), the air is cold and contains little moisture. A cold air mass weighs more than an equal mass of warm, moist air. Consequently, this cold air exerts more pressure on the surface of the earth than the warmer air, and it develops a clockwise spiral, heading toward areas of lower pressure. This is caused by gravity and the earth's spinning. Our barometers—instruments that measure air pressure—will show higher readings when colder air is above the Cape and Islands. Weathermen call this type of air mass a high. Highs usually bring fair weather and light winds.

COLD FRONTS AND WARM FRONTS

High-pressure zones will keep building in the north until so much cold air accumulates in this circular pattern that it spills over and begins to move south, continuing its clockwise spiral pattern (this pattern is reversed in the Southern Hemisphere). The colder air—because it's heavier—forces its way under the warmer, more moist air near the earth's surface. The front edge of this advancing cold air mass (the place where cold air meets warmer air) is called a cold front. The front edge of the warmer moist air is called a warm front.

When moving air is extremely cold, the temperature of land it passes will drop dramatically, by as much as sixty degrees in northern parts of the United States. Local meteorologists call such winter winds Alberta clippers when they arrive over the Cape and Islands.

LOW-PRESSURE ZONES

As these cold rivers of air flow farther south toward the equator, they are warmed by the lands and bodies of water they pass—the farther south, the warmer the water. This infusion of heat speeds up evaporation and warms the passing air above, which now carries more water vapor. This causes the air to expand. When this happens, the air mass presses down on the land below with less force. In other words, the air pressure is lower. This is what meteorologists call a low. Because of the spin of the earth and the forces of gravity, incoming winds in a low-pressure zone curve counterclockwise in the Northern Hemisphere toward the center of the low (clockwise in the Southern Hemisphere). Lows usually bring cloudy skies with rain or snow. Winds are generally strong.

STATIONARY FRONTS

There are times when two air masses stall as they travel across the earth. When this happens, the difference in temperature, air pressure, and moisture between the two is slight. Weathermen often have trouble determining where one air mass ends and the other begins. This kind of vague, hard-to-determine boundary line is called a stationary front. Weather on either side of the front will be similar.

OCCLUDED FRONTS

An occluded front occurs when a mass of warm air is overtaken and forced higher above the surface of the Cape and Islands by a mass of faster-moving, colder, drier air. Weather on both sides of an occluded front will most likely be cloudy, damp, and often rainy (but no major cloudbursts) and will not change until the front moves out of our area.

How Fronts, Jet Streams, Winds, and Clouds Affect Weather

Understandably, residents and visitors on the Cape and Islands are more interested in the weather these fronts create than in their definitions. Here's what to expect as you read the weather map over morning coffee.

COLD FRONTS

Precisely what happens when a cold front arrives depends on the speed the front is traveling and whether or not the air mass has collected much water vapor. Excess water vapor condenses as rain, snow, or some other form of precipitation. The faster this occurs, the greater the chances that stormy weather will be accompanied by shifting gusts or squalls of wind. Rapid clearing begins soon after a cold front passes, and the wind shifts to the north or northwest—the origin of the front. Ground temperatures also drop, sometimes quickly, and air pressure rises—dissipating humidity on the Cape and Islands.

But if the temperature difference between incoming air and the ground air is slight (five degrees or less), the showers will be light, the clouds patchy, and the wind almost still. In such cases, about the only way you can tell a front has passed is by checking your barometer carefully.

WARM FRONTS

Clouds form in the sky as warm air begins to cool during the advance of a warm front. The clouds become darker and heavier as water vapor is condensed to form rain. Because a warm front moves slower than a cold front, the bad weather lingers longer. But once the front passes, the temperature rises, wind direction changes, the barometer drops, precipitation ends, and the sky clears.

Often, a stationary mass of colder high-pressure air in the middle of the North Atlantic—called a Bermuda high—blocks masses of warm air over the Cape and Islands from moving out to sea. When this happens, the region is in for warm, rainy, foggy, cloudy weather until this Bermuda high loses some of its punch.

OCCLUDED FRONTS AND STATIONARY FRONTS

Occluded and stationary fronts usually bring periods of prolonged cloudiness, fog, or precipitation. Neither front brings severe weather, just weather that will not gladden the heart of the Chamber of Commerce. If you're caught in an occluded or stationary front, the best you can hope for is the swift arrival of another air mass to drive the front out to sea.

JET STREAMS

The path that high- and low-pressure areas take as they move aross the earth is determined, for the most part, by high-altitude wind "rivers" flowing west to east called jet streams. These wind rivers race across the United States at speeds in excess of 150 miles an hour. Responding to air pressures weathermen are just beginning to understand, these narrow wind belts meander north and south over the landscape in their headlong dash across the country. Knowing the exact position of these jet streams will facilitate the forecast of weather.

WINDS

Winds are created by temperature and air pressure differences between two air masses. Warmer air contains molecules that have more energy than colder air. As a result, currents of the warmed molecules, called convection currents, begin to flow across the land. Colder, heavier air fills the vacuum left by the warm air. Simply put, this flow of warm and cold air molecules is called wind. Winds will continue blowing until there is no difference in temperature and air pressure between adjacent air masses. The bigger the differential in temperature and air pressure, the stronger the winds.

When surrounding seas are significantly colder than the land, winds will blow off the water toward the land and cool it. For centuries, such delightful winds have been called sea breezes, or offshore winds. If the land temperature drops below the water temperature, the winds will blow from the land toward the sea, creating a land breeze, or an onshore wind.

But on some days winds on the Cape and Islands are so light they don't even disturb the surface of the ocean, let alone our ponds. On such days, the locals talk of the water looking like glass. Other days the glass is shattered into ten thousand fragments by the wind.

When meteorologists forecast winds, they always name the direction the wind is coming from. A northeast wind, for instance, blows from the northeast. An so it is with northwest, southeast, and southwest prevailing winds.

In winter, prevailing winds over the Cape and Islands blow from the northwest. In April and May they begin to change direction, and by midsummer they are blowing from the southwest. In September they begin shifting to the northwest again. The most feared winds are those from the northeast, and they are usually caused by powerful storms, often three-day blows, off the coast that can do much damage. These storms are called northeasters. One such storm in the winter of 1978 caused millions of dollars in damage and was dubbed the worst storm of the century. Nature is still recovering from that storm.

CLOUDS

An unwelcome sight in summer, clouds are formed by water vapor collecting on solid particles in the atmosphere. There are six basic types of clouds—cirrus, altocumulus, stratus, nimbostratus, cumulus, and cumulonimbus. Clouds that form near the ground at the shoreline create fog.

Cirrus, thin wisps of white clouds high above the Cape and Islands, are the first sign that an approaching warm front is less than twenty-four hours away. These clouds, resembling the long, thin hairs of a mare's tail, are made of ice crystals formed at altitudes as high as 20,000 feet.

Altocumulus clouds, which appear in the sky shortly before the arrival of a warm front, form at altitudes of 5,000 to 10,000 feet and look like small, stretched-out wads of cotton. Fishermen and sailors say these clouds remind them of mackerel scales. Those who live by the sea have long known that mackerel skies mean rain and wind are on the way—hence the old sailor's rhyme, "Mackerel clouds in the sky. Expect more wet than dry."

On the heels of the mackerel sky comes a cloud that resembles a giant dirty gray sheet drawn across the horizon. This cloud, called a stratus, sags closer and closer to the earth as it accumulates more and more droplets of water and turns a darker gray with black clots. This is an indication that a nimbostratus is forming and that rain will fall soon. In summer, nimbostratus clouds are the source of showers that accompany most warm fronts. In winter, they bring snow.

Without mare's tails, a mackerel sky is a sign that a cold front is on the way. With the approach of colder air, these altocumulus balls of cotton will appear to get thicker, looking more like great wads of wool. These are called cumulus clouds.

When cumulus clouds become thick to the point it appears a giant hand is pulling this wad of wool higher and higher into the sky, you are witnessing the formation of a cumulonimbus cloud. Popularly called thunderheads, these clouds are giant energy machines creating enormous electrical energy surges within sections of the cloud, which result in lightning discharges and thunderstorms with heavy rain or hail and strong winds.

Weather's Temper Tantrums

Weather, like an incorrigible child, often throws fits—temper tantrums that can be costly. Locally, these tantrums come in the form of line squalls, gales, hurricanes, and an occasional tornado. An explanation of each follows.

LINE SQUALLS

Line squalls are severe storms that develop along the boundary line between two air masses. These squalls are caused by the mixing of cold dry air with warm moist air and result in heavy rain, lightning, thunder, and gale-force winds. Squalls, however, only last a short period of time and are followed by rapid clearing.

GALES

Gales are strong winds, caused by adjacent high-pressure and low-pressure air masses. The bigger the difference in air pressure between the two masses, the stronger the winds. Technically, an average wind speed of thirty-nine to fifty-four miles an hour is considered a gale. Average wind speeds between fifty-five and seventy-five miles an hour are called whole gales. An average wind speed in excess of seventy-five miles an hour is a full-scale hurricane.

HURRICANES

There are times late in the summer or early fall when a large mass of moist air, usually a low-pressure zone south of the Florida coast, begins spinning in a circular pattern. The more heat energy this air mass absorbs from the ocean, the faster the air spins. The faster the air spins, the lighter the air becomes at the center of this air mass. This warm air takes the shape of a column, spinning higher and higher and faster and faster—helped by the rush of nearby colder air from a high-pressure zone. When wind speeds reach seventy-five miles an hour, a hurricane is born. This giant energy machine now begins moving across the face of the ocean, its path dictated by neighboring air masses. If a Bermuda high is in place over the Atlantic, it may block the Cape-bound path of a hurricane, as it often has. A hurricane, in this case, will take the path of least resistance and spin west toward land or east into the open ocean. But if a Bermuda high is not in place to block this disturbance, a hurricane—using the warm waters of the Gulf Stream as a highway to gather speed and intensity—will head up the East Coast with a vengeance.

TORNADOES

The major difference between a hurricane and a tornado is the diameter of the mass of revolving air at the center of the storm. While the center of a hurricane can be measured in miles, the core of a tornado is often just a few feet wide, yet it can cause catastrophic damage. Excessively low air pressure at the center of a tornado can cause a building to explode when air pressure outside the structure is suddenly lowered.

Fortunately, tornadoes are rare in these parts, but many fishermen and sailors have experienced a cousin of the tornado—the water spout. Water spouts are columns or funnels of water whipped up by the same forces—but on a smaller scale—as tornadoes. Vessels in the path of a water spout face the triple danger of low air pressure, high-velocity circular winds, and a wall of water.

Warning Signs on the Horizon

Along with the highs and lows, cold fronts and warm fronts, line squalls, and hurricanes, high-altitude winds also carry a cargo the environment of the Cape and Islands could do without. Gaseous garbage from millions of smokestacks, open fires, and automobile exhausts rises up into the atmosphere every day and is carried east by prevailing winds and the jet stream. This toxic cargo is dumped along our coastline and in our ponds in the form of acid rain. (This is discussed in detail in Chapter 5.)

But by far the biggest threat is not what falls on the ground, but what remains in the air—a buildup of gases that have depleted the protective ozone layer and have trapped heat from the sun, triggering what scientists fear will be a worldwide rise in temperature and sea levels. Scientists call their prediction the greenhouse effect, which is discussed in the question and answer section to follow.

Q & A

Q What is sea snow?

During the winter the air near the shoreline often becomes full of subtle sparkle and glint, as though static electricity were everywhere going off. This meteorological phenomenon—called sea snow—is created when cold air along the coast passes over the relatively warm ocean, crystallizing the vapor being given off from its surface, and precipitates it inland in the form of light, cloudless snow. It is the opposite of the process that forms the thick fogs so characteristic of our wet, chilly springs when warm moist air masses move over a still, cold sea.

Sometimes significant accumulations of an inch or more of sea snow will fall in a band that may extend only a few hundred yards inland; it is usually brought on by a shift in the wind.

Q *What causes dew? What is the dew point?*

Dew is caused by condensation; it is moisture in the air that condenses on colder surfaces after a warm day in the form of tiny droplets of water that appear on the ground and those surfaces. Notice the wet grass late at night or early in the morning or the beads of moisture on the windshield of a car.

The dew point is the temperature at which dew begins to form or vapor condenses into a liquid. The dew point varies, depending on the amount of moisture, or humidity, in the air. The higher the humidity, the higher the dew point.

Q *What causes fog?*

Fog is a cloud of moisture that forms just above the surface of the ground, often over a body of water. Chatham, Nantucket, and Menemsha on Martha's Vineyard, to note just a few, are famous (or infamous) for their pea-soup fogs.

Fog is formed when excess water vapor in the air begins to condence as the temperature reaches dew point, but the water droplets are not heavy enough to fall. Hence a cloud of mist forms. When this mist forms just above the surface, we call it fog. The air is still and saturated; fog cannot form in a steady wind, which disperses moisture.

Q *What is the difference between dew and rain?*
What causes rain?

The major difference between dew and rain is that dew condenses on land, while rain condenses in the air.

Rain is caused when air filled with water vapor is cooled and becomes so heavy that the air can no longer hold moisture, and drops of condensed moisture fall to the ground. The amount of rain and the intensity with which it falls is determined by several factors, among them air temperature, wind, the amount of moisture in the air, and how quickly it condenses.

Q How often does it rain on the Cape and Islands?

In summer, it rains an average of seven to nine days a month; in fall, an average of nine days a month; in winter, an average of twelve days a month; in spring, an average of eleven days a month.

As you can see, winter and spring are our wettest months.

Q How much rain falls a month on the Cape and Islands?

In summer, an average of 3.4 inches falls a month; in fall, an average of 4.0 inches falls; in winter, an average of 4.4 inches; and in spring, the average is 4.1 inches.

During the course of a year, a total average of 47.7 inches of rain falls on the Cape and Islands.

Q What is humidity? What does relative humidity measure?

Humidity is moisture or dampness in the air. Moisture or dampness makes air heavier, stuffier, and harder to breathe. Because the Cape and Islands are often blessed with an ocean breeze, humidity here in summer is tolerable compared to humidity in Boston, New York, Washington, D.C., and points south.

Relative humidity is expressed in percentages and measures the amount of moisture in the air compared with the amount of moisture the air is capable of holding, given its temperature (the higher the temperature, the greater the moisture capacity). When relative humidity, for example, reaches 100 (meaning the air contains all the moisture it can hold), rain will likely fall. When the relative humidity is low (in the twenties or thirties), the air is dry, crisp, and visitors can expect a clear day since there isn't enough water vapor in the air to produce many clouds.

Q By season, what is the average daily relative humidity on the Cape and Islands?

In summer it is 77 percent (weathermen usually drop the word "percent" in their forecasts); in fall, it is 73; in winter, it is 65; and in spring, it is 68.

Q How often are the Cape and Islands hit with thunderstorms?

The region is whacked with thunderstorms an average of eighteen days a year—an average of about two thunderstorms a month in summer, one a month in fall and winter, and two a month in spring.

Q What causes hail?

Hail begins as rain. But as it falls, updrafts of air currents stronger than gravity pull these drops of water higher into the atmosphere where they freeze. Since ice weighs less than water, winds take these ice crystals even higher, where they often pass through clouds containing more water vapor. The vapor condenses on the top layer of these crystals, turning them almost to slush. Air currents carry this slush still higher, where it freezes a second time. The process of freezing, adding another layer of water, then freezing again makes these crystals so heavy they finally fall to the ground. Hail often occurs in severe thunderstorms with high winds.

Q How windy does it get on the Cape and Islands?
What month does the wind blow the strongest?

In summer, the wind blows an average of eight miles an hour, usually from the southwest; in fall, it blows an average of nine miles an hour, usually from the southwest to northwest; in winter, it blows an average of ten miles an hour, usually from the northwest; and in spring, it blows an average of ten miles an hour from the northwest to west-southwest.

Winds hit their average peak gusts of seventy-three miles an hour in September. Average peak gusts range from thirty-eight miles an hour to sixty miles an hour the rest of the year.

Q In terms of extremes, what are the hottest and coldest
times of the year on the Cape and Islands?

August is generally the hottest month, with an average peak temperature of 97 degrees Fahrenheit, although a few times a summer the temperature may reach over 100 degrees Fahrenheit.

The coldest month, in terms of peak temperature, is December—not January or February, as you might expect. The coldest extreme temperature in an average December is just below zero.

The good news is that extreme temperatures on the Cape and Islands, whether highs or lows, usually last only a day or two at the most.

Q *By season, what is the average high temperature on the Cape and Islands? By season, what is the average low temperature?*

In summer, the average high temperature is seventy-six degrees Fahrenheit; in fall, it is sixty-one degrees; in winter, it is thirty-nine degrees; and in spring, it is forty-six degrees.

In summer, the average low temperature is sixty-one degrees Fahrenheit; in fall, it is forty-six degrees; in winter, it is twenty-five degrees; and in spring, it is thirty-eight degrees.

Q *What causes sleet? What causes snow? What is the difference between sleet and snow?*

Like hail, sleet begins as rain. Simply put, sleet is rain that freezes as it falls, or seconds after it reaches the ground, coating everything with a sheet of ice. Sleet occurs when air temperatures near the ground are in the high to mid-thirties Fahrenheit. Sleet often falls on the Cape and Islands in winter, making driving conditions here hazardous.

Snow forms as crystals (as opposed to ice pellets that form hail) when the ground temperature is at or near thirty-two degrees Fahrenheit, supercooling the water in the air above the surface and freezing it almost instantly. The formation of sleet, given higher air temperatures, is a more gradual process. Snow, while slippery, is much easier to drive on than sleet, but like rain, you never have to shovel sleet. You chip it or salt it.

Q *Do fish, plants, and animals sense a change in season? What season offers the most dramatic examples?*

For many, fall is the favorite time of year. The crowds have gone from beaches and trails, and fish, plant, and animal kingdoms are bracing, in ways dramatic to the eye, for the coming of winter.

Shorebirds, for example, are aware well in advance of the change in seasons. These tundra nesting birds depart for their South American wintering grounds early—passing over the Cape and Islands in late July and reaching a migratory peak by mid-August.

Fall brings with it a certain amount of excitement. It is a period of stress and testing for many species. Add to this the increasingly inclement weather associated with this time of year, and you have the potential for unusual occurrences. If you are a beach walker, there are many things to look for at this time of year, depending on which shoreline you walk. On the ocean side, a steady easterly wind will often blow piles of luminescent purple jellyfish ashore. Also drifting in on easterly winds are gooseneck barnacles, with long leathery necks; the shell portion of the barnacle is attached at the end of the neck.

On Cape Cod Bay, fish frequently wash ashore this time of year. The most bizarre is the ocean sunfish, which looks like a 300-pound bullet (ocean sunfish can actually grow as large as a ton). Basking sharks, twenty-five feet long and weighing several tons, also wash up with regularity. The toothless, plankton-eating shark is an incredible sight.

And if you are boating late in the season on Cape Cod Bay or Nantucket Sound, there is always the possibility you will cross paths with our largest reptile, the leatherback sea turtle. This time of year leatherbacks are returning south from a summer spent feeding on jellyfish near the Artctic Circle around Iceland and Norway. Unfortunately, the leatherback is constantly ensnaring itself on lobster pot lines. They have been known to tow as many as twelve pots.

Q *What is a halo?*

When the summer sun sports a ring or halo, enjoy the good weather while it lasts. Rain is likely on the way. The halo is a tip that cirrus clouds, the first sign of an advancing rain front, are present six miles or more above the earth. These clouds, made of ice crystals, act like thousands of small prisms, bending sunlight so it appears to come from a white ring around the sun. At night, the same halo effect will appear around the moon, indicating an 80 percent chance of inclement weather.

Q *What is the ozone layer? Why is it so important?*

Everyone today is talking about the ozone layer, but not everyone understands what it is. The ozone layer is the outer layer of our atmosphere. It shields the earth from many of the dangerous radiations, such as ultrviolet rays, that are being generated continuously by the sun and other stars. As long as this ozone blanket remains thick, much of the harmful radiation is either reflected from the earth or trapped in the outer layer.

You can see why researchers became so concerned when their studies several years ago indicated there were holes in the ozone over the North and South poles—holes that may have already allowed enough radiation to seep through to cause genetic damage to plants and animals and an alarming increase in skin cancers and eye damage. Scientists blame this ozone depletion on the increased release of chlorine-based chemicals (chlorofluorocarbons), which are most often used in making fluids for refrigeration, plastic foam compounds, and aerosol cans. It takes five years for such gases to work their way up to the ozone layer, but they have a life span of 100 years—a century of breaking down this ozone mantle. Chlorofluorocarbons, or CFCs as they are often called, also contribute as much to our global warming as carbon dioxide (see following question and answer).

If predictions of scientists are true, some day the ozone shield, if we aren't more careful, may resemble a piece of Swiss cheese. If this occurs, no one will be able to step outside safely unless fully protected from the sun's dangerous rays. A day at the beach will be a thing of the past.

Q *What is the greenhouse effect? What is its probable impact on the Cape and Islands? Is it too late to reverse this effect?*

The greenhouse effect is the common term used for a projected global warming trend that may raise temperatures an average of five degrees Fahrenheit in the next sixty years, ironically much more in the polar regions. The term refers to the trapping of heat from the sun by a buildup of carbon dioxide, methane, and other gases and pollutants in the sky. This gradual buildup began during the Industrial Revolution and has progressed unchecked.

If scientists' predictions are true, those who live near a coastal area or visit one will have to make adjustments in their life styles. A global warming trend of this scale will accelerate the melting of polar ice packs at both ends of the earth, causing a dramatic worldwide rise in sea levels. Ocean waters eventually will claim many of today's bathing beaches and dock facilities, not to mention homes, shopping malls, restuarants, and favorite night spots.

While a five-degree increase in temperature doesn't sound like much, it will cause the release of more methane compounds, one of the culprits of this warming trend. Methane compounds now chemically trapped in the ocean bottom and in marsh and swamp sediments will bc released in greater quantities as warmer water and its increased energy exert more pressure on those sediments.

Warmer ocean waters will also result in the release of more carbon dioxide, which also holds heat and increases warming, although to a lesser degree than methane. This increase in carbon dioxide trapped in the atmosphere by a bubble of gases—an invisible greenhouse—will cause plants to grow faster by speeding up food production, or photosynthesis. Those plants that cannot adjust to a warmer world with more carbon dioxide will die off faster. Single-celled animals will feed on the decaying plant materials, releasing more heat-absorbent carbon dioxide.

Forests will also begin to fill in and grow faster and farther north. The limit of tree growth will be pushed closer to the poles. These trees will absorb more heat than ice and snow and cause even further warming.

Is it too late to reverse this effect? Scientists say it is not too late to at least slow it. Worldwide attention, they insist, must be focused on this problem to cause governments to work together to limit the release of these gases.

Q Why are winter storms so severe on the Cape and Islands?

Three factors determine the severity of a storm: the season, the position of the sun and moon, and the storm itself.

During January and February, the sun is closer to the earth than at any other time of year, although the Northern Hemisphere is tilted away from the sun during this period, resulting in colder temperatures and harsher weather. The proximity of the earth to the sun causes tides to be higher in winter; the gravitational pull of the moon during these months also causes higher tides, particularly when there is a full moon or a new moon. This combination of gravitational pulls, along with a powerful storm, can cause severe damage to the shoreline. Storms in winter often blow in off the ocean from the northeast in a pattern that resembles a roundhouse punch, picking up precipitation and strength from the sea. Such was the case in February of 1978, when the "storm of the century" struck—winds, blizzard conditions, and a storm surge caused millions of dollars of damage to the shoreline.

A storm surge is a wall of water, almost a mini-tidal wave, that is created by low pressure in the center of a storm. The lack of pressure allows sea level to bulge or rise higher than normal. Hence, the larger the storm and the lower the pressure, the greater the "bulge" or surge of water. Powerful storm surges on the Cape and Islands can travel hundreds of yards inland, destroying almost everything in their paths.

Q   *What is the easiest way to predict the weather?*

Note the wind's direction. Fair weather follows winds from the northwest, west, and southwest. Foul weather follows winds over the water from the northeast, east, and south. Also, if there is early morning fog, or if there is frost or dew on the ground, that means there will be no rain during the day.

Q   *Why is the color of the sun often different when it nears the horizon at sunset?*

Our atmosphere is filled with clouds, smoke, dust, and pollution. During the day, the sun's rays pass vertically through this relatively thin film. As the sun dips to the horizon, its rays must now pass horizontally along this plane of particles and pollution. Only red light waves—the longest waves in the color spectrum—can penetrate this plane, resulting in a horizon colored by a beautiful shade of red at sunset. The best spots on the Cape and Islands to witness this phenomenon are: on Cape Cod Bay, Corn Hill Beach in Truro, Eastham's Thumpertown Beach (at low tide), Cold Storage Beach in Dennis, and Barnstable's Sandy Neck; on Martha's Vineyard, Menemsha Beach; on Nantucket, the shoreline east of Madaket.

Q   *How much rain and energy can a single thunderstorm generate?*

A single thunderstorm, in 20 minutes, can dump more than 120 million gallons of water and generate enough electrical energy to supply a large city for a week.

Q   *How are rainbows formed?*

Rainbows are the result of light rays passing though rain drops, which make visible (to the eye) the color spectrum in consecutive bow-like bands. The rain drops act as a prism refracting this white light, which travels in different wave lengths. The colors of the spectrum are: red, orange, yellow, green, blue, and violet. Red is produced by the longest light wave, violet by the shortest. You are most likely to see a rainbow on the Cape and Islands after a storm.

Q What is the "January Thaw"?

The "January Thaw" on the Cape and Islands is a period (a week or two) in mid-to-late January or early February of unusually warm temperatures in the 50s or even 60s. Mid-winter weather patterns pump up this warm air from the south, which melts ice-covered ponds and thaws frozen fields—creating a muddy mess. Still, the thaw is a welcome relief to residents, and a tease that spring is not far away.

Part III

Everything You Wanted to Know about Nature and Didn't Ask:

A Guide to Intriguing Questions Pondered at the Cape Cod Museum of Natural History and the Cape Cod National Seashore

by Mary Loebig, Robert Cousins, and Greg O'Brien

Observation, as Thoreau once pointed out, "is not what you look at, but what you see."

Our eyes, ears, and feet are windows to nature on Cape Cod and the Islands. Naturalist Henry Beston was acutely aware of this when he wrote his classic book, *The Outermost House*, "Listen to the ocean; it has many voices. Really lend it your ears, and you will hear in it a world of sounds; hollow boomings and heavy roarings, great watery tumblings and tramplings, long hissing seethes, sharp, rifle-shot reports, splashes, whispers, the grinding undertone of stones and sometimes vocal sounds that might be the half-heard talk of people in the sea."

To hear nature, to see and feel it, we must be in sync with it. The child in all of us must witness the majesty, desire the discovery, of the unique and fragile world around us. Discovery begins with a question about change, or with a curiosity about the difference between a scallop and a quahog, a gribble and a gooseberry, an Indian pipe and an insect gall.

Nature on the Cape and Islands is in flux, as it is everywhere. Change, writes contributor and naturalist Robert Finch, "is the coin of this sandy realm, and as long as we are not too close to it, such change delights us." One of the hazards, Finch notes, of living on Cape Cod is not always knowing where we are. "The sea fog that rolls in occasionally over the flats and the marshes is not entirely to blame for our chronic disorientation. The winter storms that break through barrier beaches, destroying parking lots, silting up harbors and claiming waterfront property, are not the only things that dislocate us either.

"Nature has no guile, and that is one of the things that makes it hard for us to see her. The bare, uncompromising face of the land is too much for us to behold, and so we clothe it in myth, sentiment or simply human terms. How many of us have seen, or held a clam except in terms of a rather limited set of actions we call clamming?"

In the pages to follow, we attempt to pique your curiosity about nature, to disrobe some of the myths, with a guide to intriguing questions asked at the Cape Cod Museum of Natural History and the Cape Cod National Seashore.

We begin with honey bees.

Q Does the term "Queen Bee" mean honey bees are matriarchal?

Yes. Male bees, called drones, exist for the pleasure of the queen, who mates with the drones and produces up to 2,000 eggs a day. Worker bees, which are sterile females, clean and build the hive and produce the honey; they also force drones from the hive after the drones mate with the queen. Sounds almost like a James Bond thriller!

Q What should birds be fed in a backyard feeder?

In feeding birds, take measures to protect them from disease and other problems. Pay attention to the seed you use, the way it is delivered, where and how it is stored. Seed should be kept in a dry place that is free of moisture and harmful substances. Damp seed is suseptible to molds that can cause disease. Seed that has been sprayed with, or stored near, pesticides can absorb and transmit these substances, which can be harmful—even lethal—for birds. Seed should always be placed in an elevated feeder; ground-level seed will attract cats and other predators.

Suet and other fatty products can create a different type of problem. Suet should be put out only during colder months because it can harm birds when it becomes warm and milky—the oily substance adheres to the bird, weighing it down and interfering with the insulation properties of its feathers. Consequently, suet can impair a bird's flight and reduce its ability to keep warm. Peanut butter is another fatty product that could cause problems. Some birders fear peanut butter can cause the beaks of smaller birds to become glued shut. The National Audubon Society advises against the use of peanut butter as a bird food.

Q How do I keep squirrels away from my backyard bird feeders?

It isn't easy to outwit squirrels. But clever devices have been produced over the years that will keep squirrels from invading a bird feeder or birdhouse on a pole. One device is a baffle—a circular, cone-shaped device placed midway up the pole that prevents a squirrel from trying to scale it. Another device is a spring perch which dumps any squirrel or other animal that places its weight on it. In some parts of the country frustrated residents have resorted to placing wide strips of unsightly but effective sheet metal around the base of trees. The sheet metal strips, about six feet wide, prevent squirrels from scaling the trees.

Q What are those green and blue boxes placed on stilts in local salt marshes?

These boxes are a unique and chemical-free way of dealing with the unruly behavior of the pesky Greenhead Fly (*Tabanus nigrovittatus*), which attacks beachgoers with a vengeance on the hottest summer days. Though Greenheads serve an important role as a food source for swallows and other birds, the bloodsucking behavior of the female Greenhead is despised by summer visitors. During the summer, the female lays her eggs on grass stems in the marsh, then seeks the blood of warm-blooded animals to develop her eggs. The eggs eventually hatch into inch-long maggots, which winter in the mud at the base of the marsh, feeding on insects, worms, snails, and other Greenhead larvae. The following summer, the maggots emerge from their larval stage as the dreaded fly.

The special boxes placed in the marsh entice adult females with welcome shade and relief from the sun. Once inside the box, an intricate maze of screens makes it impossible for them to find an exit. It is estimated that the boxes, if placed correctly, can rid a marsh of more than 50 percent of its Greenhead Fly population.

Q Are there coyotes on Cape Cod?

Coyotes arrived on the Cape 12 to 14 years ago the same way most visitors get here today; they crossed the bridges. These carnivorous, dog-like animals first appeared on Otis Air Force Base in the Sandwich-Mashpee area, and are now thought to be thriving in all 15 Cape towns. Although sometimes called "coydogs or brush wolves," these animals are true coyotes. They are the size of a German shepherd dog, but have longer, thicker fur. Cape coyotes have bushy, black-tipped tails, slender snouts, and pointed ears. Their pelts range from the more common grayish-black to a less common blonde. Females weigh up to 40 pounds, and males weigh up to 50.

Mostly nocturnal, coyotes are keen hunters. They feed on a wide range of animals, including rodents, deer, and some plant material. There has been local speculation that coyotes have attacked dogs. Like dogs, coyotes can be found in small family groups, consisting of a mated pair and their young offspring; dens for pups are usually built in concealed areas, along heavily vegetated slopes and under banks. If you have any questions regarding coyotes, call the Cape Cod Museum of Natural History at 508-896-3867.

Q How do woodpeckers stay parallel to a tree while boring their holes?

Woodpeckers, common to the Cape and Islands, can move about in an unlikely fashion by the use of a unique set of adaptations. Most species of birds have long legs with four toes on each foot—three toes facing forward and one backward, an ideal configuration for perching on horizontal branches and wires. The woodpecker, however, has stubby legs with two toes in front and two toes in back. These feet, coupled with extremely stiff tail feathers, allow the bird to brace itself against the tree trunk when climbing.

Other intriguing adaptations include an unusual tongue and skull. The woodpecker can dart its tongue in and out of narrow holes it has drilled. Its skull is particularly thick and hard, allowing the bird to drill while hunting or excavating nesting cavities without damaging its brain. It is thought that woodpeckers have protective air sacs in their heads. Scientists in the safety helmet field have been studying the woodpecker's head, hoping to discover ways of improving the construction of helmets.

Woodpeckers commonly found on Cape Cod include the northern flicker, the downy woodpecker, and the hairy woodpecker. Downy and hairy woodpeckers resemble one another, with both displaying distinct black and white body markings with a small red spot on the back of the head. The hairy woodpecker is slightly bigger than the downy, reaching ten inches in length. The northern flicker is larger than the other two, with gray, black, white and red markings and yellow underwings that are most obvious during flight.

There have been reports of poisonous brown recluse spiders
Q *in Truro; what do they look like and how do you recognize their bite?*

These reports are difficult to confirm. The brown recluse spider is one of a variety of spiders known as violin or brown spiders, all of which are venomous. They derive the "violin" name from the fiddle shape that appears on their heads. These spiders are fairly common in the southern United States where the warmer weather they prefer prevails. It is believed, however, that they have recently made their way into more temperate climates, via shipments of industrial and manufactured materials from their native habitat. In northern climates, the spiders survive by living in homes and temperature-controlled buildings; they do not appear to be very common in New England. But despite their rarity it is always advisable to err on the side of caution. Brown recluse spiders prefer dark, warm areas and will bite and flee when startled. Be careful to check and shake things out that have been in storage, especially in closets.

If you have been bitten by a spider, monitor the bite for telltale symptoms—a distinct bull's eye with a black center and red, white and blue rings. Other symptoms include nausea accompanied by aches and pains. Call a doctor immediately.

Q *Are there poisonous snakes on Cape Cod?*

There are no poisonous snakes on the Cape and Islands. In fact, the only two poisonous snakes found in Massachusetts—the eastern timber rattlesnake and the copperhead—are extremely rare even in their preferred bedrock habitat on the mainland. This is not to say there are no large, aggressive snakes in our area. Two in particular—the water snake and the black racer (found near the water)—can grow to lengths of six feet and will bite vigorously if bothered. Occasionally, these snake bites can break the skin and introduce localized infections into the wound. But the infection is caused by bacteria, not venom. On balance, Cape Cod snakes are beneficial because they consume insects, slugs, and rodents.

Q How fast do the wings of hummingbirds flap?

A hummingbird's wings can flap an amazing 55 strokes a second. The amount of energy this requires may seem excessive, but as a nectar feeder, a hummingbird's ability to "hover" is necessary for its survival. Most nectar feeders, such as butterflies, moths, and bees, are able to gather nectar while resting upon the flowers from which they feed. The hummingbird's comparatively heavier body makes it impossible for any flower or plant to support its weight. By flapping its wings rapidly in figure-eight configuration (made possible by incredibly flexible shoulder joints), the hummingbird is able to suspend itself in midair. Hovering enables the hummingbird to gather its food without stressing the flower.

Q How serious and how common is a case of rabies?

Rabies is a painful disease of the nervous system. It is caused by a virus that is spread through saliva from the bite or scratch of an infected mammal. If left untreated, it is almost always fatal. Though rabies is no longer commonly found on Cape Cod, there is evidence of a recent outbreak in the western portion of the state, and it is possible that it could spread to other sections of Massachusetts.

Raccoons appear to be the most affected by the present outbreak, followed by foxes, skunks, and bats. The likelihood of contracting rabies from a wild animal is not nearly as great as catching it from a domestic pet infected by the disease. To be safe, keep your pet vaccinations current. Avoid handling unfamiliar pets and report suspicious, overaggressive behavior to your local animal control officer.

Q Where do insects go in the winter?

Like reptiles and amphibians, insects are ill-suited for winter because they are cold-blooded and require warm temperatures to be active. Cold temperatures cause their regulatory mechanisms to slow down to a virtual standstill, a stage known as diapause. Triggered by the short days of autumn, diapause is a period when virtually all activity and growth cease. Insects survive the winter by burrowing into a leaf litter, the ground, or the crevices of rocks and logs. One insect home fairly visible after the leaves have fallen is the gall; it is formed when an insect uses the surface of a twig or leaf for food and shelter for its offspring.

Q Do insects serve a purpose in nature?

In spite of their reputation for spreading disease, inflicting pain, and destroying crops, insects play a key role in nature—from pollinating plants and vegetables, to providing products like silk and honey, to serving as an essential food source for fish and birds.

Q Can animals and insects see in color?

Experiments have determined that most mammals are color blind across a wide spectrum of colors. They see the world in varying shades of light and dark. Since many mammals hunt at night, color vision is not essential to them. Many insects and birds, however, are able to discern color. Bees, for example, use color vision to detect certain flowers. Although it is believed that bees cannot discern the color red, they can detect ultraviolet—a color humans cannot see naturally. Birds, on the other hand, appear to require color detection for mating and other interactions; the brightly colored plumage of male birds attracts female birds. Birds also use their color vision for hunting and avoiding predators.

Q What are bird pellets and where can they be found?

The pellet of an owl or gull (and less commonly of a hawk or eagle) is a conglomeration of the indigestible pieces of its prey. Pulling one of these pellets apart can be an informative pastime, revealing a great deal about the diet of the animal that produced it. A pellet is what remains after an owl has eaten. Unlike hawks and eagles, who tear meat from their victims' skeletons, an owl consumes its prey whole. Since portions of its prey are not digestible, the owl regurgitates a small packet. Generally, these pellets are elliptical in shape and can range from one to three inches, depending on the bird. The best way to find these pellets is to search under a known roost of an owl; for example, the mature white pines that great horned owls prefer. When pulling the pellets apart, look for the skulls and small bones of the bird's victims. The owl's prey are generally easy to identify because the skeletons are relatively intact. Gull pellets tend to be larger and often contain quantities of plastic and other human litter, an indicator of the scavenging nature of the gull's appetite as well as human carelessness.

Q *What are those small tunnels, more than an inch in diameter, that crisscross grass meadows and lawns?*

These intricate tunnel networks are generally the work of meadow voles, a small mouse-like rodent common throughout New England and Canada. Voles are shy creatures who will disappear the moment they are spotted. A quick way to discern a mouse from a vole is to compare its tail to its body; a vole's tail is shorter than its body. Voles also have much smaller ears than mice and longer fur.

Meadow voles are active year-round, and feed on grass, seeds, and insects in the summer, and in winter on bark and leaf litter. Like other rodents, voles have four gnawing teeth—one pair above and one below that continue to grow throughout their lifetime. This adaptation prevents the wearing down of their teeth, which they use constantly.

Q *What are "digger" wasps and where do they live?*

Just as the name implies, digger wasps live in underground burrows they dig. They are members of the bee, wasp, and hornet family, and consume other insects. If you observe one of the many digger wasp colonies throughout the Cape and Islands, you will notice that wasps often return to the nest carrying the bodies of their prey, which are stored in the colony's extensive tunnels as food for larval wasps that thrive below.

Q *What are those baffling animal signs on mud flats at low tide?*

The region's extensive flats, particularly on Cape Cod Bay, offer an enthralling, easy walk for amateur naturalists. Favorite areas include: Skaket Beach in Orleans, Paine's Creek Beach in Brewster, and Cold Storage Beach in Dennis.

Many shellfish leave a multitude of clues marking their presence. Small holes in the sand, for instance, reveal the location of razor clams, soft-shell clams, and quahogs just below the surface. Several snail species leave tracks on the flats—short, random ribbons of sand drawn by the animal's body as it traverses the flats in search of food. The periwinkle is generally seen at the end of the track as it forages for algae and detritus, while the moon snail's trail often appears to end in the middle of nowhere. Dip your hand below the surface at the end of this trail, however, and you might scoop up a globe-shaped shell with its lavender digging foot extended. Also, look for snail eggs. A snail lays its eggs in a semi-cylindrical configuration—approximately one inch in height and made up of eggs, sand, and a sticky mucus. This forms what is called a moon collar, shaped by its formation around the body of the egg-laying snail. When the process is complete, the snail crawls away leaving the collar to harden and sit until the eggs hatch.

Another track, most frequently seen from mid-May to mid-June, is the broad linear track left by a pair of mating horseshoe crabs. The female will drag the male, who is attached to her back by his front claws, onto the flats where she will lay the eggs. Often she will burrow into the sand, creating the impression that the male is alone. A quick check below the sand's surface will reveal the female, which should discourage the curious from disengaging the animals from one another.

Q *Where do you find bullfrogs?*

Bullfrogs are the largest amphibian found in our area. Their size, coupled with a distinctive call, makes them far easier to spot than many smaller, more furtive relatives. During summer evenings, many Cape and Island ponds resound with the bullfrog's loud sounds, which resemble those of a bass fiddle. Bullfrogs usually sit quite still on vegetation near the edge of a pond or float on the pond's surface with only their large eyes peering above the water; camouflage colors of brown and green allow them to blend into their surroundings.

Male bullfrogs are distinguished from females by comparing the size of their ear membrane (the distinct round spot behind the bullfrog's eye) to the size of the eye. Those bullfrogs possessing ear membranes larger than their eyes are almost always male. As with other amphibians, the bullfrog's cycle is characterized by several distinct stages—growing and changing from egg to tadpole, then to fully metamorphosed adult, a process that takes about two years.

Q *Why are ponds on the Cape and Islands so round?*

The roundness of kettle ponds is the result of shoreline currents, powered by the wind, that sweep and redistribute the shoreline sands. Over thousands of years, most shoreline irregularities have been softened and rounded over by this redistribution of unconsolidated sand.

Q *Are river otters found on the Cape; recently what appeared to be a river otter was seen on Scargo Pond in Dennis?*

River otters have been spotted in Dennis, Brewster, Falmouth, Mashpee, and Sandwich. Nationwide, the number of river otters is declining because of a loss of their habitat, excessive trapping, and water pollution. The Cape, in some ways, offers otters more protection.

A member of the weasel family, a river otter—as its name implies—is a water lover. Living along streams, rivers, and marshes, the otter's primary food source appears to be fish and crustaceans, though otters have been known to eat turtles and an occasional muskrat. Otters are playful and are endowed with good humor; they are graceful and swift underwater swimmers, and love to slide in snow or down sand banks. Otters have a distinctive face with long whiskers, a prominent nose pad, closely spaced eyes, and a sleek, dark, oily, insulated fur coat. Their tails are long and broad, ending in a point.

Q *What nature walks are best suited for children?*

For a short and easy walk that offers an incredible variety of plant and animal life, try the Hallet House trail (behind the Yarmouth Port Post Office on Route 6A). You can take a side path down to a small pond and wetland area where you will hear a cacophony of bullfrogs and other creatures. The trail is maintained by volunteers, and costs 50 cents for adults and 25 cents for children.

The Cape Cod National Seashore also offers a variety of walks for little legs: Coast Guard Beach and Nauset Light Beach, both in Eastham, are terrific places to walk. Be careful to stay off the dunes and away from protected nesting areas.

In addition, the Seashore offers boardwalk access to two swamp areas that might otherwise be inaccessible to small children. The first is a path over the Red Maple Swamp at Fort Hill in Eastham (follow the signs that lead you from Route 6A). The walk offers a glimpse of large maples and their attendant birds and creatures. Take a magnifying glass and examine some of the unique fungi. If your children are not tired after this walk, take them over to enjoy Fort Hill's spectacular view of Nauset Marsh. Read them a brief account of the Native American and early settler history that is associated with the area; in the lower parking lot you will find a printed guide to the trail.

Another unusual Seashore swamp trip, accessible by boardwalk, is the Atlantic White Cedar Trail near the Marconi Station in Wellfleet (follow the signs off Route 6)—a beautiful example of an increasingly rare habitat; the pathway and boardwalk allow you to walk the trail ithout inflicting any damage. The children will love it.

For inexpensive family entertainment, try Nickerson State Park off Route 6A in Brewster; the park offers great camping sites, bicycle trails, hiking trails, and magnificent freshwater swimming and fishing ponds.

Also take in the Cape Cod Museum of Natural History up the road near the Dennis town line. The museum offers children's exhibits, hiking trails, and nature classes. For more information, see the section on nature trails and sanctuaries.

Q Where have all the bluebirds gone?

The eastern bluebird was once common on the Cape. Unfortunately, several factors led to a 90 percent decline of its population — commercial development, loss of forest habitat, and the introduction of the European starling in the early 1900s. The canary nature of the starling, combined with its prodigious birth increase and a tendency to live in large flocks, allowed the species to compete successfully with the more docile bluebird for nesting cavities and food. Starlings have spread in large numbers throughout the United States.

Q Are there any wild turkeys on the Cape today, as there were in the days of the Pilgrims?

Turkeys served at the first Thanksgiving in Plymouth were hunted by a party of Pilgrims, as a contribution to the feast, while the Wampanoags provided deer and other game, history tells us. The Wampanoag tribe also had offered the Pilgrims the knowledge of how to grow corn, making possible the first Thanksgiving—a celebration of a successful corn harvest.

In the days of the Pilgrims, wild turkeys—with their colorful plumage—were common on the Cape. But during the past few hundred years, the gobblers have fallen victim to an increase in hunting and a loss of natural habitat. Today, there are only scattered pockets of wild turkeys in the United States; most turkeys are confined to turkey farms where they are slaughtered and sent to market. In Massachusetts, where the last wild turkey died in 1851, a turkey conservation effort is in full swing. For example, in March 1989, 18 wild turkeys captured in the Berkshire Mountains in the western part of the state were released in the woods of the 21,000-acre Massachusetts Military Reservation off Barlow Road in Sandwich. The release was part of an effort to reestablish wild turkey flocks that were once common throughout the Cape, and marked the first time in 300 years that wild turkeys walked the woodlands here. The results have been encouraging to date.

Q How many working lighthouses are there on the Cape?

There are eight working lighthouses on the Cape, mile-for-mile one of the largest concentrations of working lighthouses in the world, according to information provided by the Cape Cod National Seashore. Cape Cod is the sort of place you would expect to find lighthouses. Sweeping far out into the ocean, the Cape is a substantial obstacle to navigation. In the last 300 years, there have been more than 3,000 documented shipwrecks along Cape shores. A tour of Cape lighthouses will take you from Woods Hole to Provincetown. You can visit all of them. The lighthouses include:

Nobska Light—located on Nobska Point overlooking Woods Hole harbor, the light warns mariners away from two dangerous shoals, the Hedge Fence and L'Hommedieu. The first light station was built here in 1828; it was a keeper's house with a light tower on top. In 1879, a new metal tower, the same one you see today, was built in Chelsea (outside Boston) and shipped in four sections to the Cape. The iron tower was lined with brick and a new keeper's house was added. Like all Cape lighthouses today, Nobska Light is unmanned. It was automated in 1985, and stands 87 feet above the sea. Its light flashes every six seconds and can be seen from 16 miles at sea. Mariners in safe water see a white light, while those near the shoals see a red light.

Bass River Lighthouse—Bass River Lighthouse today forms the center of an historic inn in West Dennis, the Lighthouse Inn on Nantucket Sound. The lighthouse was built in 1850 to mark the entrance to Bass River, once an important entrance to the Mid Cape for commercial boats; at one time, Bass River was considered as a site for the Cape Cod Canal. The lighthouse became a private residence in 1915 after it was de-commissioned. It is now one of the few privately-owned lighthouses on the East Coast.

Chatham Light—The first lighthouse was established in Chatham in 1808. It consisted of two brick towers and a keeper's house. The two towers were built to help mariners distinguish the light from other lighthouses, a problem in early days before light technology created distinctive flashes. Ultimately, it was decided that Chatham's two lights were too costly to maintain because of the additional fuel, personnel, and supplied needed. So one light—the north tower— was moved in 1923 to Nauset Beach in Eastham, and the south tower was moved back from the bluff to its present location next to the Chatham Coast Guard Station, near the mouth of Chatham Harbor.

Nauset Light—Distinctive with its handsome red stripe around the top of its tower (called a daymark), Nauset Light off Ocean View Drive in Eastham can be distinguished during the day from other Cape Cod lighthouses. Today it is threatened by erosion and the Nauset Light Preservation Society is seeking to move it back from the edge of a sand cliff. Donations to the society are greatly appreciated; call Eastham Town Hall at 508-255-0333 for more information.

Cape Cod Light—Cape Cod Light, or Highland Light, as it is sometimes called, also is perilously close to the sea. Off Route 6 in Truro (follow the signs), Cape Cod Light was established in 1798 and is the Cape's oldest lighthouse. For transatlantic sailors, Cape Cod Light was the first light seen on voyages from Europe. The present brick lighthouse and associated buildings were built in 1857. Standing 66 feet tall and located high on a clay cliff, the light's beacon shines 183 feet above the ocean and can be seen 20 miles out to sea. The beacon flashes a white light every five seconds, and can be seen by motorists at night from Truro to Provincetown.

Race Point Light—Accessible on foot, by four-wheel drive, or by boat, Race Point Light is about two miles west of Race Point Beach in Provincetown. The light was built in 1816 to help ships navigate the dangerous knuckles of the Cape's fist on their way into Provincetown Harbor. Between 1816 and 1946, more than 100 vessels were shipwrecked on the beach and offshore shoals. So treacherous is the area that Race Point Light is equipped with a foghorn to warn ships in times of poor visibility. The keeper's house and lighthouse currently on the site were built in 1876; the 40-foot tower is 41 feet above the ocean and its white light, flashing every 15 seconds, can be seen 16 miles out to sea.

Wood End Light and Long Point Light—The best spot to view Wood End Light and Long Point Light is from the breakwater by the rotary at the end of Commercial Street in Provincetown. It is a half-hour walk to the tip of Cape Cod where Long Point Light marks the entrance to Provincetown Harbor. During the summer, a private shuttle in the town center offers service to Long Point.

Wood End Light, visible at the far end of the breakwater, is the twin of Long Point Light. Unlike other Cape lighthouses, Wood End Light is a square white tower; built in 1873, it is now powered by the sun and flashes a red light every 15 seconds.

Part IV

A Listing of Nature Trails and Sanctuaries on Cape Cod and the Islands

by John LoDico and Greg O'Brien

Knowledge and discovery are synonymous; you can't have one without the other when it comes to nature. Now that you have learned all about the unique ecosystems on the Cape and Islands, you need to go out and explore them.

The region offers some of the finest, most varied nature trails in the country—some of them paths wisely preserved down through the years. Others are within the boundaries of our many parks and nature sanctuaries, like the Cape Cod Museum of Natural History on Route 6A in Brewster, Brewster's Nickerson State Park (considered the jewel of the state park system), the Massachusetts Audubon Society's Wellfleet Bay Sanctuary off Massasoit Road in Wellfleet, the Cape Cod National Seashore, the Felix Neck Wildlife Sanctuary and the Cedar Tree Neck Sanctuary on Martha's Vineyard, and Nantucket Conservation Foundation lands.

The trails offer something for everyone in the family—from Provincetown's ghostly beech forests, to the owl-haunted seclusion of Wellfleet's Great Island, to the spirit-heavy Dennis Indian lands, to the Audubon Society's spacious Ashumet Holly and Wildlife Sanctuary in Falmouth, to Sandwich's Thornton Burgess Museum and Old Briar Patch (a favorite among children), to the pristine shoreline of the Vineyard's Long Point.

There are also bike trails, chief among them the Cape Cod Rail Trail—eighteen miles of winding trails through forests; around ponds, bogs, and swamps; and past rivers—and bike trails that criss-cross the Islands. And don't miss the world-renowned Center for Coastal Studies in Provincetown, where you can learn about nature's "gentle giants" and hook up with whale-watching cruises aboard the *Dolphin Fleet.*

The trails that follow are special places. Walk lightly, don't litter, and please don't pick the plants. Enjoy your journey into solitude. We begin with trails on the Upper Cape, followed by the Mid-Cape, the Outer Cape, and the Islands.

The Upper Cape

BOURNE

Bourne Scenic Park

The camping area at Bourne Scenic Park, bordering the Cape Cod Canal and under the Bourne Bridge, has some walking trails along its length. Although not especially rich in flora and fauna, the park allows hikers access to the man-made canal—a good fishing spot. Since the canal is salt water, a fishing license is not needed when casting off its rock-lined banks.

Bourne Town Forest

This parcel off County Road has some hiking trails and allows walkers to explore plant life in the westernmost portion of Cape Cod.

FALMOUTH

Ashumet Holly and Wildlife Sanctuary

The forty-five-acre parcel in Hatchville was given to the Massachusetts Audubon Society in 1964. The extensive American holly that grows throughout the parcel was propagated by Winifred Wheeler, the state's first commissioner of agriculture.

The flat trails lead around a grassy pond, the Wheeler Memorial, a patch of Oriental and English holly, and past the tallest holly on the property. Special attention should be paid to the Franklinia, an unusual fall-flowering shrub around which the sanctuary holds a festival each autumn. In winter the trees produce colorful berries. Also, each April a colony of barn swallows returns to nest in an old barn on the property, a natural ritual repeated for over fifty years. The Audubon Society holds a day camp for children at the reservation throughout the summer.

Goodwill Park and Town Forest

Just off Route 28, Goodwill Park occupies eighty-six acres around Grews Pond. There are hiking trails. The Falmouth Town Forest, or Gifford Woods, is adjacent to Goodwill Park and surrounds Long Pond. It is a much larger parcel than Goodwill and contains a variety of freshwater plant life.

Beebe Woods

Occupying 400 acres off Depot Road (just off Route 28) the woods are intersected with hiking trails.

Washburn Island

On Waquoit Bay, this large island is owned by the state, which allows overnight camping with permission.

SANDWICH

Shawme Crowell State Forest

Shawme Crowell consists of 2,756 acres off Route 130 in Sandwich. Park staff offer interpretative programs during the summer; guides conduct night walks and stargazing trips and hikes to Scusset Beach. The general public, not just campers, is welcome on the walks.

Scusset Beach State Reservation

Off Scusset Beach Road, this 380-acre parcel offers hiking, and interpretative programs are offered in season.

Wakeby Conservation Area

The small Wakeby Conservation Area in South Sandwich borders Wakeby Pond, off Sandwich-Cotuit Road. Trails in the area take hikers past cranberry bogs and holly trees.

Mill Creek

Mill Creek by Sandwich Harbor (off Town Neck Road, off Route 6A) contains a boardwalk that leads hikers over marshland and tidal inlets. Shorebirds and sea life abound in the area.

Talbot's Point Salt Marsh Wildlife Reservation

This state wildlife reservation is located off Old County Road, opposite the East Sandwich Post Office on Route 6A. The trail through the marsh overlooks cranberry bogs and the state game farm.

Thornton Burgess Museum and Old Briar Patch

The great children's book writer Thornton Burgess lived here. Near the Shawme Pond house that serves as the Burgess Museum, the Briar Patch conservation lands take up fifty-seven acres.

Trails through the area show different locales from the stories such as Smiling Pool and the Crooked Little Path. Maps of the land are available at the museum.

The Mid-Cape

BARNSTABLE

Barnstable allows public use on over 3,400 acres of conservation land. A map detailing the publicly owned land is available from the Conservation Commission at town hall. Some of the more notable parcels follow.

Sandy Neck Conservation Area

Magnificent. That's the best word to describe this 1,332-acre spit of barrier beach, dunes, and salt marsh on Cape Cod Bay. From Route 6A, take Sandy Neck Road north to the ranger station. A list of regulations and maps of individual trails are available there.

Sandy Neck is home to many protected wildlife species and is the site of many ongoing research projects. Pay attention to the signs along the way and keep off restricted areas. A great way to experience the beach is to take a boat out from Barnstable Harbor and anchor off the easternmost point, which is off-limits to the many beach buggies that crowd Sandy Neck.

Otis-Atwood Conservation Area, West Barnstable

Off Route 6, Exit 5, take a left and then head west at the sign for the service road. Or from Race Lane, head north on the Crooked Cartway to reach this 1,224-acre parcel.

Popple Bottom Road cuts across the parcel's middle. To the north, the land is described as knob-and-kettle topography typical of glacial moraines. White pine and holly grow in the southeast corner. Watch out for the shooting range north of the power lines.

Arnold Property at Long Pond

This 37.5-acre parcel borders Long Pond in Marstons Mills. From Newtown Road follow Lakeshore Drive west.

The land contains large open fields and a mature, mixed upland forest.

Crocker Neck Conservation Area

This attractive parcel is on Popponesset Bay and is accessible from School Street to Crocker Neck Road, south to Cotuit Cove Road.

By walking the length of its ninety-seven acres one can experience salt marsh on the eastern and southern borders and a freshwater marsh on the northeastern border.

"1776" North and South

For the south parcel, travel from Route 149, then east on Church Street, and park across from the cemetery. The north parcel is located off Route 6A.

The interesting south parcel is distinguished by old open fields and swamplands, as well as wet woodlands and scattered hummocks of upland forest. Wetlands and salt marsh are also included.

Darby Property

For a good look at two kettle ponds side by side, the 103-acre Darby Property is the place to go.

From Main Street in Osterville, head east on Pond Street, then take a quick right on Tower Hill Road to park.

Joshua's and Micah's ponds lie side by side with trails around and between them. Pitch pine, oak, and holly mark the area.

Hathaway's Pond Area

Off Phinney's Lane, a road leads to Hathaway's Pond Recreation Area. Two ponds actually share the same name. A typical array of pitch pine, oak, and small wetlands dots the area. The ponds are also known for their excellent trout fishing.

YARMOUTH

A guidebook prepared by Yarmouth's Natural Resources Department and the private Yarmouth Conservation Trust describes the town's five main hiking trails. The booklet is available at the town hall.

The trails are open from a half hour before sunrise to a half hour after sunset. Camping is permitted with Conservation Commission approval and with prior notification to the police and the town's Natural Resources Department.

Meadowbrook Road Conservation Area

This short trail leaves the end of Meadowbrook Road (off Winslow Gray Road) and travels along a boardwalk, through swamp and marsh, to Swan Pond. Poison ivy abounds, as do cattails, bayberries, ferns, blueberries, and wildflowers. A single red cedar stands among red maples and dead, vine-entangled trees. Benches along the end of the boardwalk at the pond's edge provide a scenic rest stop from which to observe freshwater marsh plants and waterfowl.

Raymond J. Syrjala Conservation Area

This 3,540-foot trail off Winslow Gray Road, about a half mile from Route 28, loops around to begin and end at a parking lot. The trail passes by a boggy, shallow pond—the remnant of a glacial kettle hole. At the top of the trail, you'll find a bench among a clump of sassafras. Two-foot bridges cross swampy areas where mushrooms and other fungi grow. Among the various plants red maple, pitch pine, blueberries, ferns, pepper bush, as well as sour gum trees (*Nyssa sylvatica*), abound.

Horse Pond Conservation Area

This 3,100-foot trail, with side paths, runs along the edge of Horse Pond from Higgins Crowell Road. From the parking area, it passes through blueberries and mixed oak and pine woodlands, then over small hills and through pine groves. The main trail bears right after crossing a small stream, while the shorter side path loops around to join up farther on. Sassafras, with its mitten-shaped leaves, grows in this area. A side trail soon bears right, down to the pond and benches. Farther on, the path terminates at the end-of-trail sign.

Dennis Pond Conservation Area

The main trail of Dennis Pond and its side trail wind their ways between Willow and Summer streets in Yarmouthport. Parking is available off both streets. From Willow, proceed down a steep slope through an old bog that now sustains a stand of red maple. Much moss grows here.

The trail then climbs through poison ivy and then white pines with their long, narrow cones. By a small kettle hole and across a rundown stone wall, the trail emerges near Dennis Pond. Bullhead lilies grow on the water; frogs inhabit the area. Near the end of the trail on Summer Street the path passes by a red maple swamp. The side trail, which runs along the pond's edge, is noted for its numerous beech trees.

Callery-Darling Conservation Area

Almost 2.5 miles of trails cut through upland and along salt marsh and old cranberry bogs in Yarmouthport. Parking is located along Homers Dock Road and at Gray's Neck Beach. Along the wetlands, great blue herons, marsh hawks, ducks, and other birds are often spotted. Grouse, pheasant, and quail share the trails with walkers. Sea lavender grows in the area, as do poplars, pitch pine, and glasswort. At Gray's Neck Beach, a boardwalk extends into the marsh along Chase Garden Creek.

Yarmouth Botanic Trail

Administered by the Historical Society of Old Yarmouth, this sandy trail pases through fifty acres of land behind the Yarmouthport Post Office on Route 6A. A map is available at the gate house. Lady's slippers, an herb garden, and Miller's Pond and its wildlife are all sites to see along the sandy, none-too-difficult trail.

DENNIS

Crowe's Pasture

Off South Street, at the end of Quivet Cemetery in East Dennis lies the road leading to the fifty-plus acres of Crowe's Pasture. Old dirt roads of about 2.5 miles round-trip lead out to this property fronting Cape Cod Bay, where seals sometimes frolic and oftentimes marsh hawks and other birds patrol. Look for wild apple and wild cherry trees, too.

Simpkins Neck and the Romig-Jacquinet Conservation Area

These two contiguous parcels are upland islands almost entirely surrounded by marsh. The path to the land is off New Boston Road, two houses past Berrien Studios on the left. The wide, level trails lead to the marsh edge, where, with a little pluck getting through the underbrush, one can walk out onto the marsh. There birds rest in the tall grass and small fish swim in the channels. The Romig parcel is known for its blueberry bushes, while Simpkins Neck, saved from development in 1986 by a municipal land buy, hosts deer, raccoons, birds, and other wildlife.

Fresh Pond Conservation Area

Off Route 134, this eighty-seven-plus-acre parcel is woven through with four trails of various lengths. Wild cranberries, blueberries, ducks on the pond, and other wildlife abound on the land.

The Indian Lands Conservation Trails

Perhaps Dennis's most impressive hiking trail, the Indian Lands at the end of Riverdale South, on Bass River, contain a wealth of natural resources. The short trail passes along river land, salt marsh, a cove, and upland. Hikers may even stumble upon Indian artifacts from the native Americans who lived there centuries ago.

The Outer Cape

BREWSTER

Brewster is graced with Nickerson State Park (1,779 acres) and the town-owned Punkhorn Parklands (roughly 800 acres). Other walking trails include the John Wing Trail, Spruce Hill, and paths maintained by the Cape Cod Museum of Natural History.

Camping is permitted in the Punkhorn with prior approval from Brewster's Conservation Commission. A rough map and a clear plastic overlay are available from the town hall for one dollar apiece. Maps of John Wing and Spruce Hill are also available in the town offices, while the Nickerson rangers station provides a map of the state park.

Nickerson State Park

This large wooded tract of land, with 420 campsites, was once the estate of Roland C. Nickerson and his wife, Addie. She donated the land to the state in 1934.

Literally miles of trails crisscross the park, with some of the most interesting encircling the two main ponds—Flax and Cliff. Higgins Pond, which is at the far end of the park from Route 6A, near a portion known as Area 7, is a renowned bird-watching site. This migration stop plays host to ducks, Canada geese, cormorants, great blue herons, sometimes the common loon, and other waterfowl. Thrushes, wrens, warblers, and other woodland birds inhabit the park, as do owls, hawks, and osprey.

The best way to see Nickerson is to pick up a map and choose any trail, applying what you have learned in this book. Or better yet, participate in one of Nickerson's extensive interpretative programs conducted by park staff. Having an expert along will make the task of identifying Nickerson's many rare and endangered plant species easier.

Punkhorn Parklands

The result of major municipal land acquisitions between 1985 and 1987, the Punkhorn and its many and complex hiking trails remain protected from development.

Once sheep-grazing land and then a thriving cranberry-producing region, the Punkhorn contains a maze of trails. The town-produced map may help hikers locate their position.

One way to see the Punkhorn is to park a little past where Run Hill Road changes from asphalt to dirt. Trails leading east where Run Hill meets Westgate Road lead to an Archimedes screw pump on Upper Millpond. Paths are confusing here, so just head toward the pond and walk along its edge, being careful not to trample plants. The pumps were used by cranberry growers to flood their bogs. Old car engines powered some of the pumps, such as the one on Seymour Pond.

Punkhorn Road, off Westgate, passes between a quaking bog and another marshy area (see Chapter 4). Deep depressions, or quarries, also mark the Punkhorn.

John Wing Trail

Named for Brewster's first European settler, the one-mile John Wing Trail runs from Route 6A just west of the museum's parking lot—through 140 acres of upland woods, salt marsh, and beach—to Wing's Island on Cape Cod Bay. The trail takes about forty-five minutes to walk, but during high tides the causeway to the island is impassable.

At the edge of the upland and salt marsh when traveling from Route 6A, one encounters many different species of plant life, the most notable being the tall grass to the right of the trail—salt reed grass—officially listed as a species of special concern by the Massachusetts Natural Heritage Program. Next comes the high salt marsh where herons and marsh hawks lurk. Drainage ditches past the main causeway are dug to prevent standing water in which mosquitoes breed. A short spur trail off the main trail leads to a plaque marking John Wing's homestead. Next comes an open field in which species such as New England blazing star and sickle-leaved golden aster flourish. Beach plums and bush clovers grow here, too. Soon the trail emerges to an overlook of the bay. In the nearby creek, small shrimps dart about; green crabs and minnows thrive. On the margin, black grass, salt meadow hay, and sea lavender grow. Watch for raccoon and bird tracks when the creek is low. The trail ends at the wrack line on the beach.

Cape Cod Museum of Natural History Trails

Like the Wing Trail, two shorter paths begin at the Cape Cod Museum of Natural History. The north trail is only one-quarter mile long and serves as an introduction to common plant species. The south trail, on the opposite side of 6A from the museum, is about three-quarters of a mile long. It moves through a cattail marsh and mature American beech. Lots of poison ivy grows here, too.

Spruce Hill Conservation Area

This twenty-five-acre parcel was bought from the Castiglioni family in 1985. The half-mile trail begins at the homestead of the Keeler family, the town's first Irish immigrants. Tall, non-native Norway spruces stand in back of the house. The trail is an old carriage road leading to Cape Cod Bay. Lady's slippers bloom in season. The wetland farther on is a freshwater one that contains tupelos—twisted, gnarled trees. Past the woods, in back of the dunes, plants that thrive in drier soils grow. Past the dunes on the beach, fish weirs are visible on the water. Stay on the trails near this delicate area.

HARWICH

Bells Neck Road Conservation Area

Park your car along Bells Neck Road in Harwich and walk along the marked yellow and orange paths to witness some of the best birding on the Outer Cape.

Here one may view in short succession—amid the herring runs, marshes, rivers, and reservoirs—swans, cormorants, ospreys devouring freshly caught fish, and numerous other hawks, warblers, and, perhaps, even a yellow-billed cuckoo.

The Cape Cod Bird Club often leads free walks through this area.

WELLFLEET

Wellfleet Bay Wildlife Sanctuary

The Audubon Society's 700-acre sanctuary in Wellfleet is a one-stop naturalist's laboratory, with enough self-guided and expert-led activities to give an interested person a solid background in Cape Cod naturalism.

Paying a nominal fee allows one to enter the sanctuary and walk its trails. For a few dollars more, one can take advantage of naturalist-led talks on topics as diverse as whimbrel watches, bat walks, or canoe cruises through Nauset Marsh.

More independent individuals may walk along the Goose Pond Trail, a 1.5-mile path. The Audubon Society provides an indispensable thirty-two-page booklet at the trailhead to help hikers interpret the walk. On first sight many of the wildflowers and grasses marked for identification—species such as phragmites and dwarf sumac—seem unremarkable, but closer inspection reveals the individuality and singular beauty of each hearty stalk.

The booklet also contains a handy list of about 250 birds spotted at Wellfleet Bay—a great way to begin a "life list" of species.

The Cape Cod National Seashore

The Cape Cod National Seashore was created in August 1961 and encompasses 44,600 acres. Within its boundaries are many self-guided and ranger-guided walks, all of them extremely special in one way or another.

Ranger-guided acitivities are numerous but change each season. Call either the Salt Pond Visitor Center in Eastham (255-3421) or the Province Lands Visitor Center in Provincetown (487-1256) to get times and dates of hikes. There are nine self-guided trails, with leaflets describing the walks available at the trailhead, summarized below.

EASTHAM

Fort Hill Trail (including the Red Maple Swamp)

Following signs from Route 6, drive to the lower Fort Hill parking lot or the upper spaces overlooking Nauset Marsh and Coast Guard Beach. Part of the roughly 1.5-mile trail traverses boardwalks and mild slopes.

Bird-watchers will delight in this trail; many local birding groups conduct walks at Fort Hill. Look for the black-crowned night heron, the great blue heron, and, during the highest tides, the elusive Virginia rail.

Skiff Hill

Reached by footpath from the Fort Hill parking lot or by a paved walkway from Hemenway Landing, Skiff Hill offers magnificent vistas of Nauset Marsh. Exhibit panels describe marsh life, Native Americans, and explorer Samuel de Champlain's visit to the area in 1605. Skiff Hill also contains a sharpening rock used by Native Americans to maintain primitive tools.

Buttonbush Trail

Only one-quarter mile, this trail has texts along the way in Braille and large type. Look for the white guide rope near the Salt Pond Visitor Center's amphitheater.

Nauset Marsh Trail

This trail begins to the right of the Visitor Center's amphitheater.

A classic marsh-side trail, this path winds around the edge of Salt Pond and Nauset Marsh, crosses fields and a bicycle trail, and returns to the Visitor Center.

Doane Loop Trail

A paved, wheelchair-accessible trail that meanders through an emerging pine-oak forest. A mixture of upland vegetation includes concentrations of bearberry, bayberry, and beach plum. The trail, located off Doane Road, begins at Doane Rock, the largest exposed glacial boulder on Cape Cod.

WELLFLEET

Atlantic White Cedar Swamp Trail

At the traffic light on Route 6, turn right to Marconi Station. Follow signs to the swamp. The trail is somewhat difficult for senior citizens, with steep stairs, a boardwalk, and soft sand.

Great Island Trail

This is the longest trail in the National Seashore and perhaps the most interesting. From the center of Wellfleet, turn left on Commercial Street.

At the town pier, turn right on Kendrick Road and left on Chequessett Neck Road.

For four miles, one way, this trail leads out to Great Island, past tidal inlets, fields, and through woods. Owls are known to nest here, as well as many other woodland and shorebirds.

TRURO

Cranberry Bog Trail

Off North Pamet Road, the one-half-mile trail is easy walking, with part of it over a boardwalk.

Small Swamp Trail

An interesting trail to walk because of the interpretative signs along the way that point out and explain interesting sites. Turn right at the Pilgrim Heights area sign.

Pilgrim Spring Trail

The story goes that the Pilgrims, recently landed in America, found the spring along this trail and took their first New World drink. This trail is three-quarters of a mile long.

Pamet Cranberry Bog Trail

A short, half-mile walk at the Ballston Beach overwash off South Pamet Road, the trail offers a scenic overlook of the knob-and-kettle landscape that gave rise to the cranberry industry on the Outer Cape in the 19th century.

PROVINCETOWN

Beech Forest Trail

Turning north at the Race Point Road traffic signal, follow the road to the parking lot on the left. For one mile, this trail leads through the strange Beech Forest landscape. A sometimes steep and sandy walk, this trail is worth the extra effort.

Bike Trails and Whale Watching

Provincetown Center for Coastal Studies

The center has been studying whales that visit Massachusetts waters for more than a decade. The public, by taking whale-watching cruises aboard the *Dolphin Fleet* (check the phone book), helps support the research.

Members of the center's research team accompany each excursion onto the bay and Stellwagen Bank, where humpbacks, fin whales, and the rare right whale frolic. Researchers are so familiar with their subjects that the whales have been identified individually.

Cape Cod Rail Trail

If you'd rather bike than hike through nature, the Cape Cod Rail Trail, extending from Dennis to Eastham along an abandoned railroad right-of-way, provides an interesting trip.

Between fifteen and eighteen miles long, the rail trail passes by the Herring River, the cranberry bogs by Hinckley's Pond in Harwich, and by the second largest freshwater lake on the Cape—Long Pond in Brewster on the Brewster-Harwich line. Then, pedal through Nickerson State Park and by the Red Maple Swamp. Namskaket Creek and Boat Meadow River are two other natural highlights along the way.

Nauset Trail

A 1.6-mile trail from the Cape Cod National Seashore's Salt Pond Visitor Center in Eastham off Route 6, the path runs to Coast Guard Beach through scenic forests and meadows. Access also is possible at the Doane Rock picnic area.

Head of the Meadow Trail

A two-mile trail accessed at High Head Road in Truro, the path runs to Head of the Meadow Beach. The trail skirts meadows and a former salt marsh, and offers glimpses of various birds and wildlife.

Province Lands Trail

The Province Lands Trail in Provincetown is a five-mile run with three spurs: a one-mile spur to Herring Cove; a half-mile spur to Race Point Beach; and a quarter-mile spur to Bennett Pond. Access is possible at the Province Lands Visitor Center, the Race Point Beach parking area, the Beech Forest parking area, and the Herring Cove Beach parking area.

The Islands

MARTHA'S VINEYARD

Felix Neck Wildlife Sanctuary

With 200 acres and four miles of scenic, self-guided walks, Felix Bay on Edgartown Road is run by the Massachusetts Audubon Society. Like other Audubon centers, Felix Neck offers staff-guided walks and interpretative programs. But along the self-guided trails one can enjoy the best of the Vineyard's beauty and watch ospreys and common terns, ducks, geese, and even wild turkeys. The sanctuary is also known for its wildlife, such as otters and turtles.

Cedar Tree Neck

Run by the Sheriff's Meadow Foundation, Cedar Tree Neck occupies 250 acres of meadows and headland on the north shore of the Vineyard, off Indian Hill Road. Marked trails guide hikers through the area.

Long Point

Five hundred and eighty beautiful acres in West Tisbury on Tisbury Great Pond, various coves, and the south beach make up Long Point. The area is run by Trustees of the Reservations and is free to enter. Picnicking is allowed. This area is a good place to get an up-close look at the shore environment.

Cape Pogue and Wasque Reservation

These adjacent conservation areas (Pogue, 489 acres; Wasque, 200 acres) lie on Chappaquiddick Island. Many four-wheel-drive fans get permits from the trustees to traverse this stretch of beach. But walking the area is better, of course.

Peaked Hill

One of the highest hills on the Vineyard, Peaked Hill, off Middle Road in Chilmark, offers an incredible, panoramic view of the island and surrounding waters. Along the walk to the top of the 300-foot summit, you'll pass grasslands, woodlands, and a large bedrock boulder left by the glacier.

State Forest

Access to this 3,900-acre preserve is off the Vineyard Haven-Edgartown Road near the high school. The access is known as Airport Road; there is a blinking light at the intersection of Airport and Vineyard Haven-Edgartown roads. Follow signs for the nature trail.

Roth Woodlands

This 26-acre nature sanctuary is on the south side of North Road in Chilmark. The sanctuary offers spectacular wetlands and trails.

Gay Head Cliffs

The Gay Head cliffs on the west end of the island are considered one of the island's top attractions. Formed during the Ice Age, the steep, clay cliffs offer breathtaking views of the Atlantic, Buzzards Bay, and Vineyard Sound. The cliffs are located near the intersection of Lighthouse Road and South Road. Parking is available.

Hugh and Heather Sadlier's *Short Walks on Cape Cod and the Vineyard* (Globe Pequot Press) is a good guide to have.

NANTUCKET

Nantucket Conservation Foundation Lands

This private group was formed in 1963 to preserve and protect places of natural and historic significance on the island. Through purchases, gifts, and conservation restrictions, the foundation has preserved over 7,700 acres of land which the public may enjoy.

Maroon posts with the Conservation Foundation's logo mark property boundaries and help identify parcels. A map of all properties is available by writing Nantucket Conservation Foundation, P.O. Box 13, Nantucket, MA 02554.

One of the more interesting parcels is the Windswept Cranberry Bog located off Polpis Road (where parking is available). This working bog and natural area consists of three parcels totaling about 240 acres. The Windswept Bog is a good place to view plant succession and meadow and marsh life, all in short order. Two hardwood forest communities are located south of the parking area. One of the American beech trees here is close to 200 years old and the American holly is one of the largest on the island. A booklet produced by the foundation contains a handy checklist of species.

Epilogue

by Robert Finch

We live on a land that is disappearing. Traditional estimates give the Cape and Islands 5,000 to 6,000 years before   as the Puritan cleric Cotton Mather graphically predicted—"shoals of codfish be seen swimming on its highest hills." More recent predictions, based on accelerated rates of sea level rise, have shortened that considerably. Nantucket, in fact, may have less than a millennium. Whatever their actual life spans may turn out to be, we know that these lands age and change at rates that, at least on small scales, approximate those of human life itself. Major alterations in the coastline—erosion, storm breakthroughs, creation of new spits and islands—occur over very short time periods. Geological change is no abstraction here but a daily occurrence, visible even to the casual observer, and one that the house builder ignores at his or her peril. In fact, this vulnerability to change, this openness to adaptation, this sense of imminent mortality may form a part of these landscapes' attraction for us, by engendering an unconscious empathy with their fate.

We also live in a time where any appreciation of a natural landscape inevitably includes a sense of threat. Almost all of the chapters in this book temper their fascination and celebration of particular habitats with a litany of losses and present threats. Especially in a place like this, where natural beauty is at once fragile and in increasing demand, there is a certain poignancy in almost everything we observe, almost as if while appreciating something, part of us wonders if this might be the last time we will see it. There is an uncomfortable element of accuracy in this feeling. Much has indeed been lost, diminished, impoverished, exploited, and overwhelmed.

The modern era of environmental history on Cape Cod and the Islands began after the end of World War II and is characterized by an ever-accelerating dependence upon and influencing by off-Cape and off-Island forces. Though tourism had become a major factor in the Cape's economy in the decades between the world wars, automobile travel increased dramatically during the postwar years. The building of the Mid-Cape Highway during the 1950s changed the nature of vehicular traffic to the Cape as much as the Cape Cod Canal had changed navigation around it a half century earlier. With the expansion of the postwar economy, the first waves of permanent immigrants in over a century began to arrive over the bridges and on the ferries, and with them came the demand for what has been the single greatest influence on our environment in the last fifty years: development, with a capital D.

The growth of Barnstable, Nantucket, and Dukes counties (incorporating the Cape and Islands) has been obvious to anyone living here for even a short time. A few figures, however, are telling. By 1980 Cape Cod's year-round population had increased to 147,925, while the summer population had grown to 441,003. Today, the year-round population is in excess of 175,000; and there are more than a half million people here in the summer. Other figures reflect not merely the increase in population but corresponding effects on the environment. From 1951 to 1971 residential land area on the Cape increased from 5 percent to 14 percent of total acreage, while agricultural and other open field habitat decreased from 15 percent to 8 percent. During the past twenty years an average of 5,000 acres a year has been developed, an area roughly the size of Provincetown.

Corresponding with, though lagging behind, this exponential postwar growth has come an increasing awareness not only of the importance of the Cape's environment to both the tourism industry and the quality of life of those who live here but also of the threat to that environment that runaway development poses.

It was not until after the Second World War that there was any widespread sense of a need to preserve land or to restrict the use of it. Though several large tracts of land had been set aside as public property, these were either lands that had always been in state ownership (the Province Lands) or municipal ownership (Barnstable's Sandy Neck), that were acquired by the federal government for non-conservation purposes (Edwards Army Base, later Otis Air Force Base, in Falmouth), or that were gifts of private estates to towns or to the commonwealth (such as the Nickerson family's gift of Nickerson State Park in Brewster in 1936).

Monomoy Island was acquired as part of the United States National Wildlife Refuge System in 1944 and was later designated as a national wilderness area in 1970. The 1960s saw the establishment of conservation commissions in most of the townships on the Cape and Islands. In addition, several towns have acquired significant portions of their wetlands; one of the first to do so was the town of Dennis, which in 1967 acquired over 1,400 acres of wetlands. Private conservation trusts have formed in most local municipalities and have purchased or received as gifts many environmentally sensitive areas. In recent years the commonwealth's Department of Environmental Management has purchased some of the last remaining significant parcels of salt-waterfront property on the Cape: South Cape Beach in Mashpee, Washburn Island in Falmouth, and Camp Monomoy in Brewster.

Environmental legislation has also matured in the last two decades in the plethora of state and local wetlands regulations, zoning bylaws, scenic road acts, growth control bylaws, and other legal measures designed to counteract the increasing development pressures. And with the signing of the Cape Cod Commission Act by Governor Dukakis in 1990, Barnstable County may at last acquire the power to address the environmental impacts of development on a regional basis. There is no doubt, however, that the single most important piece of environmental legislation on the Cape and Islands was Public Law 87 126, passed by the United States Congress and signed into law by President John F. Kennedy on August 7, 1961, which officially established the Cape Cod National Seashore. This act gave permanent federal protection to some 27,000 acres of the most spectacular and desirable oceanfront property on the Lower Cape from Orleans to Provincetown. That this was done none too soon is illustrated by the example of the Fort Hill overlook in Eastham, now one of the jewels in the necklace of public access areas within the seashore, which had already been subdivided, with house lot stakes and bulldozer tracks marking the site, when the seashore was established.

It is not only development pressures but many specific environmental problems that appear to originate more and more from outside the county itself. The issue of acid rain is discussed in Chapter 5. In addition, oil spills along our shores have been a chronic problem since the early part of this century. Henry Beston noted this "wretched pollution" on Coast Guard Beach during his stay in the Outermost House in the 1920s and recorded that "the shores of Monomoy peninsula were strewn with hundreds, even thousands of dead fowl, for the tankers pumped out slop as they were passing the shoals . . . ." Today it is still the chronic dumping of bilge oil at sea that presents the greatest threat to seabirds, whose feathers become matted with oil, losing their insulative value, so that most oiled birds die of pneumonia. But in September 1969 a fuel oil barge spill covered a large portion of Wild Harbor Marsh in West Falmouth. Intensively studied by the nearby Woods Hole Oceanographic Institution, the effects of this relatively small spill on marsh vegetation and animal life can still be traced two decades later. Even more dramatic was the wreck of the *Argo Merchant* tanker off the Nantucket Shoals on December 15, 1976. Only a fortuitous shift in the wind kept some 7,600,000 gallons of crude oil from ending up on the Cape's ocean beaches. No major spills have occurred on the Cape and Islands since then, but the recent Alaskan disaster of the Exxon *Valdez* should remind us how vulnerable our beaches and estuaries remain to the effects of oil transport and offshore drilling.

Perhaps the best example of the complexity of the Cape and Islands' environmental makeup and the increasing difficulty in distinguishing between local and outside forces is the fate of our tern colonies. These graceful birds return each spring from their wintering grounds in Central and South America to nest in dozens of colonies in our outer beaches and dunes, skillfully skimming the shallow offshore waters and estuaries and making shallow dives to catch sand eels, silverside minnows, and other small prey.

When Drs. Oliver S. and Oliver L. Austin began their pioneering studies of Cape Cod terns in the 1930s, they estimated some 60,000 pairs of common, Arctic, and roseate terns. By 1982 the number had dropped to about 10,000. The precipitous decline in tern numbers over the last fifty years has been due largely to the development and/or disturbance of suitable nesting habitat and to the explosive growth of populations of herring and black-backed gulls, larger and more aggressive birds, which drive out the high-strung, easily disturbed terns. This increase in gull numbers, however, has been indirectly caused by human development, for the spread of large municipal garbage dumps has supplied these scavengers with an almost unlimited food supply.

Thanks to vigorous protection and education programs by the Massachusetts Audubon Society, the National Seashore, the Trustees of Reservations, and other conservation groups, tern populations on the Cape seem to have stabilized in recent years. But the fate of the terns is not solely in local hands. The birds are still unprotected and even actively hunted for food in some of their wintering grounds in some Latin American countries, demonstrating that in the modern era, wildlife conservation is rarely a local, or even solely a national, matter anymore.

Today visitors and residents all experience the growing congestion and crowding of our roads and beaches, villages and towns, marinas and shopping malls. But perhaps the most far-reaching effect of our growing numbers is the increasing demand on and potential pollution of our groundwater reservoir. Recent federal studies have refined Arthur Strahler's original concept of the Cape's water supply as a single uniform underground "lens" into a more complex series of "domes" and "subdomes," but the basic model of an interconnected, rainfall-dependent, and nonreplaceable source of groundwater has been firmly established and was made official in 1972 when Barnstable County accepted federal designation of the Cape's water supply as a sole source aquifer.

Mapping of public supply wells has shown that virtually every town on Cape Cod and Martha's Vineyard (Nantucket Island comprises only one town) is at least partially dependent upon aquifers in neighboring towns and is therefore dependent on the quality of that water. Provincetown represents the extreme case, having been completely dependent on neighboring Truro, though Truro itself lacks a municipal water system. A gasoline leak into the South Hollow well field in North Truro in 1971 shut down the pumping station and required expensive and lengthy cleanup procedures, an incident that demonstrated dramatically how fragile and vulnerable water quality may be, even when water supplies may be abundant.

Where private wells have been driven close to the shore, problems with saltwater intrusion have been common. Wastewater plumes from sewage treatment plants at Otis Air National Guard Base have posed a hazard for Falmouth's reservoir; and sanitary landfills, which are decades old in many towns and which for years carried little or no restrictions on the dumping of toxic wastes, may pose future time bombs for the water supplies of several communities. If there is any one problem that demonstrates the essential oneness and interdependency of our environment here, and points to the need to confront our problems on a regional basis, it is that of protecting our common aquifers and handling the growing problems of septage (human waste) and refuse disposal.

It is one of the great ironies of the recent rapid growth of the population of the Cape and Islands that the very people who most deeply appreciate the unique environment and rich natural life of their chosen home or vacation spot now represent its most active threat. The biggest threat to wildlife today is not the wanton tree cutter but the wildlife lover whose house is one of several thousand new homes each year that increasingly displace local deer, grouse, box turtles, whippoorwills, meadowlarks, and other species sensitive to human presence. The biggest threat to our wetlands and ponds is no longer the wholesale drainer and filler of swamps and marshes but the pond-view lover whose new beach and dock destroy bordering wetland vegetation and whose new septic system is one of several dozen ringing a small shallow pond, thus accelerating its aging process abnormally. The threat to our shorebirds is no longer the hunter but the beach lover, whose mere innocent presence during the nesting season limits the options for terns, piping plovers, and other threatened species.

On the other hand, it is the increasing awareness and concern for our local environment by its new residents and visitors that has led to support for protection and acquisition programs and to the establishment and support of homegrown environmental education organizations. The Cape Cod Museum of Natural History in Brewster, the Greenbriar Nature Center in Sandwich, the Wellfleet Bay Sanctuary in South Wellfleet, the Association for the Preservation of Cape Cod in Orleans, the Nantucket Conservation Trust, and the Felix Neck Wildlife Sanctuary in Edgartown are only some of the many local environmental organizations dedicated to the understanding and protection of our limited and irreplaceable resources.

Meanwhile, as we both add to and seek to alleviate environmental pressures, the forces of wind and wave that have always been the ultimate determinants of the shape of this land continue to create new forms and destroy old ones. Perhaps the most dramatic natural event of the last half century was the Great Blizzard of February 6–7, 1978. Dubbed the Storm of the Century, it brought fourteen-and-one-half-foot waves and ninety-two-mile-per-hour winds to the Cape and Islands for two days. Though we escaped the wholesale destruction of property and loss of life experienced elsewhere along the Massachusetts coast, the storm effected major changes in shoreline configuration. Monomoy Island was cut into its present two sections by storm surges. At Eastham's Coast Guard Beach, nearly the entire line of barrier dunes was flattened, destroying the National Seashore's parking lot and bathhouse and carrying off several beach cottages, including Henry Beston's Outermost House. The sea also broke through the beach at Wood End in Provincetown, cutting off vehicle access to Long Point.

Other less-dramatic, but equally pervasive, changes continue to take place here at nature's hands on a daily basis. Willets and oystercatchers, for instance, are nesting again after a long absence, and ospreys, responding to the setting up of artificial nesting platforms, are returning to the Cape and Islands after their decimation in the 1960s from DDT poisoning. Opossums, cattle egrets, and perhaps even coyotes have made recent forays into our area. Who can say what or who is next?

As always, the ocean bluffs continue to fall into the sea a few feet each year. Ponds continue to silt in, salt marshes expand their ranges, barrier beaches lengthen or contract, and the sea level continues to rise.

In the end, the greatest threat to our quality of life here may not be any specific threat such as acid rain, oil spills, or water pollution. Rather, it may be the growing paradox that in order for large numbers of us to live here, it is becoming more and more necessary to cut ourselves off from direct and unfettered contact with the environment that we love. The challenge is not so much to keep Cape Cod and the Islands nominally livable—to ensure drinkable water, breathable air, and other necessities of physical survival. It is not merely to protect endangered habitats and rare species of wildlife, though their fates may be linked more directly to our own than we may recognize. It is not even to preserve those less-tangible qualities of our landscape—what our chambers of commerce and boards of trade are fond of calling rural seaside charm and what we residents more fervently but no less vaguely defend as our towns' characters.

No, the real challenge seems to be not so much to preserve and protect the environment in the sense of insuring it against damage or of avoiding change (both of which are inevitable with or without our help) as it is to learn once again how to live with natural change and allow for it in our own lives, to restrain our own numbers and demands on the land, and to keep wide enough natural margins for our own communities and individual lives that we may continue to share and not merely observe, in carefully restricted and officially prescribed ways, the natural life of our surroundings. If we can do this, we will reclaim the birthright of contact that has nurtured us in the past, so that we may continue to live in, and not merely exist upon, these incomparably lovely lands by the sea.

Index

Acidity of ponds, 137, 143, 149, 150-151
Acid rain, 150, 200, 248
Agassiz, Louis, xi, 100
Age of dinosaurs, 19
Age of mammals, 19
Alewives, x, 41-42, 44, 51-52
    diet, 51
    in ponds, 148
    spawning migration, 51-52, 137
Algae (phytoplankton)
    in ponds, 137, 139, 141, 144-146, 149
Altpeter, H. Stanford, 171
Anglerfish, 54
Animal signs on mud flats, 220-221
Animal species, 150, 251
    endangered, xiii
    matching habitat to species, 187
Aquatic habitats, 116 See also Wetlands
Aquatic insects, 141
Aquatic plants, 150
Archeological artifact inventory, xiii
Arnold Property at Long Pond,
    Marstons Mills, 213
Ashumet Holly and Wildlife Sanctuary,
    Falmouth, 230-231
    for family bird-watching, 60
    holly trees at, 169
Association for the Preservation of
    Cape Cod, Orleans, 251
Atlantic White Cedar Swamp Trail,
    Wellfleet, 167, 240, 223
Austin, Dr. Oliver L., xii, 249
Austin, Dr. Oliver S., xii, 249
Austin Ornithological Research Station,
    South Wellfleet, xii

Bald eagles, 69, 141
Ballston Beach, Truro
    washovers, 32
Barnacles, 100-101, 205
Barnstable, 232-233
Barnstable Conservation Commission, 232
Barn swallows, 230-231
Barrier beach, 25, 36, 232, 252
    formation of, 17, 24
    hooking of, 25

Barrier dunes, Eastham
    blizzard of 1978, 251
Barrier islands, 25, 26
    migration of, 17, 31
Bass, 138, 141
Bass River Lighthouse, Dennis, 224
Bat, 43, 44, 45, 49-50
    echolocation, 44, 50
    species worldwide, 49
    uses of, 50
Bay beaches, 81
Bay scallop, 102
Beach erosion
    collapse of a house, 27
    at Nantucket, 29
    rate per year, 28
Beach grass, 83
    plants associated with, 84-85
Beaver dams, 150
Bedrock, 18-19
    igneous rocks, 18
    metamorphic rocks, 18
    sedimentary, 17-19
    stones on beaches, 18
    till, 19, 20, 22
Bedrock boulder
    at Eastham, 18
    on Martha's Vineyard, 243
Beebe, William, 50
Beebe Woods, Falmouth, 168-169, 231
Beech Forest Trail, Provincetown, 176, 241
Beech trees, 235, 238, 241, 244
    American (*Fagus grandifolia*), 169, 177
Bees, 39, 214, 218, 219
Beetlebung tree, 168
Beetles (whirligig), 44, 139
Bells Neck Conservation Area
    Harwich, 238
    bird watching at, 60
Benthic plants and animals, 79-80
Berries (heath land), 174
Beston, Henry, 213, 248-249
    Outermost House, 213, 252
Bike Trails, 242-243
Billingsgate Island, 27
Biological clock, 38

Bioluminescence
  defined, 45
  process, 46-47
Bird migration, 37 See also Migrating birds
  biological clock in, 38
  in fall, 61, 204
Birds For description of species see family
name
      i.e., Heron, Owl. *See also* Migrating birds.
  at backyard feeders, 59, 214-215
  in fall, 61, 204
  land birds, 57-58
  marsh-feeding birds, 114, 118
  need for living space, 172-173
  nesting areas, 59, 60
  open-habitat species, 173
  near ponds, 140, 141
  shore birds, 57, 58, 60, 61
  sighting spots, 57-58
  songbirds, 60, 61
  speed of flight, 65
  in spring, 59-60
  in summer, 60-61
  in swamps, 121
  threats to, 57, 59-60
  times of stress, 56
  in winter, 58-59
  young or injured, 63
The Birds of Massachusetts, 62
Bird-watchers
  activities, 55-56
  advice to, 56
  sites, 236, 238, 239, 241, 243
Black alder (*Alnus glutinosa*), 170
Black birch, 177
Black cherry trees, 179-180
Black ducks, 121
Black gum tree See Tupelos
Black locust (*Robinia pseudoacacia*), 168
Black racer snake, 217
Black rush, 111
Black scoters, 67
Black skimmer, 68-69
Blueberries, 234, 236
Bluebird
  decline of, 223
Blue crab, 79, 87
Blue heron, 59, 61, 69, 118, 140
Blue mussels, 102
Bourne Scenic Park, 230
Bourne Town Forest, 230
Box turtles, 41
Bradford, William, 156, 158
Brewster, 236-238
  ice-contact head in, 22
Brewster: A Cape Cod Town Remembered, 154
Brewster Conservation Commission, 236

Brewster Mill Sites, 155
Brown recluse spider, 217
Bullfrog, 221
Bullhead lilies, 235
Burgess, Thornton, 232
Burls on trees, 179
Bushy rockrose, 173
Butterfly, 44, 46, 218
Buttonbush Trail, Eastham, 240
Buzzards Bay
  mean tidal range, 75
Buzzards Bay Moraine, 20, 22

Callery-Darling Conservation Area,
    Yarmouth, 215
Camping areas, 231, 234, 236
Canada geese, xiv, 146, 236
Cape Cod
  attractiveness of, xi, 193
  becoming an island, 32
  challenge to humans, x-xi, 253
  cut-throughs, 29, 32 See also Coastal erosion
  distinctive environments, 45, 163, 249
  geologic origins, ix, x See also Ice ages
  historic role of forests, 153-154, 158, 161, 164
    See also Trees
  hydrology of, x, xi
  impassable thickets, 157-158, 162
  lands acquired by state, municipal, or
    federal government, 247-248
  need to restrict land use, x, 247-248
  postglacial era, 154
  post-World War II tourism and off-Cape
    influences, 248
  residential land increases, 248
  rich topsoil, 158-159
  threats to, x-xi, xiii, 252
  a vanished forest, 154-155
  vulnerability, 247, 249-250, 252
  water temperature, 91
  way station, 39
    for birds, 55
    for turtles, 40-41
    for whales, 39-40
  weather, 191-192
Cape Cod Canal, 248
Cape Cod Light (Highland Light), Truro, 225
Cape Cod Museum of Natural History,
    xii, 223, 252
  archeological artifact inventory, xiii
Cape Cod National Seashore, 61, 239
  established by Public Law, 87-126, 248
  guided walks, 120
  opposed to use of jetties and revetments,
    30-31
  owls at, 68
Cape Cod plants listing, xii

Cape Cod Rail Trail, 242
Cape Pogue and Wasque Reservation,
    Martha's Vineyard, 243
Cape Pogue Lighthouse, 31
Carbon dioxide, 206
Carnivorous plants, 122, 129-130
Carp, 105
Carson, Rachel, 74
Catbrier, 157, 162
Cattails, 117, 125-126, 150
Cattle egret, 193, 253
Cedar-apple fungus, 180
Cedars, 156, 157, 159-160 *See also* Swamp
    cedars
  Atlantic white, 167, 176
  cedar-apple fungus, 180
  Eastern red, 166-167, 176
  flavoring for gin, 182
  galls on red cedars, 180
Cedar Tree Neck, Martha's Vineyard, 243
Champlain, Samuel de, 104, 156, 240
Chappaquiddick Island, 31, 243
Chatham, 27
  coastal erosion at, 28, 29, 31, 32
  reforestation, 161
  reports of forests, 156
Chatham Light, 225
Children's nature trails, 222
Chlorofluorocarbons (CFCs), 206
Civilian Conservation Corps (CCC), 177
Clam chowder, 101
Clams, 86, 101-102, 220
  freshwater, 149
Clam worm, 48, 88
Coastal erosion, x, xii *See also*
    Environmental pollution
  accelerated, 30, 247
  attempts at control, 30-31
  sinking caused by silt, 28
  towns affected by, 28, 36
Coastal plain pond shore, 122-123
Codfish, 155
Cold Storage Beach, Dennis, 220
Collecting instinct, 35, 89
  protective measures, 90
  rules for civilized collecting, 91
Collecting tools, 90
Colonial algae, 149 *See also* Algae;
    Ponds, algae in
Color vision, 219
Comb jellies, 99
Common reed (*Spartina alterniflora*), 78, 86
Common skate, 43
Conservation Areas See Nature trails
Conservation commissions, 249, 250
Conservation issues
  international scope of, 251

Continental glaciers, 15, 17
Cord grass (*Spartina alterniflora*), 78, 86
    110-113 *passim*, 114, 125
  at Nauset Marsh, 124
Cormorant, 70, 140
Coyotes, 216
Crabs, 86, 87, 90
Cranberry bogs, 119-120, 231, 232, 235,
    236, 237, 241
  effect of draining swamps, 160
  plants in, 120, 129
  water level, 119
  Windswept Bog, Nantucket, 244
Cranberry Bog Trail, Truro, 241
Crane Wildlife Management Area,
    North Falmouth, 174
Crayfish, 148
Crickets, 43, 114
Crocker Neck Conservation Area,
    Barnstable, 233
Crowe's Pasture, Dennis, 235
Crows, 59
Crustaceans, defined, 99

Danforth Property, Marstons Mills, 174
Darby Property, Barnstable, 233
Day camps, 231
DDT, 71, 253
Deer, 107, 186-187
  need for living space, 173
  size, 186
Deer tick, 187, 188
Dennis, 235-236
  coastal erosion at, 28
Dennis Pond Conservation Area,
    Yarmouth, 234-235
Dew, 201, 208
Dew point, 201
Diapause, 218, 219
Digger wasp, 220
Doane Loop Trail, Eastham, 240
Doane Rock, Eastham, 18
Dog tick, 188
Dogwood trees, 177, 193
Dolphins, 40
Downy woodpecker, 217
Dragonfly nymphs, 139
Duck Pond, South Wellfleet, 151
Ducks, 65-68, 121
Dune Bog, 119, 120
Dune grass, 25
Dune ponds, 136
Dunes See also Sand beaches; Seashore
  aspects of dune environment, 82-85
  different types, 82
  dune water table, 82-83
  formation of, 17, 24, 80

Dunes (cont.)
  growth rate of, 83
  plant and animal dwellers, 83-85
  sand surface temperature, 84
  shaped by wind, 25, 77
Dwight, Rev. Timothy, 160

Eagles, 69, 141
Eastern hemlock, 177
Eastham, 239-240
Eastham Salt Pond, 24
Eastham woods, 158-159
East Harbor, Provincetown, 105
Echinoderm, 97
Ecosystems
  research into, xii-xiii
The Edge of the Sea, 74
Eelgrass, 78, 79
  as food, 86
  habitat, 102
Eider duck, 66
Elizabeth Islands
  end moraines on, 20
  glacial deposits on, 17
  Naushon Island's oak-beech forest, 170
  trees sighted in 17th century, 156
Environment
  adaptation to (salt marsh), 109
  efforts to preserve, 26, 108, 252
  man's encroachment on, 90-91, 251-252
  need for knowledge of, ix-xiv
  restrictions on use of, x, 247-249
Environmental educational organizations,
  252
Environmental ethics
  love and, x, xiv
  six rules for protecting the environment,
  91
Environmental legislation, 249
Environmental pollution, x, 26, 90-91
  acid rain, 150, 200, 249
  groundwater and, 251
  oil spills, 249-250
Erosion control, 26, 30-31 *See also*
  Coastal erosion
European linden (*Tilia europaea*), 170
Eutrophication, 145-146, 149
The Evergreens of Cape Cod, 171

Falmouth, 230-231
  coastal erosion at, 28
  mean average tide, 75
Felix Neck Wildlife Sanctuary, Martha's
  Vineyard, 243, 252
  marshland, 109, 124
  threat of erosion, 29-30

Fiddler crabs, xiv, 38, 86, 87, 126-127
  habitat, 86, 113
  life cycle, 127
A Field Guide to the Birds, 56
Finch, Robert, 213-214
Firefly
  mating flights, 45, 46-47
  used in scientific research, 36, 47
Fish *See also* Fish migrations
  eggs, 42-43, 104
  marsh inhabitants, 113-114
Fish and game laws, 91
Fishing holes, 230, 233
Fishing industry, 159
Fish migrations, 41-43
  alewives, 41-42, 51-52
  codfish, 43
  eels, 42, 45
  flounder, 42, 43
  mackerel, 43
  skate, 43
Flax Pond Conservation Area, South
  Dennis, 167
Flora of Cape Cod, xii
Forbush, Edward Howe, 62, 128
Foredune, 104
Forest fires, 162, 163
"The Forests of Cape Cod," 170
Fort Hill Trail, Eastham, 239-240, 249
  for bird-watching, 60-61
  red cedars at, 167
Franklinia, 230
Fresh Pond Conservation Area,
  Dennis, 236
Freshwater lake, 242
Freshwater lens, 134-135
Freshwater marsh, 233, 238
  most interesting marshes, 125
Freshwater ponds, 134-135
Freshwater wetlands, 115-124
Frogs, 37, 45, 118, 139, 221
Frost, 208
Fuelwood industry, 161-162
  pitch pine for, 165
Fungal injury to tree, 179

Galls, 186, 218
Gannet, 63-64
Garbage dumps, 146, 250, 251
Gay Head Cliffs, Martha's Vineyard
  224
  erosion at, 31
  fossils on, 19
  glacial deposits on, 18, 19
  high tide at, 75
  moraine on, 22

Ghost shrimp, 99-100
Giese, Graham, 29, 32
Gin, flavoring for, 182
Glacial geology, xi, 15-26
    bedrock, 18-19
    coastal landforms, 17, 24-26
    formation of:
        end moraines, 20,22
        glaciers, 15
        ice-contact head, 22
        kettle holes, 22, 24
        moraines, 17, 20, 22
        outwash plains, 17, 20, 22
    glacial deposits, 17, 19-20
    glacial landforms, 20-24
    glacial streams, 19-20
    man as a geologic factor, 26
    marine deposits, 24
    meltwater streams, 19, 20, 22
Glassworts, 114-115, 235
Global warming trend, 28, 200, 206-207
Goodwill Park and Town Forest,
    Falmouth, 231
Goose fish, 53-54
Grasshoppers, 43, 114
Grasslands, 173, 175
    rare plants in, 173-174
    threat to, 68
Great black-backed gulls, 92, 140, 250
Great Island Trail, Wellfleet, 240-241
Great Marshes, Barnstable, xii, 109, 110, 124
Great Outer Beach (Wellfleet-Truro), 24
Great Pond, Truro, 143
Greenbriar Nature Center, Sandwich, 252
Green crabs, 238
Greenhead fly (*Tabanus nigrovittatus*), 215
Greenhouse effect *See* Global warming trend
Gribbles, 100
Groundwater, 112, 134-135, 146, 147
    basic model of source, 251
    increasing demand for and pollution of,
        251
Gulf of Maine, 88
Gulfweed, 85
Gulls *See* Herring gulls
    pellet, 219, 220
Gypsy-moth infestations, 171

Hairy woodpecker, 217
Harlequin duck, 67-68
Harwich, 238
Hathaway's Pond, Barnstable, 233
Hawk, 43, 59, 61
Head of the Meadow Trail, Truro, 242
Heath lands (moors), 173, 174-175
Hen or surf clams, 86, 101
Herbivores, 85

Hermit crab, 87, 89, 93, 102
Heron *See* Blue heron
Heron family, 118
Herring gulls, 59, 91-92, 137, 140
    feeding habits, 149-150
    increasing population of, 146, 249
Herring River, West Harwich, 117
Hewlett-Packard field, East Sandwich, 174
Hickory trees, 177
High Head, Truro, 25
Hitchcock, Edward, 155
Holly trees, 169, 230, 231, 232, 233, 244
    American (*Ilex opaca*), 169, 177
Horse Pond Conservation Area,
    Yarmouth, 234
Horseshoe crab, 47-49, 87
    diet, 48
    life of, 36-37, 48
    mating of, 221
    skeletons, 82
    threat to, 49
    use in scientific research, 36, 48
Humidity, 192
    defined, 202
Hummingbirds, 218

Ice age forests, 142, 143
Ice ages
    Cretaceous period, 19, 22
    Holocene, 15, 24
    Laurentide ice sheet, 15, 17, 18, 22, 133
    mammals of, 17
    Tertiary period, 19, 22
    Wisconsinan Glacial Stage, 15, 17, 19
Ice sheets *See* Glacial geology; Ice ages
Indian Lands Conservation Trails,
    Dennis, 236
Indian pipes, 182-183
Indians' slash-and-burn agriculture, 157, 158
Insects
    animals feeding on, 181
    carnivorous plants and, 122, 129-130
    in dunes, 84-85
    in freshwater marshes, 118
    in ponds, 139, 141
    role in nature, 219
    in salt marshes, 114
    in winter, 218-219
    in wrack, 81
Intertidal flats, 85-87
    collecting in, 89-90
Intertidal zone, defined, 85
Iron foundries, 161

January Thaw, 209
Jellyfish, 88-89, 205
Jeremiah's Gutter, 32, 66

John Wing Trail, Brewster, 237-238

Kame and kettle surface, 22
Kennedy, President John F., 249
Kettle hole, 235
  depth of, 142
  formation of, 22, 24, 140
Kettle ponds, x, 233 See also Ponds
  average size, 136
  formation of, 133
  at Polpis, Nantucket, 170, 178
Knob-and-kettle topography, 232
Knobbed whelk, 87, 89

Lady's slipper, 183, 238
  transplanting, 183-184
Lampblack, 161
Lampyridae, 45
Lateral line (in fish), 44
Leopold, Aldo, x
Lichens, 84, 130-131
Lighthouses, 224-226
  Bass River, 224-225
  Cape Cod (Highland), 225
  Chatham, 225
  Long Point, 226
  Nauset, 225
  Nobska, 224
  Race Point, 225-226
  Wood End, 226
Liming of ponds, 151
Linear dune, 104
Lion's mane, 88
Lobster (*Homarus americanus*), 96-97
  habitat, 96-97, 148
  industry, 96
Long Point, Martha's Vineyard, 243
Long Point Light, Provincetown, 226
Long Pond, Barnstable, 233
Long Pond, Brewster, 242
Longshore current, 77, 78
Low tide
  shell collecting at, 75
Lowell Holly Reservation, Mashpee, 169
Lunar cycle, 75
Lyme disease, 187, 188
  symptoms, 188

Maine, 96
Marconi, Guglielmo, 28
Marine Biological Laboratory, xi
Marine cliffs (scarps), 77-78
Marine deposits, 24
  longshore drift, 24, 25
  salt marsh, 24
Marine invertebrates, 78-79

Marine research, xi-xiii
Marsh birds, 114, 125, 235, 237
  heron family, 118
Marsh grasses, 110-113
Marsh hawks, 114, 128, 235, 237
  courtship display, 128
Marsh plants, 234, 238
  effects of oil spill on, x, 243-244
Martha's Vineyard, x, 243-244
  beetlebung trees at, 168
  coastal erosion at, 29, 31
  end moraine on, 22
  fossils on, 19
  moraine on, 20, 22
  post oaks on, 178
  woodland destruction on, 159
Mashpee, 28
Mashpee River
  freshwater marshes, 117
Massachusetts Department of
  Environmental Management, 249
Massachusetts Natural Heritage
  Program, xiii
Meadowbrook Road Conservation Area,
  Yarmouth, 234
Meadow vole, 220
Meiofauna (sand dwellers), 80
Melville, Herman, 155
Mergansers, 65
Mermaids' purses, 43, 81, 89
Mid-Cape Highway, 248
Migrating birds
  effect of overuse on, x
  food for, 37
  long-distance record, 65
  sea ducks, 65-68
  study of, xii
Mill Brook, Martha's Vineyard, 117
Mill Creek, Sandwich, 231
Millenium Grove, North Eastham, 166
Milt, 104
Minke whale, 40
Moby Dick, 155
Monarch butterfly
  migration, 46
Monomoy National Wildlife Refuge,
  Chatham, 60, 249
  dune bog, 120
  effects of 1978 blizzard, 252
  owls at, 68
Monomoy Point
  mean average tide, 75
Moon
  influence on tides, 74, 75, 207
  phases of, 74
Moon jellyfish, 88

Moon snail, 35, 49, 79, 81, 86, 221
Morris Island, Outer Cape, 60
Mosquito infestations, 147
  control ditches, 112
Mosses, 84, 130-131
Moth, 44, 218
Mourt's Relation, 157
Mud flat, 78, 86, 220
  animal signs on, 220-221
  species on, 86-87, 220-221
Mud shrimp, 100
Muskeget meadow vole, 114
Muskrats, 119, 150
Mussels, 113, 139, 148-149
Mycorrhiza, 183, 184

Nantucket,
  coastal erosion at, 29, 31
  Eel Point, 124
  end moraine on, 20, 22
  glacial deposits, 17, 19
  hidden forests, 170, 178
  high cliff in village, 25
  moors, 174-175
  moraine on, 20
  Sankaty cliffs, 31
  tidal ranges, 75
  treeless, 155
  woodland destruction, 159
Nantucket Conservation Foundation Lands,
  175, 244
Natural beauty
  fragility and threat to, xi, 247-248, 253, 253
Nature
  complexity of, 35, 36, 42, 250
  explorers of, 45-46
  predictable events, 37
  scientific research into, 36
Nature trails
  in Barnstable, 229-244
  in Bourne, 232-233
  in Brewster, 236-238
  in Dennis, 235-236
  in Eastham, 239-240
  in Falmouth, 230-231
  in Harwich, 238
  on Martha's Vineyard, 243-244
  on Nantucket, 244
  in Provincetown, 241
  in Sandwich, 231-232
  in Truro, 241
  in Wellfleet, 239, 240-241
  in Yarmouth, 233-235
Nature writers, xii
Nauset Beach, 66
Nauset Light, Eastham, 225
Nauset Marsh, 109, 124, 223, 239, 240

  tern colony, 95
Nauset Marsh Trail, Eastham, 240, 242
New Alchemy Institute, Hatchville, xii-xiii
Nickerson State Park, Brewster, 50, 169,
  176-177, 223, 229, 236-237
Nickerson, William, 156
Nobska Light, Woods Hole, 224
Noctiluca, 45
Northern flickers, 217
Norway spruce, 238
"No-see-um" insects, 53

Oak trees, 156, 157, 162
  most common, 171, 173
  old-growth, 166
  100 years from now, 181-182
  other oaks, 165
  red oak, 177, 181
  scrub oaks, 165, 175
  survivors, 165-166
Ocean Arks International, Falmouth, xii
Offshore, 77
Oldale, Robert, 28
Old Briar Patch, Sandwich, 229, 232
Old-man's beard, 130-131, 167
Opossum, 50, 253
Opuntia, 193
Orchids, 118, 121, 122 *See also* Lady's slipper
Orioles, 59
Ornithology, xii
  study of Cape Cod birds, xii
Osprey, 60, 71, 140, 253
Otis-Atwood Conservation Area,
  West Barnstable, 212
Owls, 59, 68, 241
  great horned, 140-141
  pellet, 219-220
  saw-whet, 173
  short-eared, 68, 114
  snowy, 59, 68
Oystercatchers, 253
Oyster leaf, 184
Oysters, 102
Ozone layer, 108, 200, 205-206
  defined, 205
  wetlands and, 108

Paine's Creek Beach, Brewster, 220
Pamet, xi, 134
Pamet Cranberry Bog Trail, Truro, 241
Pamet River, Truro, 32, 134, 174
  freshwater marsh at, 117
Pamet River Valley, Truro, xi
Panne pools, 114
Pannes, 125
Parabolic dune, 104-105
Parula warbler, 167

Peaked Hill, Martha's Vineyard, 243
Peat, 119, 129
  analyses of, 154
  as fuel, 162
  at Great Marsh, 124
Peat moss, 121
Pelagic plants and animals, 79
Pellets, bird, 219-220
Penikese Island, xi
Periwinkle, 35, 79, 93, 113, 221
Peterson, Roger Tory, 56
Phoebe, 37, 59
Phosphorescence, 45
Pilgrim Lake, Orleans, 134
Pilgrim Spring Trail, Truro, 241
Pilkey, Orrin H., Jr., 31
Pine barrens
  birds of, 173
Piping plover, 60, 61-62
  threatened species, 60, 62, 252
Pitch pines (*Pinus rigida*), 143, 154, 161, 162,
    233, 234, 235
  flexibility, 165
  multiple trunk, 178-179
  other qualities, 163-165
  overtaken by oaks, 171
Plankton, 45, 51
Plants
  endangered species, x, xiii, 237
  near ponds, 123-124, 129, 143
Poison ivy, 120, 184-185
  as erosion control agent, 185
  treatment of rash, 185
Poison sumac, 185
Polypores (mushrooms), 179
Ponds
  acidic, 135, 143, 149, 150-151
  aging of, 149
  algae in, 137, 139, 144-146, 149
  in autumn, 140
  becoming a marsh, 117
  brackish, 134, 136
  clarity of water, 144
  coastal plain pond shores, 122-124
  definition of, 133-134, 135
  definition of "great pond," 134
  fish in, 138
  forces of sun and wind, 136, 140
  formation of, 133, 141-142
  fossil studies of sediment, 142
  freshwater lens, 135
  freshwater ponds, 134-135
  human threat to, 144, 145, 151
  ice formation, 148
  inhabitants of limnetic zone, 144
  number on Cape Cod, 133
  nutrient loading of, 145-146

plants and animals in littoral zone, 143-144
plants on pond shores, 123-124, 129-130
predators, 137, 138, 139
role of streams in, 147
saltwater ponds, 135-136, 146
smallest forms of life in, 149
source of fresh water in, 147
in spring, 136-138
stagnation in, 138
in summer, 138-140
vegetation, 144
water level fluctuations, 123
water table, 135
water temperature, 141
in winter, 140-141
zones, 143-144
Pond succession, 142, 144-146
Portuguese man-of-war, 88
Post oak, 178
Poverty grass, 184
Property boundary lines, 179-180
Province Lands Trail, Provincetown, 242-243
Province Lands Visitor Center, 104
Provincetown, 241
  effects of 1978 storm, 252
  efforts to stop tree cutting, 160
  erosion of center, 28
  sand invasion, 160-161, 176
  1620 reports of forest, 156
  water supply, 251
Provincetown Beech Forest, 169
Provincetown Center for Coastal Studies,
    29, 242
Provincetown spit, 25, 104
Punkhorn Parklands, Brewster, 237

Quahog, 101
Quaking bog, 121-122, 237
Quarries, 237

Rabies, 218
Race Point Light, Provincetown, 225-226
Railroad ties, 163
Racoons, as carriers of rabies, 218
Rain forests, 175
Raymond J. Syrjala Conservation Area,
    Yarmouth, 234
Reading the landscape, 180
Red cedars, 166-167, 176
Red cedar tea, 182
Redds, 138
Redfield, Dr. Alfred, xii
Red maple swamps, 130, 131, 145, 167, 234,
    235, 239, 242
Red tide, 90, 104
Rhythms
  in plants and animals, 38-39

River otter, 222
Rodents, 114, 181
Roe, 104
Roth Woodlands, Martha's Vineyard, 244
Rugosa rose, 29
Rushes, 111, 150

Sadlier, Hugh and Heather, 244
Salamanders, 121
Salt marsh, 108-115, 232, 233, 235, 236, 237, 239, 240
  acreage lost, 108
  development of, 17
  formation of, 24, 78, 109-110
  functions of, 107-108
  harsh habitats, 109, 113
  inhabitants, 109, 113-115
  marsh-feeding birds, 114
  most interesting marshes, 124
  plants and grasses, 110-113, 114-115
  predatory animals, 114
  sandy floor (substrate), 110
  scientific study of, xii
Salt marsh mosquito, 114
Salt marsh plants, 24, 26, 108, 110-113
Salt meadow grass (*Spartina patens*), 110-112, 114, 124
Salt meadow hay, 111, 238
Salt pond *See also* Ponds
  formation of, 24, 133
Salt Pond, Eastham, 104
Salt reed grass, 26, 237
Salt spray horizon, 181
Salt water, 113
Saltwater ponds, 135-136, 146
Saltworks, 159, 161
Sand and gravel pits, 26
Sandbar
  formation of, 78, 85
  plants and animals on, 85-86
Sand beaches
  vs. bay beaches, 81
  composition of sand, 80
  as habitat, 80-82
  plants, 81
  unstable habitats, 81
Sand dollar, 92, 97
Sand dune, 104-105
Sand launce, 114
Sandpipers, 65
Sand-plain gerardia, 173-174
Sand shrimp, 100
Sand spit, 78, 109
Sand terraces *See also* Dunes; Seashore
  summer and winter berms, 77
Sandwich, 231-232
  coastal erosion, 28

Sandwich glassworks, 162
Sandwich moraine, 20, 22
Sandy Neck Conservation Area,
    Barnstable, 109, 120, 232
  hardwood forests at, 169
Sanitary landfills, 251
Sargasso sea, 42, 85
Sassafras, 234
Scallops, 44, 79, 86, 102
Schall, Donald, 171
Scoters, 67
Scusset Beach State Reservation, Sandwich, 231
Sea
  effect on temperature, 192
  Gulf Stream, 192, 199
  Labrador current, 192-193
Sea birds, 238, 241
  list of, 239
  oil spills threat, 250
Sea cliffs, 77-78, 253
  formation of, 17, 24-25
  loss of shore land, 78
Sea cucumber, 103
Sea ducks, 65-68
Sea gooseberries, 99
Sea gull, 91-92
Sea hare, 103
Sea lavender, 115, 235, 238
Sea level
  rise in, 17, 24, 28, 108, 110, 200, 206, 253
    accelerated, 247
    cause of coastal erosion, 31
    coastal development and, 108
    long-term effects, 206-207
    salinity of ponds and, 146
Seals, 93, 235
Sea mouse, 103
Sea nettle, 88
Sea potato, 103
Seashore
  attractions of, 74, 108
  complex ecosystem, 73
  description, 73
  dredging process, 77
  encroachments on, 90
  plant and animal habitat, 73, 78-80, 83-85, 90
  power of waves, 76-78
  sand surface temperature, 84
  zones, 76
Sea snow, 198-199
Seasons on Cape Cod
  autumn, 192, 203, 204
  average high and average low temperatures, 204
  constants in nature, 36
  hottest and coldest times of year, 203

Seasons on Cape Cod (contd.)
  migration of birds and, 37
  spring, 192-193, 203, 204
    rainfall, 202
  summer, 192-193, 203, 204
  winter, 192-193, 197, 203, 204
    average snowfall, 192
    rainfall, 202
Sea turtles, 40
Sea urchin, 94, 97
Sea wattle jellyfish, 88
Seaweeds, 79, 85, 114
  black wrack, 81
  green fleece, 87
Sengekontacket Pond, Martha's Vineyard
  threat of erosion, 29, 30
Senses
  in fish, 42, 43
  hearing, 43
  sight, 43-44
  smell, 42, 44-45, 52
Septage problem, 251
"1776" North and South, Barnstable, 233
Sewage treatment plants, 251
Sharks, 205
Shawme Crowell State Forest, Sandwich,
  177, 231
Shelled mollusks, 79-80, 82, 100
Shellfish *See also* Clams, Crabs, etc.
  attempts at erosion control, 30
  effects of loss, 66
  Martha's Vineyard shellfish beds, 29, 30
  species on Cape beaches, 101-102
Ship-building industries, 157, 159, 160
Shipworm, 89, 100
Shoreline
  basic elements, 109
  configuration changes due to 1978 storm, 252
  erosion, 145
  retreat, 28
Short Walks on Cape Cod and the Vineyard,
  244
Shrimp, 86, 87, 113, 118
  species, 99-100
Simpkins Neck and Romig-Jacquinet
  Conservation Area, Dennis, 235-236
Skaket Beach, Orleans, 220
Skiff Hill, Eastham, 240
Skunk cabbage, 130
Sloane, Eric, 158
Small Swamp Trail, Truro, 241
Snails, 86, 87, 113, 118, 138, 220-221
  See also Moon snail; Periwinkle; Sea hare;
  Whelks
  habitat, 87
  operculum, 89

Snail's pace, 50
Snakes, 140, 217-218
Sour gum trees, 193, 234 *See also* Tupelos
Southern plants and animals, 193
Sphagnum bog, 119, 120, 121-122
  plants in, 121-122, 129, 130
Sphagnum moss, 121, 144
Spider bite, 217
Spike rush, 143
Spring
  signs of, 37, 52-53, 121
Spring peeper (*Hyla crucifer*), 37, 52-53, 121
Spruce Hill Conservation Area,
  Brewster, 238
Squid, 43, 44
Squirrels, 215
Starfish, 43, 44, 97-98
Starling, 223
State Forest, Martha's Vineyard, 244
Storms, 28, 31, 32, 110
  1978 northeaster, 197, 207, 252
  1938 hurricane, 169
  salt spray damage, 181
  thunderstorms, 198, 203, 208
  winter, 207
Storm surge, 207-208
Strahler, Dr. Arthur, xi, 251
Streams
  refuge for migrating fish and animals,
    147
Subtidal zone, 87-89 *See also* Intertidal flats
  inhabitants of, 87-89, 102
Sundews, 122, 129-130
Sunfish, 98-99, 148, 205
  life cycle, 138
Sun's energy, 15
Sunsets, 208
Surf scoter, 67
Svenson, Dr. Henry, xii
Swamp cedars, 156, 159-160
Swamp plants, 120-121

Tadpoles, 115, 118, 139
Talbot's Point Salt Marsh Wildlife Reservation,
  Sandwich, 232
Temperature
  effect on animals, 40-42
  of ponds, 141
  sand surface temperature, 84
  timing and, 38, 48
  of water, 91
Terns, xii, 94-95, 252
  Arctic, 37
  arrivals in spring, 59
  diet, 250
  hunted for food, 251

near ponds, 140
nesting area, 95, 250
nesting time, 56
population decline, 250
Thoreau, Henry David, 32, 90, 155, 164,
     184, 213
Thornton Burgess Museum and Old Briar
Patch,
     Sandwich, 232
Tidal creeks, 26, 111-112, 147
Tidal cycles, 75
Tidal flat inhabitants, 86
Tidal pools, 56, 102
Tide line, 76
Tides, 36
  birdwatching and, 56
  ebb tide, 74
  formation of salt marshes, 110
  horseshoe crabs and, 48
  neap tide, 75
  rhythms of, 38, 74-76
  spring tides, 74, 112
  tide, defined, 74
  variations on Cape Cod, 75
  watching the tide, 90
  in winter, 207
Time changes, 39
Toad, spade-foot, 115
Towhee, 70-71
Tree cricket, 38-39
Tree frogs, 37, 52-53
Trees
  causes of depletion, 157-163, 172
  causes of stunted trees, 176
  common Cape trees, 176
  critical wildlife habitat, 153-154
  dead trees as habitat, 181
  desiccants, 180-181
  dune forest, 167
  ecological value, 175
  effectsof human encroachment, 172-173
  effects of warming trend, 207
  farming and grazing interests, 157, 158, 160,
     174, 176
  fines for tree destruction, 159, 176
  forest in transition, 171-173
     process of create and destroy, 172
  forest trees of Outer and Lower Cape, 177-178
  forest trees of Upper Cape, 177
  history of Cape forests:
     18th to 20th century, 157, 160
     17th century, 155-156
     photographic sources, 154-155
  land use and forest fires, 162
  multiple trunk trees, 178-179
  100 years from now, 181-182
  reforestation, 164-168

trend to diversification, 171
use of pesticides, 171
used in ship-building industry, 157, 176
a vanished forest, 154, 157
virgin forests, 170
Trout, 138
Truro, 241
  Highland Light, 32, 225
  water supply, 251
Tube worms, 44
Tupelos (*Nyssa sylvatica*), 131, 167-168, 176,
     193, 238
Turkeys, 173, 184, 223-224
Turtles, 40-41, 118, 138, 140, 144

United States Geological Survey, 28
Urban development
  forest decrease and, 172
U-shaped dunes, 25, 104-105

Venus's-flytrap, 122, 129
Violin spiders, 217

Wakeby Conservation Area, Sandwich, 231
Wakeby Pond, Mashpee, 170
Wampanoags
  Indian myth, ix
  and Pilgrims, 223
Warblers, 37, 59, 60, 121
Warming trend, 108, 200, 206
  long-term effects, 206-207
Washburn Island, Falmouth, 231
Wash-overs, 32, 110
Wasp, 186, 220
Water density, 148
Water level, 74-75
Water quality, 147, 251
  role of wetlands, 107
  tide in wetlands, 116
Water snake, 217
Water striders, 139
Water supply
  degrading of, 26
  problems of septage and refuse disposal, 251
  threats to, 251
Water temperature, 91
Wave, defined, 76
Weather, 191-209 *See also* Seasons on
     Cape Cod
  clouds, 197-198
  cold fronts, 194, 195-196, 198
  fog, 145-146, 192, 201, 208
  gales, 199
  hail, 203
  halo, 194
  high pressure zones, 194
  hurricanes, 199

Weather (cont.)
  jet streams, 196
  line squalls, 199
  low pressure zones, 194-195
  occluded fronts, 195
  rain, 201, 202
  sleet, 204
  snow, 204
  stationary fronts, 195
  tornadoes, 199-200
  warm fronts, 194, 196, 198
  water spouts, 200
  winds, 197, 208
Wellfleet, 239, 240-241
  erosion at, 28
  Gull Pond, 134, 136
Wellfleet Bay Wildlife Sanctuary, xii, 239, 252
Wetlands, 107-131 *See also* Salt marshes
  defined, 107, 117
  federal, state, and local protection, 172, 249
  functions of, 107-108
  freshwater, 107, 115-124
    animals of freshwater marsh, 118-119
    cranberry bogs, 119-120
    plants of freshwater marshes, 117-118
    plants of freshwater wetland, 116-117
    tide, 116, 118
  pond shores, 122-124
  research on, xiii, 147
  sphagnum bogs, 121-122
  swamps, 120-121
  trails, 244
  wet meadow plants, 119-120
Wet woodlands, 233, 235, 238
Whale blubber, 159
Whales
  finbacks, 39
  as fuel or national resource, xiv
  humpbacks, 40
  mass strandings, 39-40
  pilot whales, 39-40
  study of, xii
Whale watching cruises, 39, 242
Whelks, 87, 89
White perch, 105
White pine (*Pinus strobus*), 168-169, 177
    232, 235
White-winged scoters, 67
Wild apple trees, 235
Wild cherry trees, 235
Wildflowers, 234, 238, 239
  mainland, 184
  on pond shores, 1224
  on salt marshes, 124
  unusual, 168, 169, 184
  in wet meadows, 119
Wild grasses, 237, 239

Wild Harbor Marsh, West Falmouth, 250
Wild turkeys, 173, 187, 223-224
Willets, 253
Williams Pond, Wellfleet, 145
Wind, 25, 76, 77, 197, 208 *See also* Weather
  Alberta clippers, 194
  Bermuda high, 196, 199
  effects on trees and sand dunes, 176
  northeaster, 197
  on ponds, 123
Windswept Cranberry Bog, Nantucket, 223
Wing, John, 237
Witch hazel, 130
Woodcock, 61
Wood ducks, 121
Wood End Light, Provincetown, 226
Woodpeckers, 64, 216-217
  study of, 36
Woods Hole Oceanographic Institution, xi, 250

Yarmouth, 233-235
Yarmouth Botanic Trail, 235
Yellow perch, 138, 141, 144